The Mallory Library

99 WAYS TO MAKE MONEY IN A DEPRESSION
REVISED AND UPDATED EDITION

99 WAYS TO MAKE MONEY IN A DEPRESSION
REVISED AND UPDATED EDITION

GERALD APPEL

Arlington House Pubishers
Westport, Connecticut

This book has been prepared with the aim of providing accurate and authoritative information regarding the matters discussed. However, it is sold with the understanding that neither the author nor the publisher is engaged in rendering legal, accounting, or other professional advice. Readers are urged to discuss relevant questions with their attorney and/or accountant, particularly as related to issues of taxes, tax laws, or other legal matters.

Copyright 1981 Gerald Appel.

All rights reserved. No portion of this book may be reproduced without written permission from the publisher, except by a reviewer who may quote brief passages in connection with a review.
Library of Congress Cataloging in Publication Data

Appel, Gerald.
    99 ways to make money in a depression revised edition.

    1. Investments.   I. Title.
HG4521.A65   1981   332.6'78   81-2845
ISBN 0-87000-501-4   AACR2

Manufactured in the United States of America

9 8 7 6 5 4 3 2

Editorial and Production Services by Cobb/Dunlop Inc.

DEDICATION

To Judy, Marvin, and Marion—still the best cure for any depression

TABLE OF CONTENTS

Preface		ix
Preface to the Revised Edition		xi
1	*The Early Warning Signs of An Economic Collapse*	1
2	*A Broad Blueprint For Survival: The Master Plan*	12
3	*Diamonds: The Ultimate Doomsday Investment?*	18
4	*From Treasury Bills to Municipals: At Least You'll Be As Safe As The Government*	26
5	*Corporate Bonds: Straight Income Plus Some With a Possible Equity Kicker*	36
6	*The Money Funds: Safe As The Bank, With Double The Return?*	49
7	*Gold: Another Hedge Against Total Calamity?*	57
8	*How to Prance Through a Bear Market Smiling*	72
9	*Sifting For Short Sales*	92
10	*Stock Options: A Low-Cost Means of Playing a Depression (And Bull) Market*	113
11	*Real Estate: During the Coming Depression? No! No! A Thousand Times, No! But After—? Now, That's A Different Story Altogether*	125
12	*Some Sundry Realty Investments . . .*	137
13	*How To Profit From International Misfortune: Trading In Currency Futures*	147
14	*Coins: The Ultimate Weapon Or The Ultimate Rip-off?*	169
15	*Art, Antiques and Autographs—No "A"s, However, During The Coming Depression*	179
16	*From Batman to Bordeaux—Collectibles and Such*	188
17	*Miscellaneous Money Matters: Some Ways to Save Dollars No Matter What*	203
18	*How To Tell When The Depression's Coming to An End and How To Take Advantage Of The Turn*	209
19	*Epilogue*	214
20	*Epilogue to the Epilogue*	216
	Index	219

PREFACE

Depression: in economics "a period of low general economic activity marked by mass unemployment, deflation, a decreasing use of resources, and a low level of investment" (Webster).

Or, to put it another way—breadlines, apples, bankruptcies, panic, riots in the streets, anxiety, foreclosures, depletion of capital, bank failure, ruin, worry, joblessness, hunger. For 70 to 90 percent of the population, perhaps, that will be the coming depression.

Would you prefer to believe it another way for yourself? How about opportunity, profit, increased purchasing power, maintenance of capital, better living, relaxation? *Believe it or not, you do have the choice!* There is no way to avoid business cycles, boom and bust, ups and downs. There are, however, ways to ride the crest—and even to profit during times of general distress; to seize aggressively the opportunities afforded by difficult economic climates, or, if you're more conservative by nature, simply to employ safe, available cash havens in which to ride out the storm.

But isn't it illegal to profit from general economic calamity, or immoral at the least? Well, is it immoral to buy stock cheap and to sell dear? To sell short? To pick up undervalued real estate? To place your money in the safest debt instruments available? In short, is it illegal or immoral to protect yourself, your family, your life savings, the production of a lifetime? Is it not only immoral but imprudent to ignore the warning signs: to risk the welfare of your loved ones—even to risk personal bankruptcy, inability to meet your obligations, perhaps, at the worst, becoming a public charge? Which is the greater immorality?

If you believe that fate, luck, or the federal government should take care of you, then ignore this book. If you believe that fate helps the person who helps himself, that, in the end, your personal destiny will be guided by you—if you prefer, at least, to try to master your own fortunes—then you will see what you can learn in these pages.

From my end, I've tried to put together an armamentarium of ideas, strategies, tactics, concepts, and devices by which you can meet the adversary, depression, head on—coming out ahead in the end. In these pages we will be discussing the following areas:

1. How to Recognize the Early Signs of Depression.
2. Protective Action for Survival
3. Aggressive Action for Profit
4. How To Recognize the End of the Depression
5. Opportunities for the Coming Upturn

More specifically, we will consider the following questions:

1. Which will be the safest cash havens during the coming depression?
2. How can you profit from other nations' misfortunes?
3. Which stocks should you buy when the turn comes?
4. How can you make money *fast* during falling markets?
5. How can you profit during indecisive climates?
6. Which are the safest realty ploys during a housing slump?
7. How can your life insurance policy help you build a future—while you're still young enough to enjoy it?
8. How can you make money on a stock that stands still?
9. When should you enter the art and antique markets?
10. Why should you beware of the best-performing investments?
11. What investments can protect you against "doomsday"?
12. What has been the "best" long-term investment of all?
13. What are your best precious metal investments?
14. Where and how can you pick up distressed property for a song?

And last, but certainly not least, we will be considering the "master plan" for survival and profit during the coming depression.

Yes, the shadow of depression does hang over the land. Will you be ready when it arrives?

GERALD APPEL

PREFACE TO THE REVISED EDITION

The first edition of *99 Ways to Make Money in a Depression* was prepared for the most part during 1974 and reached publication during 1975. Within that edition I outlined many of the reasons why I believed that this country may be heading into a major economic collapse, outlining strategies that should be followed for economic and personal survival. The book was concluded with a statement that investors probably had a few more years yet in which to put their houses in order—but very possibly not much longer than that.

And what has happened in the interim, in the years between 1975 and 1980? The economy did manage to stage a recovery during 1975—a recovery, unfortunately, that has been fueled by mounting national, corporate, and individual debt, supported by inflation as a way of life. Buy today because tomorrow things will become more expensive. Incur debt today because tomorrow you will be able to pay back with cheaper dollars.

As a result, increasing percentages of family income have become committed to servicing debt—personal debt and federal debt, confiscated in the form of taxes, tax rates rising as inflation has pushed personal incomes into higher tax brackets. The social security system, with its built-in inflation escalator clauses, has moved toward the verge of bankruptcy. Worker productivity, in the interim, has been rising at slower rates; the American worker is far from the most efficient. Our auto industry is now taking a back seat to the Japanese; Chrysler, a major corporation, exists only with government support.

The deterioration in our military position has been even more marked. American diplomats are now being kidnapped with impunity. The Soviet Union has moved into a commanding position in the Middle East, threatening 50 percent of our oil supply. There seems little that we are inclined to do about these situations, presuming that viable remedies are, indeed, available.

If anything, the economy seems to have run completely out of control. Interest rates, which rose precipitously during the early months of 1980, fell precipitously within weeks as soon as it became apparent that the country was once again entering into a severe recession (depression?), the worse since 1974, and that the 1974 recession, only five years previous, had been the worst since 1929. The figures emerging are indeed bleak. Unemployment has already approached 8 percent, with the largest proportion hitting at the young adult population, the population required to support a steadily increasing base of older persons, dependent upon social security payouts. The housing industry has been in a shambles for years; the automobile inudstry seems doomed to follow. America has long lost preeminence in the textile industry, our production hampered by outmoded mills and high labor costs.

And now, energy. Our leaders have yet to come up with a cogent energy policy, and our citizens seem hardly inclined to support any policy that calls for sacrifice of any kind. With approximately one-sixth of the national economy dependent in one form or another on the automobile industry, and with the automobile the prime victim of what will probably develop into a long-term energy nightmare, what would you guess are the chances of a major depression at some point during the coming years?

In the first edition I cited evidences of moral turpitude that generally accompany decays in civilizations and national economies. I've seen nothing over the past five years—years of Watergate, increasing crime, and diminishing national commitment—to alter my view that this country may be approaching some very serious trouble.

You may want to take your precautions while you still have time.

Reviewing Some of the Recommendations Made in the First Edition

In the first edition I made a number of recommendations for investor capital—recommendations for depression periods and recommendations for periods of economic recovery. And how have some of these recommendations fared?

The money market mutual funds, recommended for high yield and safety during both good and bad times, have proven to be among the best of investments for the typical investor. To my knowledge, not one single long-term investor has ever lost money in a money market mutual fund. Rates of return during early 1980 reached to well above 16 percent. This is still a number one selection for maximum liquidity and as a form of hedge against inflation and accompanying high interest rates.

Gold, another recommendation, moved from $200 an ounce in late 1974 to approximately $800 an ounce approximately six years later.

Coins, a prime pick as an inflation beater, have continued to rise spectacularly. High-grade Morgan Silver Dollars rose by more than 100 percent during 1979 alone.

I advised investors to familiarize themselves with currency futures in anticipation of further weakness in the American dollar. Have you tried traveling of late? Fortunes have been made by investors who heeded advice to convert dollars into Swiss francs.

All investments have been reviewed for this edition. I have weeded out strategies that are no longer viable and have retained those strategies likely to remain effective.

I do believe that this book provides many of the essential ingredients required for your financial planning for the hard years that may lie ahead. The rest, as they say, remains up to you.

GERALD APPEL

1
THE EARLY WARNING SIGNS OF AN ECONOMIC COLLAPSE

A Noneconomist Views The Economy

No, I am not an economist, and no, I did not live through the crash of '29, though I was around in the late thirties and early forties, when the war finally bailed out the country. I can't tell you too much about the international banking system, or about the footnotes in General Motors' annual report, or even about the insidious governmental economic policies that have led us to where we are today.

My publisher will no doubt take care of my credentials, probably on the book jacket, so there's no point in going into them here. However, let me just say this. I have been a financial writer. I am trying to muddle through difficult times like everyone else, and I do think I know trouble when I see it. I believe that I do see it.

In the newspapers, over the radio, on TV, in the long lines at the unemployment offices, in mounting welfare costs, in layoffs, in our international impotence, in a stock market sick since '68, in failing pension funds, in a general credit collapse—I see trouble. Some examples? Well, we can go back through the course of recent years, through a rather dismal 1974, for example, if we so choose, but why not settle for just one recent week or two? The following items came across my desk during a single two-week period in November 1974. I select them at random.

New York Times, November 26: "Pornography Fight Lags Across Nation." (Don't laugh, we'll see later why this means more than you might think.)

New York Times, November 25: "Experts Fear Growth in Costly City Debts," The gist: New York City is overextended in terms of its borrowing capacity and may have trouble borrowing money. No, no danger of default—or so they say—but a lowered credit rating (why, if there is no danger of default?) and higher interest costs to burden future taxpayers. [In April 1975 Standard and Poor's suspended New York City's "A" credit rating.]

Wall Street Journal, November 22: "General Motors Will Close Nine of Its 22 U.S. Assembly Plants for a Week or Two Next Month." "Ford Lays off 3,000 White Collar Employees." "Bethlehem Steel Won't Schedule Work for 2,600 Employees Next Week." (Need we say more?)

New York Times, November 24: "Canada, the Single Largest Supplier of Foreign Petroleum to the United States, Announced That All Its Exports of Crude Oil To This Country Will Be Phased Out by 1982." (What price gasoline then?)

New York Times, November 24: "Long Beach ... City Manager ... Warned That His City Was About $2 Million In the Red and Would Have Trouble Meeting Its Payrolls."

"Mayor Beame [New York City] Announced That He Would Dismiss 1,510 City Employees And Would Impose a Vacancy Job Freeze on Every Agency." "The City Will Take In $318 Million Less in Real Estate Taxes Than it Had Expected.... Stock Transfer Tax Running Under Budget by $65 Million." *"The Full Extent of the Problem, Many Believe, is Still to Come."* (Italics mine.)

New York Times, November 24: "President Under Pressure to Shift Economic Policy." (If at first you don't succeed....)

Barron's Financial Weekly, November 25: "Financial Time Bomb".... Loans to Underdeveloped Nations May Lead to Rescheduling of Debt, Default." (Anticipated time of explosion, 1975–76.)

Barron's Financial Weekly, November 25: "Most Commodity Prices Are Coming Down." (Why? Lack of demand of course.)

Wall Street Journal, November 29: "Economic Blight Spreads Over Europe; Jobless Millions Cause Grave Concern." ... "Alfred Schaefer, chairman of Zurich's Union Bank ... dean of Swiss bankers, sees signs of an approaching depression that ... could even be worse than that of the 1930's.... In Britain, bankruptcies ... have become epidemic.... Italy still hasn't shown how it can pay for the oil imports without going broke." (With Europe gone, can the U.S. be far behind?)

We could go on and on and on, of course—into the reports of the housing slump, layoffs at Eastman Kodak, the shooting of a German banker by Arab guerrillas, preparations for renewed hostilities in the Middle East, the failure of Franklin National Bank (one of the largest in the country), continued deficits in our national spending, problems with bauxite-producing nations, the worst crash on Wall Street since the Great Depression, and the fall in the price of a seat on the New York Stock Exchange to one-seventh its value six years ago.

We might then consider the rising tide of corporate and individual bankruptcies, the increasing defaults in personal debt, lower auto sales, spreading pessimism, political malaise, government assault on private industry, worldwide shortages of raw materials, declining liquidity, and the virtual bankruptcies of Italy and Britain—all daily newspaper fare, hardly pleasant bedtime reading.

As I said, I'm no economist, but I do know trouble when I see it.

Apparently, the government is beginning to agree publicly. (Who knows what calamities they concede in private?) On November 27, 1974, *The New York Times* noted that Treasury Secretary William E. Simon had stated that the United States may be facing the longest recession since World War II. In the same issue: "Sears Sees Growth In Sales as Less Than Was Expected," plus an article stating that the United States was planning on a continuation of high oil prices.

I guess I'll say it just one more time: I do think I know trouble when I see it. How about you?

Nor Am I Alone

Actually, when it comes to doomsday reports, in comparison to some I'm a positive optimist. At least, I believe that we *may* escape the worst this time around. I hope so—then we may all have more time to prepare for the worst. *However, there is no guarantee of a respite, and things may become far worse before they become better, so plan on getting your house in order* NOW.

Should an economic upturn develop during 1981, use it for all it's worth, but stay loose, friend. When the bell tolls it will be tolling for thee. Just to emphasize the point: Did you notice who was being laid off during last year? Auto workers? Naturally, we all know that assembly workers are expendable. White collar workers?! Well, didn't you think that GM would cover their office staff? City workers?!! I just know you thought government work, at least, was secure. NO ONE WILL BE SAFE DURING THE COMING DEPRESSION—unless you plan ahead now.

As I said, there is a chance that we may step back from the brink *this time,* in which case you won't be hurt in any event. Others, however, rate the chances of a respite as practically nil. To wit:

Business Week, November 23, 1974: "... ominous signs are cropping up everywhere ... the economy has not yet experienced the most adverse influence that intensifies downswings: inventory liquidation ... the unemployment rate has already climbed to 6% even though the recession is only beginning to bite...." (The article goes on to speculate that we *may* be in for the worst recession since the depression of the thirties.) [By April 1975 the unemployment rate had crossed 9 percent.]

C. V. Myers (an interview with the financial analyst, appearing in *Financial World*, October 9, 1974: "... there is no hope ... a complete overhauling of the standards we expect to live by—a reduction of about 50% in living standards ... you should think of how you might feed a few chickens if necessary...."

James Dines (*The Dines Letter*, October 18, 1974): "... a wave of bank failures in Europe would leap the Atlantic like wildfire ... the Treasury is going to have to print money ... in the event of widespread banking failures ... could lead to *triple* digit inflation!"

"Internationally, the situation continues to deteriorate ... Eimei Yamashita, Vice Minister of International Trade and Industry ... warned that Japan was almost certainly headed for depression."

Richard Russell (*The Dow Theory Letters*, November 8, 1974): "We are headed for trouble, and it is going to be one of the ... most difficult periods any of us has ever tried to get through.... It's a matter of survival ... the great danger lies in an international credit collapse ... panic situation which could shake or shatter the economic structure of the Free World ... if one nation topples the shock waves will carry throughout the world." [Richard Russell, *did* renounce his gloomy prognostications, however, by year-end as the stock market rallied.]

Yes, I know. You can trot out plenty of optimists with their rebutals, and I could trot out a few more bears. Believe me, I haven't even touched the big guns in the doomsday ranks (Harry Schultz, Harry Browne, Alexander Paris for instance*). And you can drag out Argus, a prestigious and bullish research company, and *Value Line* and....

But can you really argue with the facts? With Chrysler layoffs, and mounting unemployment, and general collapse, and Italy's bankruptcy, and ... well, have you tried to sell your house lately? After all, when

---

*Probably the ultimate in doom appeared in *New York* magazine, Dec. 2, 1974, "The Oil War of 1976: How the Shah Won the World" by Paul Erdman. The subject: a hypothetical scenario, 1976, driving the Western World into bankruptcy, social revolution, famine, and out of the industrialized age.

the U.S. Treasury Secretary beings to recall '29, is it only the "panic nuts" who are sounding the knell? Think about that.

How Did We Get into This Mess Anyway?

The world will probably recall Yom Kippur Day 1973 as the moment that confirmed the vulnerability of Western society. It was then that the Arabs struck at Israel, a short skirmish as wars go, but the start of a reshuffling of economic power—the massive shift of wealth from London, New York, Zurich, and Paris to Teheran, Baghdad, Kuwait, and Abu Dhabi. Arising from the war—a militant position on the part of OPEC, the Arab oil-producing cartel; a quadrupling of price in crude oil; and a movement in the succeeding year alone of some $60 billion from the Western to the Arab world. From that day forth the balance of economic power was visibly tilted.

Actually, developments in 1973 only accelerated an already burgeoning shift in the balance of oil power. Early warnings were given in 1951 when Iran nationalized its oil fields. In 1956 we collaborated with the Soviet Union in quelling a British, French, and Israeli attempt to secure power in the area, meantime keeping foreign oil out of the United States through a quota system, thereby using up our own diminishing reserves. In 1970 Libya both kicked the United States off its airfields and raised the price of crude oil. We complied with little question. Matters simply followed their natural course from that point on.

But did the Arabs really do it to us? Frankly, I doubt it. We have a profligate society—living a profligate life in our consumption, travel, expectations, and debt. And we have been borrowing, and spending, and borrowing. Even the most "stable" of our financial institutions, the banks, have been joining the "credit society," borrowing heavily themselves, spreading into other areas, speculating in foreign currency, soliciting debtors, and, in general, overextending their resources. Since 1967 loans from banks have grown far faster than bank deposits, the banks themselves relying more heavily than ever on borrowed money. Over 6,000 banks failed in the 1930s. Was the failure of Franklin National (the twentieth-largest in the country) a harbinger of events to come? (In 1967 the average bank had only 65 cents in loans outstanding for each $1 of deposits. By mid-1974 the figure had jumped to 75 cents. In 1967 the average bank showed its own borrowed money at the rate of 2 percent of assets; by 1974 the rates had grown to 12 percent. Some banks, of course, show far worse ratios.)

Nor can banks alone be cited for upping their leverage—the attempt to use borrowed money to produce profit. The entire American corporate structure has been weakened over the years by an ever increasing reliance on borrowing rather than equity financing—creating a huge mountain of corporate debt, interest charges, and the danger of a massive domino fallout. All this, of course, the result of declining productivity, high labor costs, shortages of raw materials, international involvement, government spending, and lower profit margins, even as earnings deceptively continued to rise.*

The final outcome: A national economy top-heavy with debt, built upon continuing consumption of raw materials from producer nations, as always tied tightly to automobile sales (as GM goes . . .), and just ripe for any event or series of events to tip the scales. Did the Arabs really do it to us? Or were the seeds firmly implanted years ago, the coming depression truly presaged by the real top in stock market prices in 1968? (The Dow made a new high in 1973, but the average stock peaked in price fours years earlier.) In any event, the time has come to pay the piper.

The purpose of this book is not to philosophize regarding the sequence of events that have led us to the brink, but rather to chart a course of action during the years ahead. I refer those interested in pursuing further the question of how we got here to *The Failure of the New Economics* by Henry Hazlitt (1959) and *America's Coming Bankruptcy* by Harvey W. Peters (1973), both published by Arlington House, Westport, Connecticut, and to *The Conspiracy Against the Dollar* by Peter Beter (1973), George Braziller, New York.

The Eleven Early Warning Signs of a Coming Depression

Forwarned is forearmed. As I said before, we just may squeeze through this time. I hope so; this is one time I'd rather be wrong than

---

*Business Week (October 12, 1974), in a special issue on "The Debt Economy," pointed up some grisly statistics—all illustrating the mountain of debt under which our major corporations are laboring. As of June 1974, 23% of the companies surveyed carried more debt than equity, an increase of 24% over the previous decade. Some typical examples: Zenith Radio debt-equity ratio is running more than 2,000% higher than its 10-year average. McCrory's debt-equity ratio is up by 327%; A&P's, 297%.

The huge amount of debt involved is now making it difficult for corporations to generate the funds necessary to meet interest expenses. As of June 1974, 71% of the companies surveyed had interest coverage ratios below 10, up from 38% the decade previous. Nearly twice as many companies had coverage under 5 as compared to the previous decade. Most hard hit: the airline and utility industries.

A study of total asset-liability ratios of the companies surveyed showed widespread (but not unanimous) deterioration in balance sheets. The whole mess, of course, has been compounded by heavy government borrowing, which soaks up funds otherwise available to private borrowers. Five government agencies alone, the Import-Export Bank, FHA, GNMA, Postal Service, and TVA owed, in total, more than $20 billion by mid-1974. (The Treasury announced in early 1975 that it would be forced to borrow $80 billion during the current fiscal year alone.)

right. But even if we do make it in '81, even if the upturn the sunshine boys call for does come to pass, there will be a depression sooner or later. Here are some of the early warning signs.

1. *Speculation in the Equity Markets Becomes Rampant, Spreading into More Exotic Forms of Investment.*

Examples? How about the equity binge that took place in '29 and again in '67–68? The sure kiss of death is active public participation—every cab driver, elevator operator, and housewife is talking stock. Otherwise sane businessmen plunk down thousands on tips. Men leave well-established careers to become stock brokers. Advisory services proliferate like rabbits.

The Dow is widely projected to unheard-of levels. (Even James Dines, now a prophet of doom, predicted Dow at 1500 near the top of the last bull market.)

As a corollary, with stock market profits in abundance, prices of real estate co-ops, condominiums, art, antiques, coins rise—anything that's a symbol of status and success, rationalized by the promise of a quick buck by way of capital gain. For example, wine soared in the early seventies to intoxicating heights following an art boom in low-class art a few years earlier.

No need to go into further details. When you hear nothing but get-rich schemes—prepare for the worst.

2. *Everyone's Convinced that Prosperity Will Last Forever.*

Optimism runs rampant—personified by rising installment debt, heavy consumer buying, bigger and faster automobiles, demand for consumer exotica, travel, home improvements—a general attitude that next year will be better than this year and the year after even better than that.

Such an attitude prevailed during the twenties following the war to end all wars, and again during the postwar period into the early seventies.

3. *Labor Becomes Difficult to Secure and Discipline.*

Unemployment is low, and it becomes a seller's market in labor. Workers job-hop with impunity, and worker production diminishes. Jobs are treated lightly by employees; employers have to offer "extras" to attract workers. Labor demands rise; job security is regarded as a minimal consideration in accepting employment.

4. *Inflation Begins to Get Out of Hand.*

Every postwar period has had a period of inflation, gradually rising to a crescendo, followed by deflation and recession. It happened following the War of 1912, the Civil War (Panic of '73), World War I, World War

II, the Korean War, and after Vietnam. We experienced a sharp, but short-lived, deflation in 1921, a dress rehearsal as it turned out, for the real crack later in the decade.

Need we say anything about the inflationary spiral of 1973–74, or of its breaking down into a deflationary spiral? With deflation comes inventory liquidation, plant shutdowns, recession—and perhaps depression.

5. *Stocks Stop Rising on Good News.*

The best example is 1973. The Dow collapsed even as record earnings reports were chattering over the ticker tape, head-in-the-sand forecasters announcing that no market decline could possibly take place in the face of such glorious profits. (I personally sold almost all my equity holdings during January and February 1973, moving my cash into income-producing securities, and hedged positions.)

A similar situation pertained during 1929. Earnings for the Dow Industrials rose by 25 percent as compared to 1928, which itself saw a gain of 126 percent over 1927. Perpetual prosperity? Well, 1930 saw a drop of 45 percent; 1931, 63 percent; and 1932, a loss of 100 percent. (The Dow Industrials showed an aggregate loss that year.)

6. *Everyone's Looking for a Quick Buck; Steady Income Is Considered Stodgy.*

Remember the go-go funds of '67–68? Your broker scoffing at income stocks, the cult of performance, and the Amex doubler? Anytime yields on the Dow Industrials drop to roughly 3 percent, watch out. (Data available each week in *Barron's Financial Weekly*.)

7. *Lead Economic Indicators Begin to Falter.*

The stock market is one, usually topping out before the economic cancer is detected (not always, however—1962 was a false alarm). Orders for machine tools slacken. Interest rates begin to rise sharply. Unemployment begins to rise. Retail sales flatten out. Housing starts decline.

8. *The Odds Are Likely that Trouble Will Crystallize Immediately Following a Presidential Election.*

Politicians are no fools. The party in power does anything it can to pump up the economy, to maintain the illusion of prosperity, to keep the voters happy. Election years are typically favorable years for investors; postelection years are, on balance, disasters. The depression of 1929 began the year after an election year. The significant declines during 1965 followed a Presidential election year. The crash of '69–70 followed a Presidential election year. And, of course, the bear market of 1973 practically started at New Year's following a Presidential election.

Which is why I say watch out for 1981. (Readers are referred to *The Stock Trader's Almanac* by Yale Hirsch, The Hirsch Organization, 6 Deer Trail, Old Tappan, N.J. 07650, for further information regarding seasonal indicators and the economy.)

9. *The Depression Will Start from a Cyclical Peak.*

Great events seem to occur in nature, history, and economics at regular intervals of time. Bull markets have ended at four to five-year intervals (1957, 1961, early 1966, late 1968, early 1973). Wars, revolutions, famines —all seem to occur at regular time intervals.

The Russian Nikolai D. Kondratieff, a professor, postulated in the 1920s a fifty-two year-long wave that has seemed to recur since the end of the eighteenth century. James B. Shuman and David R. Rosenau have examined the wave to determine its applicability to the United States. The outcome of their labors were presented in a fascinating book, *The Kondratieff Wave* (World, 1973).

In brief, the Kondratieff Wave is still very much alive, its impacts very much in force—and it calls for deep trouble within the *coming few years.*

The wave itself is approximately fifty-two years in length, measured from peak to peak or from trough to trough. Peak periods are marked by rising prices, prosperity, liberal political outlooks, slowly rising tensions (the have-nots want theirs), and inflation. Peaks are marked by strikes, riots, and wars. The Civil War, World War I, and the Vietnam War developed just following peak periods.

Following the peak, the national mood shifts to conservatism and calm, the precursors of the economic depression to follow. The authors see past peaks occurring in 1918–19, 1970–71—the next peak due in 1996 or thereabouts. In between we have had troughs, the last in the 1930s, the next due in the early 1980s, perhaps ending by 1983.

Interestingly, the nation psychologically now appears to be at the postpeak stage described by Shuman and Rosenau. Following the tempestuous years of 1968–70 (remember Kent State, college demonstrations, *Hair,* peace marches, race riots, LSD, and the Democratic convention of '68, complete with the Chicago riot?) we appear to have lapsed into a return to conservatism—shorter haircuts, peace on campuses, conservatives elected to office (Watergate notwithstanding), a diminution in drug abuse, relative racial calm. In fact, *The New York Times* recently reported an epidemic of neurotic symptoms in college students because of an *excessive concern with grades.* Five years ago the issue of neuroses on campus revolved around symptoms caused by the use of hallucinogenic drugs.

Lest you be reassured by the apparent return to normalcy, remember that this is just the calm before the storm.

Business Week (November 30, 1974) reported that Gilbert Hass, one of the most successful investment counselors and another student of the Kondratieff Wave, believes that the wave indicates an imminent series of two troughs, the first similar to the dip in 1921, the second similar to the crash of the 1930 period: "The potential exists for a financial crisis of greater proportions than has ever occurred before." (In the same issue of *Business Week* was an article self-descriptively entitled "The Coming Dividend Crisis.")

Another student of cycles, George Lindsay, presented a historical theory based upon time at a meeting of the Society for the Investigation of Recurring Events on October 10, 1974. In his discussion Mr. Lindsay presented evidence that the Soviet Union will be at the peak of its power between 1981 and 1989 (a nation's "magic years" occur between sixty-four and seventy-one years after a major internal revolution). He foresees aggressive action on the part of the Soviets during this time, relative impotence at our end. The magic years for the United States, incidentally, occurred between 1839 and 1846, the period that ushered in the Mexican War and our annexation of the western portion of our nation. Can our economy sustain itself against a hostile and powerful Soviet Russia, cyclically at the peak of its own power?

10. *The Depression Will Develop Following a Period of Moral Turpitude.*
And recently? For better or for worse, the condition of our accepted morality has been undergoing a radical change. Divorce is on the rise, almost chic in many circles; virginity is now taboo among young females.

11. *The European Economies Will Begin to Falter.*
In an era of intertwined economies, monetary systems, and trade the United States economy is inexorably tied to the economies of Western Europe. However, ours is basically sounder, our nation more self-sufficient in natural resources. Therefore, when worldwide depression threatens, the signs will show up first in Europe.

Britain's stock market has led our own down, during the crash of '29 and during the crash of 1973. Europe's economies, particularly in Britain and Italy, become true disaster areas months before the recession seriously hit our shores. Coverage of European markets exists in any number of financial newspapers: *The Wall Street Journal* and *Barron's Financial Weekly*, for example.

The Economic Peak Will Take Place During a Period of Liberalized Moral Codes

Ira U. Coleigh (*Happiness is a Stock That Doubles in a Year*, Bernard Geis Associates, 1968) underlined an oft-cited observation—there appears to be a definite correlation between rising hemlines and prosperity, falling hemlines and declining stock markets. Hemlines were high in 1927, very low in the 1930s. Coleigh, however, treats the matter lightly, referring to "romantic enthusiasms," "confidence," and "wolfish ogling."

It would appear that a more significant connection does exist between rising hemlines, standards of morality, sexual permissiveness, and the economy. During times of plenty, the mass psychology takes an Epicurean turn, public interest centering upon consumption, free sexuality, drugs to spice jaded appetites and away from standard convention and the work ethic. Waves of sensual excesses marked peaks in the Roman, Grecian, and French aristocracies. Is it significant that the twenties ushered in the speakeasy, bootlegging, campus hijinks and—as a mark of a new sexual freedom—the rising hemline? Is it simply coincidence that the '70s saw the proliferation of X-rated movies, topless waitresses, wife-swapping, publicly advertised prostitution, and coed dormitories? Perhaps. But then again, perhaps not.

Which is why that headline regarding the lagging pornography fight just might mean something after all.

Have the above conditions already been met? Just review events of recent years and decide for yourself. And while you're at it, consider the effects of the developing realignment of economic power from consuming countries to the countries that own and produce the world's natural resources. Look at the growing depletion of our own natural reserves and the reserves of our total planet. Can we continue to consume the earth's resources as we have, or will basic alterations have to take place in the entire standard of living of industrialized civilization? And if so, what chaos will be wrought, what economic upheaval, during the period of transition? It does make you think, doesn't it?

I said it at the beginning of this book and I'll say it again. I'm not an economist, but I do believe I know trouble when I see it.

2
A BROAD BLUEPRINT FOR SURVIVAL: THE MASTER PLAN

I certainly do hope that you don't consider me a pessimist by now. Believe me, I'm not. I do see some hope that we will manage to muddle through with nothing more than a serious recession in the cards. And I do believe that we might even be able to ride out a depression with our social order intact.

For true pessimism read C. V. Myers, who forecasts a fascist state arising from the phoenix of economic chaos. Try Harry Browne, who predicts riots, mass looting, and crime, and who tells his listeners to find an isolated country retreat, stocked with canned food, powdered milk, and well-oiled shotguns. Or heed Franz Pick, who likewise anticipates rioting in the streets, or—well, you probably get the point by now.

I do believe that our social systems will manage to survive, as they did in the thirties, until the economic upturn finally develops. And I do believe that *you* should be making plans to maneuver within the existing social system, both during the depression and after. And that, I believe, is not pessimistic.

If you believe otherwise—well, just forget the rest of this book. Your best investment will lie in a brace of carbines and some shooting lessons.

Presuming that Armageddon does *not* arrive, that the United States, democracy, and capitalism do survive—what now? THERE *ARE* STEPS YOU CAN TAKE TO SURVIVE AND EVEN TO PROSPER DURING THE COMING DEPRESSION! Which brings us to our "master plan," and to its basic survival rules.

Master Plan Rule #1: When You See the Depression Coming, Get into Cash or into Cash Equivalents Immediately!

Do not stop for "Go." Do not hesitate (all you can lose are some last-gasp profits). Do not procrastinate. Become as liquid as possible as quickly as possible. When the depression hits, there will be no buyers for your real estate, no suckers for your stock, no dealers for your antiques, no spendthrifts for your stamps, no imbibers for your wine, no collectors for your coins. If you need cash, you will practically have to give away your investments, and, even if you do manage to hold on, you may have to wait years for a full price recovery. What's more, you won't be profiting by the depression—you'll be perspiring through every miserable moment of it. Nor will you have the cash to snatch up the bargains that will prevail as less prudent folk are forced to dump stocks at bargain prices to meet margin calls, real estate at distressed levels, art, coins at below normal wholesale, wine at Coca Cola prices (and considering the price of sugar not long ago, that may come sooner than we think).

During a depression the man with cash is king! Out of the stock market, you can observe the crash with equanimity, from a safe distance, ready and *able* to step in when the time comes. Out of real estate —let somebody else worry about foreclosure. *You* will have the cash around at foreclosure auctions. I know a number of people *who had the cash* who were able to pick up real estate for a song, dirt cheap, during the thirties, who made lifelong fortunes and futures from the calamity of the times. Others snatched up GM, AT&T, and RCA at depression prices, making their futures in the years ahead. But, again, you must have the cash—otherwise, forget it.

Nor can you safely ride out the depression with the majority of existing investments. A few safe ones do exist, and we'll be seeing what *those* are. Some cases in point? The stock market began to crumble in earnest during January 1973, though its actual demise began years earlier. By October 1974, measured from the 1968 peaks, the average stock had lost more than 70 percent of its value! (From 1929 through 1932 the average stock declined by 89 percent.) Obviously, the market is no place to be during a crash.

Fine Arts? Antiques? No better—just that the collapse takes longer. The stock market is highly liquid, trading takes place daily, communication is nearly immediate—and stocks are readily associated with economic processes. Art and antiques are a bit further removed. Prime customers, the museums and the very wealthy, are hit last by depressions. Prices of fine art, antiques, autographs, and the rest of the ultrachic collector scene, continued merrily upward during a good portion of 1973, though some rumblings were felt at certain European auctions that year. (I take some pride in having pointed out the vulnerability of art prices in various places at that time—for example, refer to my book *Double Your Money Every Three Years*, 1974, published by Windsor and distributed by Arlington.) However, the bottom really fell out of those markets in mid-1974, the collapse marked by disastrous auctions at Christie's and Sotheby Parke Bernet. No, art is no haven, and, what's more, just try to sell during a depression.

Real estate? Possibly the worst. Stocks may be bad, but at least you *can* sell once you see the handwriting on the wall. You may have to give the art away, but there just might be a flush dealer around, ready to accumulate if the price is right. Under adverse conditions real estate may simply be impossible to sell at almost any price—even as its value erodes.

We don't have to belabor the point. Depression is a vortex that sucks virtually everything down into it, some things sooner, some later. And once the suction is apparent to all, it's too late to escape the quicksand.

Remember, it's far, far better to get into cash too early than too late.

Rule #2: Place At Least Some of Your Cash into Investments That Will Produce Considerable Profit Even During Depressions

We'll be getting into specific examples later on, and you yourself may prefer a more conservative approach. Nonetheless, there are means of investing—yes, even during depressions—that will not only preserve your capital BUT THAT WILL MULTIPLY IT, providing you with even more cash when THE BOTTOM FINALLY DOES ARRIVE.

For instance, did you know that you can make money twice as fast in a falling stock market than in a rising one? That certain realty ploys are probably safe enough, even during depression? That you can benefit from the weakness in the economies of other nations?

All true—and all will be discussed as we proceed.

As I said, you may prefer to concentrate on survival, content just to protect yourself. If so, fine, But other alternatives do exist.

Rule #3: Learn to Recognize the Turning Points, and Then Change Course Quickly

Depressions do not last forever, and, when the turn comes, part with that cash quickly. At economic highs, your neighbors won't want cash —they'll want your stocks, your art, your realty, your stamps. Prices have been rising, inflation's been heavy, and they'll be clamoring for "inflation hedges." Wine ran in price through 1973; buyers were looking for more, willing to part with dollars. Swell, you gave them your grapes and took the dollars. In 1974 wine prices simply collapsed.

At economic troughs things appear evil, terrible, hopeless—your neighbors will need and clamor for dollars. Swell. Let them have yours. You take back their art, realty, stocks, and stamps. Comes the next high point, you just sell those items back once again.

We'll also be discussing precisely which investments grow in value the fastest during rising economies, which are more conservative (just in case you guess wrong), and which can be safely entered into during periods of economic transition, before the evidence is clear that the depression has, indeed, ended. You will have plenty of choice.

About The Structure of This Book

We come neither to praise the economy nor to bury it. Our aim is to show you how to profit, during depression and during periods of strong economic growth as well. Subsequent chapters will cover specific investment media, those suited for depressions, those not, those suited for the turning point, those not. Each investment will be graded for its viability as a vehicle during depressions. You'll see quickly enough what to consider, which to avoid, and when. In addition, we'll consider various miscellany—tax tips, ways of making one dollar do the work of two, ways of conserving and making cash in various assorted fashions, where you can obtain further information in areas of special interest.

In short, we'll be more than trying to take care of our side of the bargain, but in the end what you do *is* up to you. We can only suggest. When the time comes, will you be ready to act?

One Sure Way to Make Extra Dollars: A Strategy for Any Economic Season

Here's a quick one, just for starters—LEARN TO MAKE THE MOST OF YOUR INSURANCE POLICY!

The majority of straight life insurance policies in effect today offer the holder the option of borrowing an amount, virtually equivalent to the full accumulated cash value of the policy at extremely moderate interest costs (in many cases at a true 5 percent rate). By comparison you'll be paying closer to 10 percent (on a true basis) for an auto loan, 18 percent on your Master Card, and more than 12 percent on your revolving checking overdraft privileges. Should you need money quickly, say, to finance your auto, why not borrow from your insurance company instead of going through your normal credit channels? Instead of making payments to the bank, regularly place an amount equivalent to your monthly payments in your savings account (drawing 5 percent interest or better). When you have accumulated the amount owed, simply pay off the loan. The interest savings can be considerable. The main point: stay disciplined in making these payments to yourself.

Another tactic: The odds are that on a long-term basis you can safely secure returns from capital well in excess of those 5 percent insurance loan carrying charges. For example, U.S. Treasury bonds, the ultimate in financial safety, were yielding as high as 9 percent (and more) at certain points during 1974, though by the end of the year, yields were down to below 8 percent. Other government agency bonds, second in safety only to Treasury issues, were yielding roughly one percent higher.

Suppose that over the years you continue to borrow out the cash value of your life insurance policy at 5 percent, investing these proceeds for a *safe* 8 percent return. (You will *not* want to speculate with insurance dollars set aside for retirement.) Each year you will net 3 percent, which, in turn, will be compounding for you. You will be liable, of course, for taxes on the returns you secure from your investments, but you will receive a tax deduction for the interest you pay on your loan from the insurance company (so long as you do *not* invest the money in tax-exempt securities like municipal bonds).

Sounds small? Consider this. Depending on your age at inception, a typical $25,000 whole life policy creates approximately $400 each year in new cash value. At the twenty-fifth year that amounts to a total cash value of $10,000. If you borrow that at 5 percent (cost of interest, $500) and invest at 8 percent (proceeds, $800), your free ride, or net gain, amounts to $300, or roughly twenty times the cost of this book—and that's during one single year alone! Set up such a program on a systematic basis, and *you can add thousands of dollars to the cash value of your life insurance policy* during the life of your holding—at no extra risk or cost whatsoever (unless, of course, you consider Hartford safer than the U.S. Treasury).

You must remember, however, not to borrow more than three of the first seven years you hold the policy. If you do, you lose the tax deduction created by the interest you pay on the loan.

How the Public Media Can Help You Time Your Investments

No, don't throw away the mail order ads—and do not pass your newsstand without a second glance. If you do, you'll be ignoring one of the best general timing tools available.

How does it work? Simple. A large proportion of financial journals and magazines relating to investment and general business advice are published by firms and edited by men who themselves are only moderately knowledgeable regarding investment. Add to these the publishers, who are sophisticated financially but still dependent upon unsophisticated reader interest to sell subscriptions. Result: *publications that follow the crowd rather than lead it.*

Magazines, newspapers, periodic market letters—all generally reflect reader interest rather than create it. As a result, they write up investments only *after* the public has begun to catch on, frequently in response to reader inquiry. And when has the public caught on? Why, *after* the investment has already advanced sharply in value, of course, usually just prior to a strong correction to the overpricing that has already taken place. Nor has this lesson been lost on savvy publishers, one of whom recently confided to me that he plans to issue a series of books on how to profit from rising stock markets. When? Why, at the top of the next bull market, naturally, when the public is most involved in securities. This rule of thumb holds for any and all investments—art, antiques, securities, gold. When your mailbox becomes jammed with advertisements detailing profit potential in the area, when widely circulated magazines promote the stuff, when *Barron's*, *The Wall Street Journal*, and *The New York Times* are unanimous, YOU GO THE OTHER WAY.

Examples? In early 1973 a panel interviewed by *Barron's* cheerfully and unanimously predicted a bull market: target, Dow 1200. *The New York Times* advertising, at the same time, was preempted by bullish stock advisories. In mid-1974, the heyday of the money funds, public seminars were offered to tell attendees how to start their own money fund. Gold has been headlined at every peak. Whisky promotion, soused up until the '60's, created a whisky glut, and wine was ballyhooed until early '74 turned up some sour grapes. In short, again, mistrust any investment that is being widely touted; go your own lonely way and let the crowd follow *you*.

3
DIAMONDS: THE ULTIMATE DOOMSDAY INVESTMENT?

Well, certainly not the most profitable. Diamonds, good years and bad, have shown only a moderate growth in value—a rate of appreciation roughly one or two percentage points above the rate of inflation. A depression hedge? Doubtful. Diamonds are a purely discretionary item, hardly the first port of call on any depression shopping trip. But a doomsday investment? Now this is quite another matter altogether.

Assuming for once that the gloomiest of doom does come to pass —rioting, looting, burning, revolution—have you ever considered just how you will cart your gold bullion, with whom you would place your buy orders, and with what you will protect your real estate? Silver coins? Will you really have the time to load those canvas sacks for the pilgrimage to your country retreat? Emigration—a retreat from the mobs, political "isms," depression? What will you take with you?

History does, in the end, teach us something. Countless refugees survived World War II because of one possession—valuable, small, readily smuggled, and easily bartered diamonds! No, you can't take stocks, buildings, gold (except in small amounts), art, and antiques with you—but you can take diamonds! Ask any number of refugees who did, and ask any number of border guards. And, what's more, what holds international value; whose price is, in fact, set by one international cartel? Well, your Mexican landlord—if that's where you should happen to land—may not understand the value of those General Motors shares left back home with Merrill-Lynch (assuming that One Liberty Plaza does survive the holocaust), but the local jeweler in Mexico City *will* understand those gems you pull from your shoe heel.

As I said, diamonds are the ultimate doomsday investment. A few stones are not likely to hurt very much, at the worst—and, at the least, they may just save your life some day.

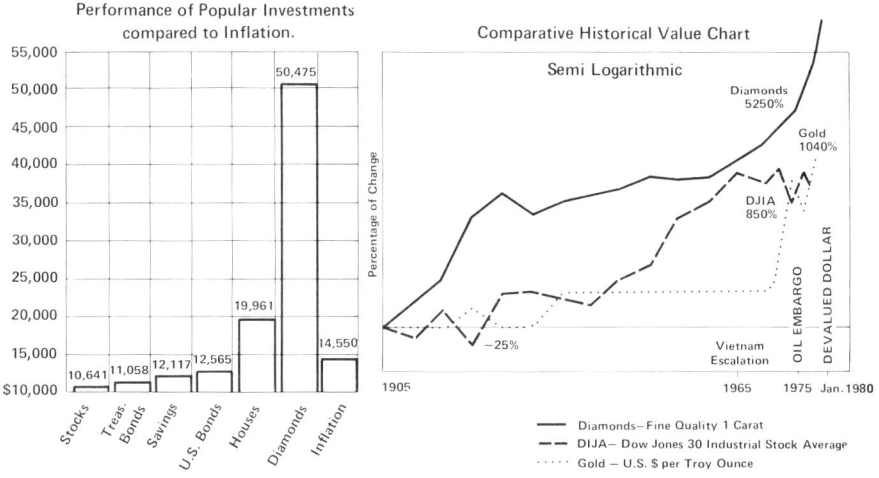

FIGURE 1
The bar chart shows the relative performance of $10,000 invested in diamonds, 1972–76. Similar trends have persisted. The chart on the right shows the price movement of diamonds, 1905–80. Larger stones generally show superior price appreciation in comparision with smaller stones.   Adopted from *U.S. News & World Report.*

The International Diamond Cartel

If you think the Arabs have a good thing going, take a look at a real cartel, De Beers Consolidated Mines Ltd., an outfit that staked a claim to nearly all the world production of diamonds roughly half a century ago, long before we associated sheiks with anything but camels, sand, and harems. Even better, De Beers maintains to this day the tightest of controls over diamond production and consumption, which does ensure that if you won't necessarily become rich, at least you're not likely to go bankrupt on your doomsday insurance.

Roughly 85 percent of the world's uncut diamond distribution is controlled by De Beers, by way of its subsidiary selling arm, the Central Selling Organization. The CSO, in turn, distributes stones to roughly 250-270 clients throughout the world, from whom the gems filter out. De Beers is in virtual total control of international diamond pricing! De Beers decides how many diamonds will enter the market, and at what price—there is no bargaining between buyer and seller—and so far no organization of buyers challenges the corporate giant (although the Soviet Union is invading the market more heavily lately). If demand slackens, De Beers simply cuts the flow, reducing supply, maintaining the price. When demand peaks, greater quantities of diamonds are released. In this way pricing of diamonds has been maintained at relatively stable levels, with an upward bias.

For example, retail prices of fine-quality, round-cut diamonds appreciated at roughly a 5 percent compound annual rate between 1940 and 1970, the larger stones gaining somewhat more in recent years than the smaller. Exciting? Obviously not, but then again when did you last make a fortune on your insurance policy? On the other hand, that 5 percent growth rate *did*, after all, beat inflation—and this was a period, for the most part, when banks were *not* paying 5 percent. In 1973 De Beers really went wild. Diamond prices jumped by some 70 percent, and by another 50 percent going to 1974, before a price correction set in. Why the rise? Probably because of the general headlong flight during that period from the stock market and from cash; 1973 was the year that truly ushered in inflation—everything and anything served as an inflation hedge. I do not anticipate rates of return in the order of 70 percent a year in the future, nor even 50 percent for the matter. I do, however, anticipate that fine-quality diamonds will continue to appreciate at a rate exceeding the cost of living in the years to come, particularly the finer, larger stones.

Caveats

Diamonds pay no dividends, no interest, and you will not want your diamonds to undergo a stock split. You will be liable for costs for insurance and storage, brokerage or auctioneering expenses (when you sell), transport, appraisal, and shopping expenses. In addition, you must allow for the handicap created by the differential spread, buying and selling, probably in the area of 5 percent or so, depending upon the size of your investment (more on this below). In short, if you do decide to enter the diamond game, expect to exercise some patience—only the diamond professional can hope to make money short-term on gems. The typical diamond investor must plan for a two to four-year holding period at the least, just to break even.

Where and How to Buy

One of the major drawbacks to smaller-scale diamond dealing is the inability to buy and sell at the going professional rate. By and large, you must anticipate purchasing at retail levels, more or less; selling at wholesale. If your tastes run to Tiffany's, you'll be in for a 30 percent markup *at the least* unless you truly purchase in quantity. Small stones generally command a markup of roughly 100 percent, wholesale to retail. If you purchase, say, $10,000 worth of diamonds at a clip, you'll probably have to pay a 60 percent markup. Real quantity, on the other hand, can be secured reasonably—at a markup of, say, 5 to 10 percent. It may even be possible to purchase from one of those 250 De Beers diamontaires, in which case $250,000 or so will net you a box of assorted rough-cut stones.

Diamond Brokers

If you're not large enough to go to De Beers, and leery of paying retail at Cartier's, you might consider playing your hand with a diamond broker who, for a fee, will secure diamonds for you at prices reasonably close to trade wholesale, and who also will act as your agent at sales time.

Possibly the best known of such brokers is Harry Gaunt, president of Investment Diamonds Incorporated, 121 West Charles Street, Muncie, Indiana 47305. He has offered, in the past, to take collect calls at 317-289-2329. Investment Diamonds has been organizing sales seminars around the country in which they claim to sell, below local jeweler wholesale, items they will select for you as part of an investment program. The firm charges a 6 percent commission for buying *and* for selling, and moreover, there is no guarantee that they'll be able to resell your stones. The minimum investment unit is $800, and for that you will receive something under a first-quality carat.

The firm appears to offer at least fair diamond value for the money, though they do seem to emphasize only medium-grade merchandise. However, you have ten full days following purchase to secure an independent appraisal, with full refund privileges, so the risk of getting badly stung does seem limited providing that you take all pertinent precautions.

La Jolla Diamond, Inc., 7911 Herschel Avenue, Suite 206, La Jolla, California 92037, will also act as a diamond broker on your behalf. La Jolla will sell diamonds as small as one-half carat for investment purposes, although it recommends somewhat larger stones for this purpose. For further information investors may contact Gary Hauser at 714-454-8806.

Kohinoor International Ltd., One Lincoln Plaza, Suite 42K, New York, N.Y. 10023 (212-595-6282), apparently deals in a better grade of stone—at least they require a higher minimum investment, $5,000 in this case. Commissions are 5 percent to buy and to sell; the firm states that they buy directly from a member of the De Beers syndicate, thereby saving customers wholesale, jobber, and retail markups. Investors receive cut, polished, and graded stones—certified by the Gemological Institute of America. Kohinoor also grants an appraisal period, limited however, to five business days. David Rosental, the president, suggests that investors concentrate on the best-quality stones they can afford, even if the purchase must thereby be limited to a single stone. Some experts suggest the accumulation of collections.

Other sources of diamonds include private sale (best if you know what to look for), auction houses such as Sotheby Parke Bernet in New York (the real big leagues), and diamond centers throughout the country, particularly the area in New York City centering around 47th Street near the Avenue of the Americas. Do be aware, however, that the basic rule at such markets is "caveat emptor"—they will not be giving anything away. However, if you do know stones and do enjoy a hard haggle, you might just catch a merchant at a time when he's desperate for ready cash. While the diamond center is strictly a trader's market, you can trust operations such as Tiffany's and Cartier's, a few blocks north, where, while you may not get bottom dollar, you can be sure of the quality claimed.

How to Sell

Major diamond merchants are generally willing to purchase quality stones—again, try Cartier's—but they will offer you a price of roughly 40-60 percent of retail value. The diamond brokers will, of course, be glad to handle resale (for a comission). You can try, yourself, to sell privately or, if your collection warrants, at auction. Auctioneering fees run at roughly 20 percent of auction proceeds. You will find stones of some quality easier to sell than inferior stones. THIS IS THE BASIC RULE OF ALL COLLECTING-INVESTING: STICK WITH QUALITY. If you plan to dispose of your holdings through dealers, secure competitive bids and stage more than a perfunctory negotiation —this, again, is a market for traders.

CUT

A well-cut diamond has 58 facets in the correct proportions.

 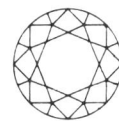 

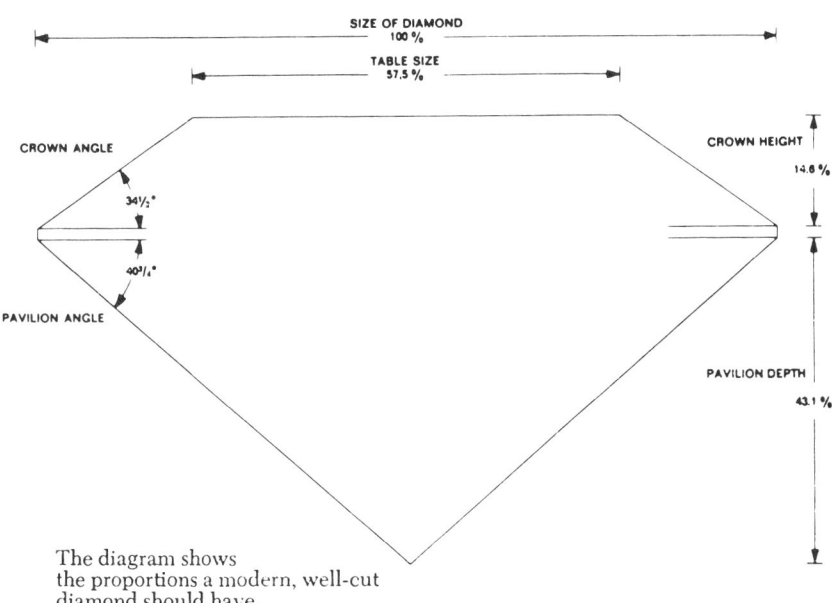

The diagram shows the proportions a modern, well-cut diamond should have.

FIGURE 2
The diagram shows the proportions a modern, well-cut diamond should have.
SOURCE: De Beers Diamond Investment Ltd.

Appraisal Tips

Diamonds are graded by color, clarity, cut, and weight (in carats), and their value is determined by the merits of the total package. The ideal diamond is "blue-white" in color, virtually transparent, a color seen in less than 1 percent of all stones. The poorest diamonds have a distinctly yellowish cast. Colors are classified into 23 grades by the Gemological Institute of America, grades ranging from D to Z. D, E, and F are the best, colorless. Z is the worst, distinctly yellow.

The ideal stone should be free of all blemishes, flaws, or specks—diamonds of ideal clarity will not be so marred. Retailers are prone to advertise diamonds as "flawless," despite the presence of flaws and despite FTC regulations limiting such claims to diamonds that show no blemishes whatsoever under 10x magnification. Clarity is classified into ten grades, ranging from the flawless through imperfect. Diamonds that show flaws to the naked eye will probably lie in the "imperfect" grade. If you require a magnifier to see specks, then the stone is likely rate a "slightly imperfect" grade.

POPULAR DIAMOND SHAPES

Brilliant—the round diamond that is a favorite in engagement rings. In tiny sizes, and with only 16 facets, this shape is called a single cut and is used as a side stone in rings.

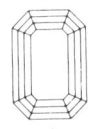
Emerald cut—so called because emeralds are often cut this way, rectangular or square, with facets polished diagonally across the corners.

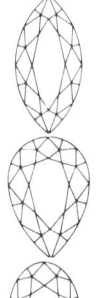
Marquise—a pointed boat shape, usually long and narrow. In a ring, it tends to make the fingers look slim. This shape costs slightly more than a brilliant of the same size and quality because of additional labor in cutting.

Pear shape—popular in rings and often used in pendants. The world's largest cut diamond, Cullinan I, mounted in the British Royal Sceptre, is a pear shape.

Oval—an adaption of the brilliant shape. The marquise, pear shape, and oval all appear to be larger than a brilliant of the same carat weight.

Baguette, meaning "little stick"—a small diamond used as a side stone in rings.

FIGURE 3
SOURCE: De Beers Diamond Investment Ltd.

Cuts vary according to style, fashion, and preference. The most "brilliant" cut was calculated roughly half a century ago, but the majority of diamonds represent, in cut, a compromise between brilliance and the saving of wastage caused by shaving to the ideal. Round stones and pear shaped occasionally achieve popularity, but are not as readily disposed of as the more typically cut stones.

Diamonds, of course, are sold by weight or carat, each carat divided into 100 points. Size alone only partially determines the value of the stones. Depending upon cut, clarity, and color, a one-carat gem can go for anywhere from $200 (at your local pawnshop) to $7,000 (and wholesale at that). Forget the cheap goods for investment purposes—seek out the truly flawless stone. And watch out for "paste," imitation diamonds, particularly the "YAG" or ythrium aluminum garnets, nearly as hard as the real thing and, when clean, nearly as brilliant. No need to worry, however, if you purchase through reliable channels. And keep in mind that the larger the stone, the more scarce a flawless example. Therefore, a two-carat flawless will sell for more than twice the price of a one-carat flawless, a four-carat for far more than double the price of a two.

FAMOUS DIAMONDS

There are more than 350 "name" diamonds, famous for their histories. These ten are among the national treasuries of seven different countries:

Table I

Name	Carats	Color	On Display at
Cullinan I	530.20	White	Tower of London
Cullinan II	317.40	White	Tower of London
Darya-i-nur	186.00	Pink	Iranian Treasury
Dresden Green	41.00	Green	Dresden Museum
Hope	44.50	Blue	Smithsonian Inst.
Hortensia	20.00	Peach	The Louvre
Koh-i-noor	108.93	White	Tower of London
Orloff	199.60	White	The Kremlin
Regent	140.50	White	The Louvre
Spoonmaker's	84.00	White	Topkapi Museum

SOURCE: De Beers Diamond Investment Ltd.

Appraisal

Unless you're personally expert with the loupe, you will want to have your diamond appraised *prior* to taking permanent possession. Be certain that your appraisor understands your purpose; diamond appraisals frequently are rendered high for insurance purposes.

If nothing but the best in appraisals will do, have the stones graded by the Gemological Institute of America (offices at 11940 San Vicente Blvd., Los Angeles, California, and 580 Fifth Avenue, New York City). The Institute's grading standards and credentials are accepted throughout the free world, from Mexico City (just in case, again) to New York. The cost of receiving a full grading is moderate. Incidentally, in case you wish to develop into one of the cognoscenti of carats yourself, the Institute offers a correspondence course.

4
FROM TREASURY BILLS TO MUNICIPALS: AT LEAST YOU'LL BE AS SAFE AS THE GOVERNMENT

Diamonds, an extra tankful of gas, some cans of food and water, a fast small boat or plane—that's about the total doomsday protection we can muster for now. So suppose we ease up on disaster for the time being? We'll still figure on the depression, if not right away, perhaps by the end of the decade. But this time around, let's assume that the government does hold, sadder but perhaps a little wiser after generations of waste and profligate spending. We'll also assume that our social institutions remain more or less intact, that the government does *not* confiscate wealth, deciding instead to reward the prudent for once instead of the puerile.

Given this set of conditions, and given our first tent of depression survival—preservation of capital—what's probably your best bet? How about government securities, ranging from the most secure to the least? If inclined, you might add to these some corporate notes—somewhat riskier in a full-fledged depression, but higher yielding if you're willing to assume the risks.

Treasury Issues: The Ultimate Protection

Not that Treasury issues will make you rich overnight—corporate bonds provide stronger yields (at least 1–2 percent more for Triple As, even greater as quality declines). Municipal bonds offer full tax shelter, plus higher yields, and convertible bonds a play on the stock market as well. However, none of these offer the complete protection of U.S. Treasury issues, which represent loans to the United States Government, repayment pledged by the full faith and credit of that government.

Keep this in mind: Banks may fold, businesses may go under, cities and states may go bankrupt. But the government cannot. If worse came to worst, the Treasury would simply print up more money. But those notes will be repaid. Guaranteed protection against inflation? Forget it, especially if payment should be made right off the printing press. Still, returns from government securities have, for the most part, remained reasonably apace with inflation. Remember that we're still geared to preservation of capital in here.

And what returns can you expect? During the peak of interest costs, mid-1974, Treasury issues were yielding as high as 9.5 percent, even somewhat more in some cases.* By the end of the year, yields had dropped to roughly 7 percent, depending upon maturity. In previous years, returns were much lower. However, Treasury issues offer one major plus—their interest is totally exempt from state and local taxation. This can result in a considerable improvement in after-tax returns if, say, you live in New York State and New York City, both of which levy local income taxes.

The Treasury issues three classes of paper:

1. Treasury Bills

Maturities range from one week to one year; minimum denomination, $10,000. They can be purchased through your bank for a modest commission, or you can submit a commission-free, noncompetitive bid at the closest branch of the Federal Reserve. Auctions take place every Monday; application forms can be secured at your branch office. T-bills pay no interest as such; their return derives from the discount from par at which they are sold. Redemption at maturity takes place at par. When you submit a noncompetitive bid, you are agreeing to buy at the average rates reached during the competitive auction. Although you are buying cheaper and selling higher, returns are treated as ordinary income, not as capital gains (ditto for any losses sustained).

Yields on T-bills (90-day) reached peaks of roughly 9 percent during 1974, but declined precipitously from late August into October to under 7 percent, partially because certain bank failures sent investors

---

*A number of references have and will be made throughout this book to the credit crunch of 1974. The record interest costs witnessed during the 1974 period were, of course, readily eclipsed during the 1979–80 expansion of interest costs—an expansion caused by both Federal Reserve action and by record rates of inflation in the United States. Money was actually easier to obtain in many instances during 1980, although the costs of borrowing were much higher.

For brief periods of time Treasury issues were providing truly munificent rates of return. Ninety-day Treasury issues were selling to yield nearly 16 percent, for example. Corporate issues provided even higher rates of return.

As usual, the laws of contrary opinion ultimately prevailed. No sooner did the public start to flock into short-term, high-yield debt instruments than the bond markets firmed. Astute investors who took the opportunity to purchase long-term, high-yielding instruments profited handsomely. Investors in short-term debt instruments received fine yields—but only temporarily.

By mid-1980 the inflation rate, running at close to 20 percent earlier in the year, stabilized—at least temporarily—at around 10 percent. I would not be surprised to see a resurgence of inflation in the near future, and with it another panic in the bond markets. I advise readers to concentrate in debt instruments of no longer than intermediate term life, perhaps four to six years at most.

scurring for safety, partially on rumors that the Arabs were putting some of their oil money to work in the area. By late 1974 rates were up a bit again, hovering from 7–8 percent. By the spring of 1975 rates had fallen to around 5.5 percent.

The short life of Treasury bills is both an advantage and a disadvantage. Since these issues mature quickly and can be rolled over quickly during periods of rising rates, they offer the opportunity of exchanging lower-yielding for higher-yielding paper at frequent intervals. On the other hand, should interest rates fall, you will not be able to enjoy high returns for any great period of time. This is no small possibility. There were periods during 1971 and 1972 when returns from 90-day Treasury bills fell to less than 3.5 percent.

2. Treasury Notes

Issued in $1,000 denominations, maturities of from 2–7 years—also exempt from state and local taxation. Like the bills, notes are offered at public auction and/or in a secondary market. However, auctions of notes are less frequent than auctions of bills. Unlike Treasury bills, however, the notes are offered with a fixed coupon; your yield depends upon how much you actually pay for the note.*

Treasury notes really hit the public eye on August 6, 1974, when thousands of investors lined up outside the New York Federal Reserve Bank to bid on 9 percent (face) coupon, 33-month Treasury notes, issued at what was then the highest rate of Treasury issue interest since the Civil War. Bidding was so spirited that the notes sold at a premium over face value, resulting in an actual yield to maturity of only 8.59 percent. The public, as usual, ended up with the short end. One day later, the

---

*To compute the current yield of any debt instrument, divide the coupon or stated amount of interest by the price you pay. For example, suppose the note or bond calls for a 7% coupon, or $70 interest per $1,000 face value, and the note sells for $930. By dividing $930 into $70 you derive an actual yield of 7.52% ($70 ÷ $930 = 7.52%). The *amount* of interest paid by the vast majority of bonds does not change, but the *rate* of interest you receive does, depending upon your cost.

Yield to maturity includes not only the current yield, but also takes into account any gains or losses resulting from purchasing a debt instrument at a price different from face value, and redeeming upon maturity at face value. For example, during late 1974, the American Telephone 4⅜s 1985 were selling at 72¼ ($722.50) to yield 6.1% currently ($43.75 ÷ $722.50 = 6.1%). However, purchasers at $722.50 stood to receive back $1,000 per bond upon maturity in 1985, deriving a capital gain of $277.50 in addition to the interest return over the years. The combined return amounted to an 8.5% yield to maturity, a more significant consideration than current yield alone. The formulae for computing yields to maturity are complicated, but your bond broker should be able to provide the information for any bond in which you have an interest.

Bond nomenclatures reflects the coupon rate, the price as a percentage of par (usually $1,000) and the date of maturity. Thus, "ATT 4⅜s 1985, price 72¼" shows the issuing company (ATT), the coupon rate (4⅜%), the year of maturity (1985), and the price, 72¼% of $1,000 or $722.50. Financial newspapers generally show the current yield of corporate and the yield to maturity of government bonds.

small investor gone, professionals were able to secure the second day's offerings at a yield of 8.75 percent. However, yields at year end 1974 were running at roughly 7 percent, so maybe those small investors on line weren't so dumb after all.

3. Treasury Bonds

Treasury bonds—interest also tax exempt from state and local taxation—range in maturities from 5½ to 25 years. They can represent excellent value if purchased during periods of high interest, "safe" returns locked in for many years to come. Yields in late 1974 were running slightly below Treasury notes.

A Special Treasury Bond That Can Add Free Dollars to Your Estate

The Treasury, in the past, issued "flower bonds," bonds with maturities ranging from 1977 to 1988 that can be redeemed at par if the proceeds are employed to pay estate taxes. For example, suppose you were to purchase one of these bonds shortly before death for $750 (these bonds, issued at low coupon rates, all sell at discounts from par) and passed away prior to redemption. Your estate could turn in this bond as part payment of your estate tax, receiving $1,000 tax credit per bond, a profit over your cost of $250.

However the gain, $250, is added to the valuation of your estate and is subject in itself to estate taxes, resulting in some nullification of the gain. The 4¼s of 1987–92 are the most actively traded flower bonds. Their yield to maturity, year-end 1974, was roughly 6.5 percent, your return should you survive the redemption date.

Stepping Down a Bit In Quality for Extra Yield

Remember that we are still in a depression, but we are *not* witnessing the dissolution of the country. Does it pay to sacrifice a bit of ultimate safety for an extra percent or so of yield? In all probability, yes, though I would *not* argue against anyone who opted instead for the utmost in safety. To repeat and to emphasize, the person who has cash near the bottom of depressions holds more than just cash. That individual holds *opportunity*. If government bonds appear unexciting, just keep in mind their virtues—regular yield, liquidity when you want to sell, and safety, not a bad package at all when Chrysler was on the verge of bankruptcy and everyone else in sight cutting dividends.

Now, about stepping down a bit in quality. We're referring, of course, to government-agency bonds—bonds issued by Federal agencies, such as the Export-Import Bank, the Federal Housing Administration, the Government National Mortgage Association, the Postal Service, and the TVA, and by government-sponsored agencies, such as the Federal Home Loan Banks, the Federal National Mortgage Association, and the Federal Land Banks. Nor is the amount of money borrowed by these agencies small potatoes; indeed, they have literally been sopping up loose capital, depriving private industry of much-needed funds. *Business Week* (October 12, 1974) estimated that these agencies could consume roughly 15 percent of all available new capital in the second half of 1974, an increase from the 11 percent recorded in 1973 and the 5 percent recorded in 1972. In total, Federal agencies owe nearly $90 billion; estimates place borrowing over the next decade into the area of $200 billion. By comparison, loans made to these agencies are not as secure as loans made directly to the U.S. Treasury itself because the guarantee is not quite so explicit. However, none have ever been in default, and, even if Congress does have to authorize special funds to pay arrearages, in all likelihood it would do so. In return for giving up just a bit of the gilt in your gilt-coated security, you can pick up anywhere from ½ percent to 1 percent additional return. In other words, you can generally anticipate yields of roughly 9 percent from agency bonds at times Treasury issues are yielding 8 percent.

Maturities and minimum denominations vary issue by issue, and not all are exempt from state and local taxation. One unusual issue is the "Ginnie Mae pass-throughs," which represent interests in a group of government-guaranteed mortgages. The monthly payments of principal and interest made by the mortgagors are passed directly to the investor. Pass-throughs are available through Merrill Lynch, which buys blocks and distributes them in $25,000 lots minimum. "Fannie Mae" (Federal National Mortgage Association) offers a convertible bond, the FNMA 4⅜s 1996, which can be exchanged for a stipulated amount of common shares of the company, trading on the New York Stock Exchange. We'll be moving further into convertibles later on, but suffice it to say at this point that the 43/8s offer a steady return from an investment-grade vehicle, plus the opportunity to achieve capital gains should the FNMA common rise in price (in which case you can exchange the bonds for the common, selling the common shares you own at an aggregate price of more than you paid for the bonds).

Many larger brokerage houses make markets in government-agency bonds. Merrill Lynch Government Securities, Inc., One Liberty Plaza, New York, N.Y. 10006 puts out excellent brochures in this area, as well as selling agency and Treasury issues. And of course you can obtain such securities through your bank.

In the meantime, the following table should give you some idea of what is available:

Table I
U.S. Treasury and Agency Issues: A Sampling

Issue	Maturity Periods	Minimum Denomination	Exempt from Local and State Taxation
Treasury Bills	Up to 1 Year	$10,000*	Yes
Treasury Notes	Up to 7 Years	1,000*	Yes
Treasury Bonds	Up to 25 Years	1,000*	Yes
Banks For Cooperatives Bonds	Up to 2½ Years	5,000	Yes
Export-Import Bank	Up to 15 Years	5,000*	No
Farmers Home Administration	Up to 15 Years	25,000*	No
Federal Home Loan Banks	Up to 20 Years	10,000	Yes
Federal Land Bank Bonds	Up to 15 Years	$1,000	Yes
GNMA, FNMA Bonds	Up to 25 Years	25,000*	No
GNMA Pass-Throughs	Approximately 30 Years	25,000*	No

*Issues backed by the full faith and credit of the U.S. Government.

Stepping Down a Bit Further for Even More Yield— But Watch Out for Some Sleepless Nights

If a number of federal bonds enjoy exemption from local and state levies, municipal bonds, issued by states, cities, and certain public authorities, go them one better—they offer exemption from federal taxation, as well as from taxation by the state and locality in which they are issued. Yields? Well, nothing is ever really for nothing, so these tax-exempt bonds have yielded less pretax than taxable bonds of similar quality. Still, for investors in higher tax brackets, the tax savings can be considerable and the after-tax returns excellent. We'll get to the caveats later—and there are many— but first let's examine the value of the tax exemption.

You can readily see the value of the tax exemption. For example, if you're in the 50 percent tax bracket, you would require a pretax return of 15 percent to equal the real, after-tax return of only 7½ percent derived municipal bonds.

Table II
The Rate of Taxable Return Required to Provide An After-Tax Return Equivalent to Municipal Bond Tax-Free Income

Investor Tax Bracket Municipal Bond Yield	28%	32%	36%	40%	45%	50%	60%	70%
			EQUIVALENT TAXABLE INCOME					
3.00%	4.17	4.41	4.69	5.00	5.45	6.00	7.50	10.00
3.50	4.86	5.15	5.47	5.83	6.36	7.00	8.75	11.67
4.00	5.56	5.88	6.25	6.67	7.27	8.00	10.00	13.33
4.50	6.26	6.62	7.03	7.50	8.18	9.00	11.25	15.00
5.00	6.94	7.35	7.81	8.33	10.00	10.00	12.50	16.67
5.50	7.64	8.09	8.59	9.17	10.00	11.00	13.75	18.33
6.00	8.33	8.82	9.37	10.00	10.91	12.00	15.00	20.00
6.50	9.03	9.56	10.16	10.83	11.82	13.00	16.25	21.67
7.00	9.72	10.29	10.94	11.67	12.73	14.00	17.50	23.33
7.50	10.42	11.03	11.72	12.50	13.64	15.00	18.75	25.00
8.00	11.11	11.76	12.50	13.33	14.55	16.00	20.00	26.67
8.50	11.81	12.50	13.28	14.17	15.45	17.00	21.25	28.33

More About Tax Exemption

The Internal Revenue Code has allowed tax exemption for the interest paid on municipal bonds, an exemption that has withstood all tests since 1913. In addition, both states and localities generally exempt interest from taxation if the bonds were issued from within their boundaries. (Bonds issued in the U.S. possessions—Puerto Rico and the District of Columbia—are exempt from taxation in all states, as well as federally.)

However, although the interest on municipal bonds is not subject to taxation, any capital gains deriving from the sale of such bonds is subject to the usual levies. For example, suppose you purchase a discounted bond, a bond selling below par value, at 80, the bond providing a current yield of 5.6 percent and maturing in 1986. You will not be liable for taxation on the 5.6 percent yield. However, should you redeem the bond in 1986 at par, or $1,000 for $800 cost to you, you will be liable for a long-term, capital-gains tax on your 25 percent capital gain.

A Tricky Tax Trap

The government, for obvious reasons, will *not* allow an interest deduction on loans taken to finance the purchase of tax-exempt securities. Moreover, the Internal Revenue Service has extended its intrepretation of that ruling to cover a broad variety of loans you may hold outstanding, concurrent with your ownership of municipal bonds, even if the loans were not taken directly for the finance of the bonds.

As an example, suppose you own municipal bonds and subsequently purchase common share securities on margin. The interest on your margin loan, normally tax deductible, may become nondeductible to the extent of your municipal holdings, on the grounds that you could have disposed of your bonds to make cash purchase. As a general rule of thumb, the IRS will disallow interest deductions elsewhere to the extent that municipals comprise a proportion of your total assets. For instance, suppose you hold total assets of $500,000, of which $250,000 consist of tax-exempt securities. You incur a $10,000 margin debt, resulting in $1,000 interest charges. You would normally be able to deduct the $1,000 in full, but in this instance you will be allowed only a 50 percent deduction, since municipals comprised 50 percent of your total assets.

This tax trap, however, does not apply to your residential mortgage payments.

Safety

During the best of times—in fact, during even middling times—the safety of municipals rarely comes into question. Simply pick up some A-rated* paper or better, and relax with your tax-free yield. However, we are *not* talking about the best of times. We are thinking about how to survive a depression—a Depression with a capital D, not a recession, business slowdown, or pause in prosperity. And in a depression you must exercise the most thorough care in order to preserve every last dollar of your capital. That, in the end, *is* the name of the game. (By way of comparison, late last year you could have drawn roughly 6.3 percent on 15-year A-rated tax-exempt bonds; 6.6 percent on BBB bonds.)

---

*Debt instruments—municipal bonds, corporate bonds, commercial paper, and so forth—are rated for safety by bond rating services, Moody's, Fitch, Dun and Bradstreet, and Standard and Poor's. S & P ratings range from AAA (best) to D (default). Moody's runs from Aaa (best) to C. Dun and Bradstreet's range from 01 (best) to 22 (worst).

Bonds of investment-grade quality command an S & P rating of BBB and better; anything below must be considered speculative, very possibly unable to ride out a major depression. Conservative investors—particularly during doomsday times—will settle for nothing less than AA or A at the least, despite the fact that increased risk does bring increased return.

During periods of prosperity, in which even marginal companies thrive, you can step down to a B rating, but go no lower.

How to Evaluate Safety

For a quick rule of thumb check the bond rating. Anything graded AA or better, perhaps even A, should be able to ride through the coming depression. However, times do change, and with them bond ratings, so you cannot rely on bond ratings alone. (For example, in April 1975 Standard and Poor's suspended New York City's "A" rating.)

The Safest Municipals

General obligation bonds, bonds secured by the full faith, credit, and taxing power of the issuing state, city, or country, are the safest of bonds, though in desperate times even these must come under some cloud. A case in point were New York City bonds, which came under intense pressure in August 1975, resulting in price declines and losses to investors and dealers alike, yields on the then-"A"-rated New York City tax-exempts climbing to more than 10 percent. All this despite the fact that the city had never defaulted on its obligations in the past and is constitutionally pledged to pay off debt obligations before employee salaries: in fact, before all other municipal obligations. Why, then, the debacle in the bond market? Adverse publicity given to city finances as a result of heavily publicized layoffs of city employees.

Nor can the collapse be attributed solely to panicky, trigger-happy investors, priming the doomsday gun. New York City has been in a steady decline in recent years—rising welfare costs, a shrinking tax base. Detroit is another trouble spot, given a major depression and the long-term shutdown of auto plants. Not to mention Newark and Jersey City—in short, any area of potentially longstanding high unemployment.

Will New York City manage to continue to pay off its notes over the years to come? Were I to hazard a guess, I'd have to say "yes"—and that a yield of around 10 percent was enticing, if you were willing to assume the risk. A risk that in late 1975 looked grave indeed.

Insofar as state issues go, general obligation bonds are almost certainly secure enough. During the Great Depression 98 percent of all states continued payment. Only Arkansas, among the states, defaulted.

Moving down the list of municipals, we come to *limited and special tax bonds*, municipals backed only by the proceeds of a specific tax; *new housing authority bonds*, bonds issued by local housing authorities but backed by the U.S. Government (high quality); *double-barreled bonds*, bonds backed by two or more guarantees of payment. *Revenue* bonds, bonds issued by special authorities created by a state or municipality, have also come under a cloud recently, the result of diminishing turnpike revenues caused by the falloff in gasoline consumption and driving.

Shopping Around

Municipal bonds can frequently be obtained in quantity at issue or in secondary markets made by dealers who advertise in the financial press, making their profit on a spread between the bid and asked prices. Spreads generally run in the area of 2–3 points, or about 3 percent, but during bond panics spreads can run to 7–8 percent and more as dealers refuse to add to inventory, except at major price concessions. Lebenthal & Co. Inc., One State Street Plaza, New York, N.Y. 10004, is one of the larger dealers, willing to send price lists of recent offerings to inquirers.

5
CORPORATE BONDS: STRAIGHT INCOME PLUS SOME WITH A POSSIBLE EQUITY KICKER

Straight Corporates

No, they offer no tax exemptions. And, no, they are *not* backed by the Federal government. And yes, there is some element of risk. But if you *will* stay with only the highest in quality (positively no less than A, preferably AA), you can draw higher returns from straight corporate issues, with little danger of succumbing to depression. In fact, if you time your purchases correctly, you can even hit a capital gain to boot —and, yes, even during or, more precisely, rather because of the cataclysm.

A straight corporate is just what its name implies, a promissory note issued by a corporation, so much interest due each month, payment of principal due on a certain date. These bonds can be obtained at issue, or in secondary markets on the major stock exchanges and over the counter. Your brokerage house will handle the trade. Spreads on actively traded bonds are slight; commissions are low.

The following is just a sampling of actively traded straight corporate bonds of AAA quality. Current yields can be found daily in *The Wall Street Journal* and weekly in *Barron's Financial Weekly*.

American Telephone	6s	2000
Du Pont	8s	1986
General Electric	7½s	1996
Illinois Bell Telephone	8s	2004
Sears, Roebuck	8⅝s	1995
General Foods	8⅞s	1990
Proctor & Gamble	7s	2002
Ohio Bell Telephone	5s	2006
Standard Oil of Indiana	9.7s	1989

Union Pacific Railroad	8¾s	1985
Wisconsin Telephone	7¼s	2007
South West Bell Telephone	3⅛s	1983

You can see that when we're playing in the Triple A league, we are dealing with substantial material, companies that should be able to weather any economic storm short of revolution. And yet, during mid-1980, these bonds were providing yields to maturity of roughly 10–11 percent on average, not a bad place, all told, in which to place cash, even during a depression.

A Worthwhile Tax Ploy for the Conservative Bond Investor

Bonds are generally priced on a yield to maturity basis, which includes both the current interest yield on the bond, plus any capital

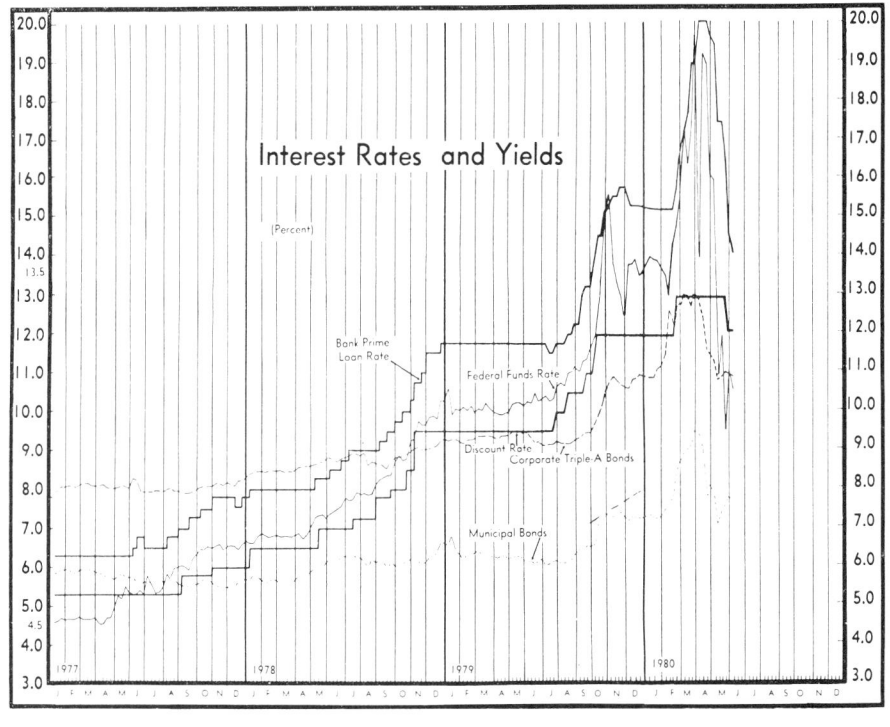

FIGURE 1
SOURCE: *The Media-General Financial Weekly,* Richmond, Va. 23261

gain or loss that will accrue if the bond purchased at current prices is held to maturity for redemption at par value.

Recent rises in interest rates have led many older issues, issued with lower coupons than current rates, to fall in price. Such issues sell at a discount from par value. For example, the ATT 2¾s 1982 bond was selling during April 1980 at a price of $870 per bond and provided a current interest yield of 3.16 percent, hardly anything in and of itself to write home about. However, were investors to purchase the bond and hold it until maturity, they would receive a 13 point, or 14.9 percent, gain; the bond, purchased at $870 would be redeemed at a price of $1,000. The total yield to maturity would have come to 10.43 percent per year. Of this 10.43 percent rate of return, *7.27 percent per year would be taxable at long-term capital gain rates*, with far more advantageous after-tax consequences than a similarly returning debt instrument whose returns developed largely in the form of interest payouts alone.

Suggestion

If you are not in need of high current income, ask your bond broker to provide you with recommendations of deeply discounted, near maturity, high-quality bonds. I suggest maturities of no longer than 2–5 years from the date of purchase. Such instruments are among the safest of investments, and one way, at least, to reduce your tax bite.

Figure 1 tells the story—a sharp rise in bond yields over recent years, accompanied by a rather long-term attrition in bond prices.*

Recent downtrends in bond prices have stemmed from a variety of forces within our economy: most notably the long-term inflation that took place following World War II, surges in corporate borrowing over recent decades, general demand for capital, weakening corporate balance sheets—all leading to increases in prevailing interest rates, declines in bond prices.

---

*Bond prices rise and fall inversely to prevailing interest rates, all other factors remaining constant. For example, suppose ATT were to issue a bond with an 8% coupon in 1981, and suppose, further, that interest rates fell so that bonds of similar quality and maturity could be issued at a 4% coupon. Naturally, buyers would flock to purchase the older bond, driving its price up until its resultant *rate of yield* matched prevailing interest rates. In this situation, the older ATT bonds would rise in price to a point somewhere between par and twice face value. Why not double face value, where their current yield would equal the prevailing 4% rate? Because the purchasers of the bonds would incur a capital *loss* when the bonds fell due for redemption, that loss would have to be equalized by a higher rate of current return.

Conversely, should interest rates rise following the issue of a bond, the bonds' price would *fall* until the yield to maturity of the issue approximated recent offerings.

American Telephone, in fact, has a number of issues outstanding with coupon rates ranging between 2⅝% and 8.8%, prices of those bonds recently ranging from approximately $600 to $1,010 for face-value $1,000 bonds. However, yields to maturity vary only slightly among the various issues.

But with depression? Depression breeds deflation (reduction of prices), slackening of capital spending, reduced borrowing. Odds favor some firming of bond prices, particularly in the highest-quality sector, a firming that can mean capital gains to you as bonds rise in price, in addition to current yield. But remember, you must stay with quality; if there is any danger at all that a company will fold, its bonds will be tough to give away.

How to Profit from a Future Upturn

If you are a speculator at heart, *if* you are adept at spotting breaks in the clouds, and *if* your sense of judgment is sound, you *can* profit from "junk" or low-rated bonds, when the depression ends. Given an era of prosperity, marginal companies will continue to pay interest and principal. During doubtful times, yields on low-rated bonds soar—investors seek quality only. However, fantastic yields are available in such issues and may be worth pursuing *as the depression comes to a close.* Such bonds have recently included, for example:

Bond			S & P Rating	Recent Price	Current Yield	Yield to Maturity
McCrory Corp.	7 3/4s	1995	CCC	$535	14.49%	15.93%
Rapid American	7 1/2s	1985	CCC	$713	10.54	16.08
Tele-Com Co	13 3/8s	1999	B	$840	15.92	16.08
United Brands	9 1/8s	1998	B	$666	10.88	14.52
Telex	11 3/4s	1996	B	$691	17.00	17.54

There is, of course, a certain amount of speculation implicit in the purchase of less-than-investment-grade quality debt instruments, but corporate failures are surprisingly infrequent. I suggest that you diversify.

Incidentally, I presented a similar list of recommendations in the first edition of this work. The United Brands bonds, listed above, were originally recommended at a price of $480, at which level they provided a yield to maturity of 19.4 percent. Had you purchased the Warner Communications 7⅝s 1994 bonds listed in the first edition at a price of $500 per bond, you would now be holding a bond whose rating had risen from B to BBB, whose price had risen from $500 to $625, and you would have received annual interest payments of 15.3 percent of your investment. Let's hope that the current crop of suggestions does as well.

Convertible Bonds: Security with an Equity Kicker

What! Equity securities during a depression? Yes—if you observe certain precautions and if you're willing to put up, again, with some increase in risk for the purpose of establishing indirect common share positions, just in case the depression does end before you are ready. We'll get to the pros and cons of convertible securities as a hedge against depression a bit further on, but first let's clarify our terms.

A convertible bond is a corporate bond that can be exchanged for shares of common stock, usually of the company that issued the bond, in lieu of repayment of the note signified by the bond. Here is how it works.

LTV Corporation has outstanding a convertible bond, the LTV 7 ½s 1977. Each bond can be converted into, or exchanged for, 95.238 shares of LTV common, trading in late 1974 at around $9 per share. The bonds, trading at roughly $970 per bond, offered, at the time, a current return of 7.7 percent, roughly 7.8 percent if held to maturity, three years distant.

Suppose, at that time, you had considered exchanging the bonds for LTV common. You would have received 95.238 shares per bond, which, at $9 per share, would represent a total conversion value of $857.14 (95.238 × 9). Obviously, it would not have paid to make the conversion, since you paid $970 for your bonds. But suppose that the LTV common had risen in value, say, to $20 per share. You would still have been allowed to exchange your convertible bonds for 95.238 shares, worth $1,904.76 (95.238 × 20), in exchange for the bond that cost you $970. Nor would you actually have had to convert your bonds to profit; the price of the bonds on the secondary markets would rise to reflect their increasing potential exchange (conversion) value.*

Let's suppose instead that LTV remained at 9 or fell, say, to 5, remaining mired at those levels. Well, as long as the company was still solvent and you were willing to exercise patience, you could not get hurt. Obviously you would not convert unless and until LTV common, the underlying shares, rose sufficiently to make conversion profitable. However, simply by holding the bonds to maturity, December 1977, you could ensure receiving your investment back, plus $30 per bond ($1,000 face value minus $970 cost), plus $75 per year interest per bond. *The price of the note might fluctuate in the interim, but, upon maturity, full face value is due you.* This is a mighty and significant plus in favor of any short to intermediate-discounted credit instrument.

---

*As a matter of fact, by the end of April 1975 the LTV common did rise to 19⅜, the convertible bonds to over $1,800 per bond.

Convertible bonds selling at or near par generally offer many advantages over the direct purchase of their underlying common shares. These advantages include:

1. *Lower commision costs:* Commissions to purchase common shares have steadily risen. Commissions to purchase convertible bonds have remained at only $5 per bond at many houses.
2. *Higher yields:* Convertible bonds generally provide yields clearly superior to their underlying common shares. For example, as I write this, the LTV common pays no dividends; the LTV 7½s 1977 yield 7½ percent.
3. *Greater downside protection:* Because of their superior yields and the promise of repayment of principal in full at maturity, convertible bonds selling near or below par decline at much lower rates than common shares. For example, between November and December 1974, LTV common dropped from 11½ to 8⅞, a decline of 22.8 percent. During that period the convertible declined from 114 to 98, a decline of only 14 percent. Remember, so long as LTV remained solvent, the *worst* you could have done with these bonds would be to earn 7.8 percent on your money, with a real chance of a major profit if the common moved up.
4. *Interest:* Convertible bonds accrue interest for each and every day they are held. Stocks pay dividends as declared. The chart

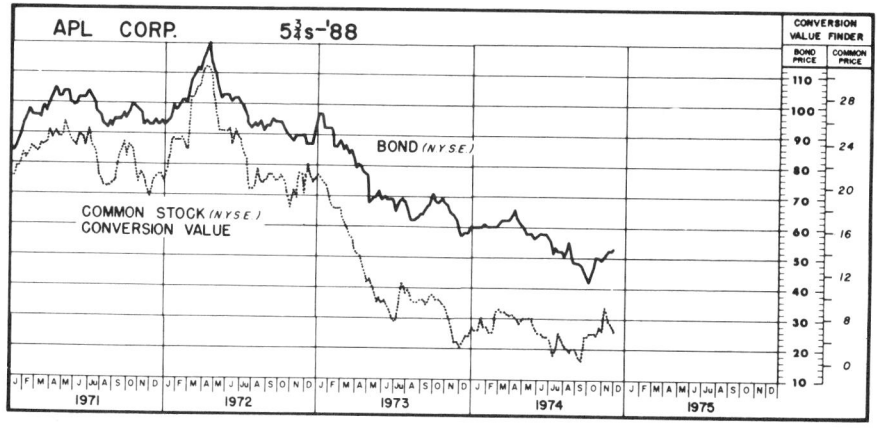

FIGURE 2
The APL 5¾ 1988 convertible bond dropped at a much slower rate than the underlying common during the bear market.   SOURCE: *KV Convertible Fact Finder*, 27 William Street, New York, N.Y., 10005.

of the APL 5¾s 1988 shows how convertibles hold up better during declining markets than their underlying common shares.

Disadvantages of Convertible Bonds

Nothing, of course, is perfect in an imperfect world. Convertible bonds are no exception. Here are some of the disadvantages and pitfalls connected with convertible securities:

1. The markets for convertible bonds are generally not as fluid as the markets for common shares.
2. If the bond sells at a deep discount, it will not rise as rapidly as the underlying common shares until the premium over conversion (the difference between the actual conversion value of the bond and its actual price, expressed as a percent of the conversion value) dissipates. For example, whereas the LTV convertible declined at only two-thirds the rate of the common while the common fell, were the shares to rise from 8⅞ to 11½ again (a gain of 29.6 percent), the bonds, returning from 98 to their former price of 114, would see a gain of only 16.3 percent. You do pay something for the downside protection.
3. You must keep abreast of developments. Companies sometimes "call in their bonds," redeeming them prior to maturity, generally at par or slightly above, plus accrued interest. If you've purchased the bonds below par, you have no problem; but if you've purchased at a premium over conversion value, above par, then you do, since you have either to redeem or instantly convert. If the bond sells above conversion value, and is above face value, you lose the premium, since you'll receive shares selling in total value below the price of the bonds.
4. During periods of rising interest rates the "floor" to convertibles, the price at which they will sell based upon yield alone, may fall, therefore disappointing investors who felt they were in a "safe" vehicle. However, during periods of falling interest rates convertibles, because of their yields, will rise in value, even if the underlying common does not move at all.

The Perfect Investment?

Disadvantages notwithstanding, the long-term purchase of discounted convertible bonds probably offers investors the most reliable opportunity of all to profit from the stock market. During market declines, convertible bonds can frequently be purchased at deep discounts from par, with yields to maturity ranging up to 12 percent and better for investment-grade paper. By comparison, the stock market, over the past century, has gained, on average, roughly 9 percent per annum (including dividends), virtually nothing at all from the middle sixties through 1974. *Remember, the only way a long-term holder can lose on discounted convertibles is for the issuing company to go bankrupt.*

Convertible Bonds as a Hedge Against Depression?

At the start of a depression, no! Near economic and stock market tops, convertible bonds, because of advances in the stock market, generally sell at levels above which their yields offer any true downside protection, even were the bonds to sell at a discount. For example, the Sprague 4¼s 1992 dropped in price from the 70s to 32 between 1973 and 1974. A safe depression buy at 75? Hardly. At 32? Now, at a 13.3 percent *current* yield, an altogether different matter.

In short, convertible bonds may prove a satisfactory depression vehicle *after* the depression has run a good part of its course, and *after* the stock market has already incurred serious decline. At that point, investors may be well advised to step into high-quality discounted bonds, averaging down at 10 to 15 percent intervals, just in case.

But Stay with Investment-Grade Paper!

Again, to restate. We're talking about a major depression—the sort of economic setback that can knock corporations over like duckpins (witness a few like Four Seasons and Levin-Townsend). You can *never* be certain just when that sort of slide can come to an end. You certainly cannot trust the perpetually optimistic pap issued from Washington or the prophecies put out by Wall Street. (Did you know that Merrill Lynch insiders were selling their own shares of MER common all through early '73, even as they were putting out their "We're bullish on America" spiel to entice the public in?)

In any case, until you are truly certain that the worst is over, *stick to investment-grade convertible bonds only.* The pickings are a little leaner here than in the straight corporate sector; companies tack on the convertible sweetener to make possible the issue of bonds at reasonable corporate interest costs. Better-grade corporations can generally issue straight corporates. Nonetheless, good, if not top-grade, issues are available. Following is a selection culled from the roster of listed convertibles:

American Hospital Supply	5¾s	1999
Bank of New York	6¼s	1994
Chase Manhattan Corporation	6½s	1996
General American Transportation	5¾s	1996
Houston Light & Power	5½s	1985
Minnesota Mining & Mfg.	4¼s	1997
Owens Illinois Co.	4½s	1992
Federal Natl. Mtge. Association	4⅜s	1996
Will Ross	4½s	1992
Xerox	6s	1995
J.P. Morgan Co.	4¾s	1998
Pfizer	4s	1997

Convertible Preferreds

Something of a cross between convertible bonds and common shares, the convertible preferred generally pays a dividend in excess of that received by common shareholders; in addition to which it can be converted into shares of common. However, dividends are generally paid quarterly, not accrued daily, and commission costs are higher than for the bonds. And, finally, the majority of convertible preferred shares guarantee no specific redemption price or time.

On the other hand, many convertible preferreds are of investment-grade quality and offer a reasonably viable alternative to the bonds. Some high-grade convertible preferreds include:

Aetna Life & Casualty	$2.00	Owens Illinois	$4.75
American Home Products	2.00	Travelers Corp.	2.00
Bristol Myers Co.	2.00	Washington National	2.50
Consolidated Foods	4.50	Continental Oil Co.	2.00

Your stockbroker can provide you with current prices, yields, terms, and special conditions concerning the above and other convertible securities.

How Leverage Can Really Perk Up Those Bond Returns

Convertible bonds can be purchased at 50 percent margin. (You put up 50 percent of the bond price; your broker lends you the rest at interest rates usually 1–1½ percent above prime.) Listed corporate bonds can be purchased at 25 percent margin (you put up 25 percent), and government issues can usually be bank financed to up to 90 percent of their value. If your timing is correct, you can really clean up by making full use of leverage possibilities. There are at least three maneuvers that can make a little bond money go a long way.

Method #1: Bet on a Price Rise in The Bonds

As we mentioned before, during periods of economic distress, investor money flows into safe havens, particularly government issues. Since depressions are generally accompanied by deflation, government securities stand to rise in price once the last vestiges of inflation vanish, and even before, in anticipation, as investors hurry purchases in order to lock up high prevailing yields.

On August 23, 1974, U.S. Treasury Bonds 4¼s 1987–92 closed at 71.22 (government issues are quoted in dollars and thirty-seconds). On December 20, 1974, the same issue closed at 76.22. Suppose you had purchased $10,000 face value notes in August, utilizing full 10 percent margin, selling in December? Here's how the workout would develop:

Cost of $10,000 face value notes at 71.22	$7,168.75
Cash required at 10% margin	$ 716.88
Interest charges at 11%, 4 months	− 236.57
Interest received, 4 months	+ 141.67
Proceeds from sale at 76.22	7,668.75
Net Gain	$ 405.10

(commissions excluded)

Based upon the amount of cash that went into the position ($716.88), your profit comes to 56.5 percent of your cash outlay—in this case, 169.5 percent on an annualized basis. In other words, if you purchase bonds on 10 percent margin and the bonds rise by 10 percent, you'll double your money (excluding interest costs). However, if the bonds decline by 10 percent, *you will be completely wiped out.* Leverage *is,* once again, a two-way street. Corporate bonds are more volatile than government issues, particularly medium-grade corporates, which can offer truly fantastic returns *if* your timing is precise.

Method #2: Deriving a 31.9P Percent Yield Return from Straight Corporate Bonds

Not exactly a depression special since this tactic generally involves less than prime-grade paper, but an excellent tactic during the period when the economy once again starts its upturn. A place, say, to put some of the cash that you protected on the way down.

As I write this, the prime rate (interest rate charged by banks to highest quality borrowers) stands at roughly 10 percent; brokers will charge margin interest at rates of roughly 11¼ percent. At this time there are a number of medium-grade corporates providing current yields well in excess of 11¼ percent, firms that will *probably* withstand depression, and are almost certain to continue to meet payments during better economic times. One such company, the American Financial Corporation, has outstanding a listed bond, the American Financial 9½s 1988, trading, as of the time of this writing, on the Pacific Exchange at a price of $580 per bond. Current yield amounts to 16.4 percent. Although the prime rate fluctuates, percentage-wise the situation remains the same.

Suppose you purchased four of these bonds at full 25 percent margin, holding for one year. We will presume that the bond's price remains stable.

Unmargined Cost of Four Bonds	$2,320.00	($580 per bond X 4)
Margined Cash Outlay	580.00	(25% X $2,320)
Interest Charges to You	195.25	(11.25% X $1740 debit balance)
Interest Received by You	380.00	($95 per bond X 4 bonds)
Net Interest Income	184.75	($380–195.25)

Based upon your cash outlay of $580.00, the annual return of $184.75 represents a yield to you of 31.9 percent! Risks? Yes. If the bonds drop in value by 25 percent, you lose your entire investment. However, if the bonds rise in value by 25 percent, you double your investment. And if the company stays solvent until redemption time, 1988? Well, you stand to receive back $1,000 for each of those bonds you purchased at $580, a capital gain of $420 per bond, $1,680 total, or 289.7 percent of your investment—in addition to the annual 31.9 percent yield.

Method #3: Playing for a 39 Percent Gain If You Win and a Steady Return (12 Percent) If You Don't

A VERY, VERY INTERESTING BOND SPECULATION FOR CONSERVATIVELY ORIENTED INVESTORS—HEADS YOU WIN, TAILS YOU MAKE 12 PERCENT....

(I first presented this situation during 1975. Some investors have probably struck it rich since then; some have probably just collected their yield while waiting for their number to come up. The deal, if anything is better now than then.)

The Position

Seaboard World Airlines has outstanding a convertible issue, the 5s 1986 convertible bond, recently selling at a price of $720 per bond, to yield 6.9 percent on a current basis, 12 percent to maturity when it is scheduled to be redeemed at par. The bond is rated "B," which means that it has to be considered as somewhat speculative, but presuming that the company pays off, the worst you can do is make that 12 percent to maturity, if you hold until redemption.

The bond has been convertible into 51.15 shares of Seaboard common, recently selling in the 12–13 region and has carried approximately a 12–13 percent premium over conversion value. As a convertible alone, it would be very well situated. However, Seaboard seemed in mid-1980 to be on the verge of being acquired by Tiger International for a package of Tiger common and some bonds. The convertible will probably then become convertible into a rather dead unit of 11½ percent debentures and some common and will have very little volatility. However, this is not the basis of our interest in the situation.

The Real Kicker—Early Redemption Via Lottery

According to the terms of the bond, Seaboard has had to institute a sinking fund to retire the bonds in certain percentages prior to maturity. Between 1972 and 1976, 2 percent of the original issue was redeemed each year, chosen at random. Between 1977 and 1981, 5 percent of the original issue is slated for redemption each year. Thirteen percent of the original issue is slated for redemption in each of the years between 1982 and 1986. The drawing for redemption is held in April, so if you buy now, you'll have to wait for the better part of a year to see if your number has come up.

And, what exactly are the odds of your cashing in early—say for a 39 percent capital gain (28 points profit on a 72 investment) + interest? The workouts chart is on page 48.

The odds are better than 50:50 that your bonds will be called by 1984, although if you hold a number of bonds some may be called sooner; some later. If you assume a maturity date of 4/1/84 and purchase the bonds on margin, assuming a 12 percent margin cost, your

	% of Original Issue to be Called	Balance of Original Issue Not Called	Probability of Being Called That Year	Probability of Being Called Since Purchase
1972–76 (2% per ann.)	10%	90%		At par
1977–80 (5% per ann.)	20%	70%		
4/1/81	5%	65%	7%	7%
4/1/82	13%	52%	20%	26%
4/1/83	13%	39%	25%	44%
4/1/84	13%	26%	33%	63%
4/1/85	13%	13%	50%	81%
4/1/86	13%	0	100%	100%

after tax return would come to nearly 16 percent per year, including all costs. Hardly, I would say, a fate worst than death, even in these inflationary times—and at very little risk at that. (For further information I suggest readers contact Murray M. Kimmel, Herzfeld & Stern, Paramus, N.J. (212) 736-2191. You can call collect. Murray is a CPA and has carefully computed all of the tax consequences of the deal.)

6

THE MONEY FUNDS: SAFE AS THE BANK, WITH DOUBLE THE RETURN?

Back in 1972 a new superhero came forth upon the financial scene. Impervious to the oil crises, thriving on inflation, fattened up by the great bear market, able to leap climbing interest rates in a single bound —the "money," "liquid assets," or "cash management" funds, as they are alternatively called, sucked up investor money during 1973, and particularly 1974, like a giant vacuum, drawing cash away from banks, the stock market, and the bond sector alike.

Phenomenal growth? An understatement! The prototype of the specie, The Reserve Fund, saw its assets grow from roughly $100,000 (May 1972) to $10 million (May 1973) to $205 million (May 1974). By the end of 1974 Reserve's assets had climbed to well over $400 million. (Reserve's management fees, incidentally, climbed from $314 (1972) to $10,368 (1973) to $384,518 (mid-1974).

Nor was the lesson lost on other fund management corporations, hurt and hurting badly as a result of net redemptions and sliding sales, the result, in turn, of the great 1973–74 bear markets. Their flight into the money management sector was inevitable. By early summer 1974 roughly seven such funds were in operation; by the end of the year more than twenty were dispensing their wares. Giants of the equity fund industry—Dreyfus, Oppenheimer, Fidelity—diversified into the money arena, growing rapidly to rival Reserve (by the end of 1974 Dreyfus Liquid Assets led the pack in size), new funds appearing, it seemed, almost daily.

By September 1974 cash was rolling into the money funds at the rate of $10 million a day. In September, twenty-odd such funds sold $304.9 million worth of shares against only $63.2 million in redemptions. The rest of the mutual fund industry, more than 500 funds in all, sold only $194.2 million worth of shares against nearly $230 million in redemptions.

Nor, too, has the growth of the money fund been incomprehensible. The period from October 1973, the start of the energy crisis, through

1974 was probably the most difficult fifteen months for investors since the start of the Great Depression. No arena was immune. The stock market? During those fifteen months the Dow fell from approximately 997 to roughly 570, a decline of some 42-odd percent. Bond prices plummeted in unison, the fixed-debt instrument a victim of the combined ravages of inflation, heavy corporate borrowing, and investor uncertainty regarding the long-term viability of borrowers. The real estate sector succumbed to rising vacancy rates, mounting operating costs, and the inability to turn over property—a whole industry, the real estate investment trusts, collapsing into virtual collective bankruptcy or near so. Art, antiques, wine—all victims of investor fear. Only gold and coins seemed able to weather the storm; that is, save for the money funds.*

With all else falling away, shareholders in the Reserve Fund saw their investments grow by 8 percent during the first nine months of 1974. Money Market Management produced gains of 7.7 percent during that period; the Capital Preservation Fund and Dreyfus, 6.9 percent. (Which recalls the time a rather well-known but herewith nameless stockbroker boasted to me that he had put all his clients in cash. "Good for you," sayeth I, "but why not direct the dough to Reserve?" "You kidding? They'll get spoiled and I'll never see that money back again.") In short, 1974 was clearly a time when Reserve holders fiddled while the rest of Rome burned. (One final point of comparison: While Dreyfus Liquid Assets Inc. was gaining 6.9 percent, the other end of the lion pride, the Dreyfus Equity Fund, was losing 29.7 percent.)

The point, I'll presume, is well made by now—cash management shareholders survived the early phases of the 1974–? recession (depression?) quite well. And how would they fare if things were to become truly grim? With care and prudence, quite well, I think. As we shall see, cash in *certain* of these funds is as safe, or even safer, than money in the bank—at considerably higher returns. An investment for all seasons? No, not really. There are times when money will be better placed elsewhere. A haven for cash during uncertain periods? Again, with some prudent selection, definitely—and when we examine what these funds actually do, we'll see why.

The Concept

The basic concept underlying the cash management funds is simplicity itself—all the more surprising that the major houses didn't beat

---

*Yield returns from money market funds, the fastest growing segment of the mutual fund industry, have continued to rise to keep abreast of inflation and generally rising interest rates. Yields in the order of 16–17% became common during early 1980, well above the peak yields of 12–13% available from these instruments during the prior credit crunch of 1974.

Reserve to the punch. Money funds are basically structured similar to the traditional mutual fund, except that, instead of investing in equities, the money funds stash their cash only in short term debt instruments —bank certificates of deposit, bankers' acceptances, corporate commercial paper, and government issues, notes and bonds. These are all vehicles available to the general public, generally (not always) yielding more than the typical savings account, but requiring more cash, if purchased individually, then the typical investor can or wishes to muster.*

By pooling investor capital then, these funds secure for the individual small investor yields generally available only to the more well-heeled investor coterie—yields that reached peaks of more than 12 percent during the tight money squeeze. (It should, however, be kept in mind that the Reserve Fund, which yielded nearly 13 percent for certain periods in 1974, managed to produce gains of only 5.7 percent in 1972 and 7.4 percent in 1973. By the spring of 1975, returns had dropped to approximately 6 percent once again.) What's more, results have thus far been consistently profitable, the funds by and large successful in protecting the investing public against poor placements and defaults on the instruments held by these funds.

Income is generally credited to shareholders compounded and reinvested daily. The majority of funds will quote current returns daily over the telephone. (Although returns are called "dividends" by the funds, they are, and are treated taxwise as, ordinary interest income.)

Liquidity

The money funds offer a unique plus—and one on which they cannot be faulted—instant liquidity. The typical fund requires a minimum initial investment of from $1,000–$5,000 (a general reduction in minimum requirements seems to be developing), charges no sales or redemption commissions (the few money funds that did charge commissions seem to be phasing out the commission load), and offers full re-

---

Certificates of Deposit are negotiable certificates issued against large time deposits in commercial banks. These are available to private investors in minimum amounts of $100,000, and are normally issued for periods of from one month to one year. Yields, during periods in 1974, exceeded 12% but, by year end, had fallen to roughly 9%. By April 1975 yields had declined to approximately 6%.

Bankers' Acceptances are time drafts drawn on banks by exporters or importers to obtain a stated amount of funds for merchandise, usually sold via international trade. The note is guaranteed by both the bank and the importer. Maturities generally are of six months or less; minimum private investment, $25,000. Yields comparable to CDs, above.

Commercial Paper includes short-term unsecured notes issued in bearer form by large well-regarded corporations. Minimum private investment, $25,000. Yields comparable to CDs.

Letters of Credit are notes jointly guaranteed by corporations and sponsoring banks. Yields run somewhat higher than CDs. Such notes are widely utilized by the Reserve Fund which, consequently, generally leads the money fund yield race.

demption upon twenty-four hours notice, funds wired directly to your bank, if you prefer.* Similar yields have been available from time to time in long-term savings accounts, but only at penalty if you withdraw before expiration of the account.** Management makes its money via management fees, charging generally in the area of one percent of fund assets.

Special Plans

A number of these funds offer regular monthly withdrawal plans for investors who wish to redeem on a systematic basis. A number also offer Keogh Plan arrangements for investors who prefer to place retirement funds into these vehicles.

Diversity

The typical cash management fund diversifies its portfolio into a melange of CDs (usually the largest banks, spread among the top twenty or so), government issues, and commerical paper. Ads to the contrary, the majority of funds have been placing only small amounts of cash into government paper—yields from government instruments are noncompetitive with bank paper and consequently with other funds. One exception has been The Capital Preservation Fund, which, taking its name seriously, has been concentrating its holdings in government issues. Some observers of the scene consider Reserve, the progenitor of the cash management group, the most speculative because of its reliance upon letters of credit. Reserve, itself, does not agree, arguing that its letters of credit are widely diversified, in addition to enjoying a double guarantee.

Safety

This, of course, is the $6-billion question: How well will these funds hold up during a massive depression? Pessimists in the crowd argue that

---

*Since the cash management funds all essentially offer the same product, they've been leapfrogging over each other with special frills to tempt investors. *Fidelity Daily Income Trust* was the first to offer special "check withdrawal privileges," the right to redeem shares by way of "checks" drawn against your fund holdings. In effect, this provides you with an interest-bearing checking account. Since then, Archer Daily Income, Dreyfus Liquid Assets, and Money Market Management have joined the free-checking brigade—minimum check permissible generally $500. By the time this book appears in print, there will doubtless be other funds offering the convenience of this means of redemption.

**Because of their instant liquidity, the money management funds may prove to be excellent vehicles for corporate money lying idle or for cash balance funds otherwise left in non-interest-bearing stock brokerage accounts.

any investor placing funds into a vehicle largely dependent upon the viability of banks is playing financial Russian roulette during periods of depression—risking the prospect of bank failures on a massive international scale. And this may, indeed, prove to be a major risk. Questions have been raised regarding the safety of debt instruments such as CDs should large numbers of banks fail, and/or whether a yield race will develop within the industry, leading the funds to scramble for lower-quality paper.

Spokesmen for the industry concede that shady or ill-informed management teams may develop new funds; but they point up that so far no investor has incurred loss, pointing to the diversification of fund placement as a prime safeguard in the event of any single bank failure. Bruce R. Bent of Reserve has advised me that in the event of massive redemptions, the fund could become completely liquid within roughly three weeks—a statement that is almost certainly true.

Certainly, Capital Preservation would appear to be virtually as secure as the U.S. Government paper it carries. The same cannot quite be said of the majority of the money funds that carry large quantities of CDs, insured by the FDIC only up to $40,000 per certificate. Any risks notwithstanding, the money funds have continued to prosper, even as their yields have declined.

Good news for money fund management? Yes, indeed. Bad news, of course, for banks already hard pressed to complete with other investment arenas.*

When queried regarding the possibility that the growth of these funds will create a "supply glut" of cash available for credit, exceeding the demand for capital, resulting in lower yields for investors, industry spokesmen, to a man, agreed that this was, at the worst, a remote possibility—the cash management funds representing just too small (roughly 1–2 percent) a proportion of the total credit market.

All told, it would appear as though nothing short of massive banking failure could result in loss to money fund investors, even during periods of heavy depression. It would seem then that sound strategy would call for the deposit of at least some of your capital into such vehicles during the coming depression, at least for so long as their returns exceed returns from such vehicles as the short-term savings account and short-term Treasury bills.

The truly prudent investor will, however, confine himself either to funds truly specializing in government instruments, or to funds, such as Dreyfus and others, whose bank commitments are limited only to the

---

*Banks, during recent periods of high interest rates, have had to face *disintermediation,* the withdrawal of cash left on deposit in banks for higher returns elsewhere—in particular, government issues, and now the cash management sector.

largest of banks. And what if the government and Chase Manhattan default? Well, I guess we can all go back to diamonds after all.

What if There Is No Depression?

The money funds actually enjoyed their phase of major growth not during depression (though the stock and bond markets were both in disarray) but rather during a period of intense inflation that frequently precedes depression—an inflationary period (1973–74) that saw interest rates reach levels not seen in over a century and bond prices collapsing to the chagrin of "conservative investors" in fixed-debt instruments. In this climate the money funds, their yields sensitive to, and able to rise with, fluctuating short-term rates, flourished—returns rising to at least match the inflationary spiral. In such a climate the money funds will thrive.*

However, during periods of falling interest rates investors will do far better by accumulating high-yielding long- or intermediate-term bonds, locking in high yields and possible capital gains while they are available. (High-yielding bonds rise in price as interest rates fall.) In such a climate the investment in cash management funds is ill-advised. And if you are uncertain as to the coming direction of interest rates? Perhaps you can hedge your bets a bit, placing some capital in long-term fixed-income instruments, some in the highly liquid money funds.

Summing Up: While management funds may not offer the panacea for all investor ills, they have at least been able to return all the cash placed into them by investors, and then some. Which, after all, is more than the rest of the mutual fund industry has been able to say.

Directory of Money Management Funds

There is little point in listing the various procedures, regulations, and features of the various funds—these have been in a continuous state of flux since this segment of the mutual industry first came to life. Do send for the prospectus of any fund in which you have interest, evaluating thereafter not simply the yield, but the quality of their portfolio, their overall philosophy, size, and past track record. And again, during the coming depression, emphasize safety above all else. Any of the following funds will be delighted to send you a prospectus upon request.

---

*Interest rates and the rates of inflation reached new peaks at the start of 1980. Rates of inflation, for a few months, approached 20% per year. Short-term interest costs approached 20% as well. Throughout, the money market funds continued to pay full interest—well surpassing 16% per annum during the early portion of the year.

Money Market Management, Inc., 421 Seventh Avenue, Pittsburgh, Pa. 15219, 800-245-2423; in Pennsylvania, 412-288-1948. *Special Features:* Will arrange for the direct transfer from your brokerage and to your brokerage of cash balances that you may want to invest in the fund.

Dreyfus Liquid Assets, Inc., 600 Madison Avenue, New York, N.Y. 10022, 800-223-5525; in New York State, 212-935-5700. Call collect away from New York City. *Special Features:* Has been among the largest of the money funds, conservatively run, "free check redemption."

Oppenheimer Monetary Bridge, Inc., One New York Plaza, New York City, N.Y. 10004, 212-825-4000.

The Reserve Fund, Inc., 810 Seventh Avenue, New York, N.Y. 10019, 212-977-9880. *Special Features:* The oldest of the money market funds and usually one of the highest yielding. There has been some controversy in the past over the quality of their portfolio, but to date the fund has always fully met its obligations to shareholders and has grown very nicely.

Fidelity Daily Income Trust, P.O. Box 193, Boston, Mass. 02101, 800-225-6190; in Massachusetts, 617-726-1650. *Special Features:* The fund has charged a low management fee but has imposed certain service charges over the years.

Capital Preservation Fund, Inc., 755 Page Mill Road, Palo Alto, California 94304, 415-858-2480. *Special Features:* Runs the most conservative of portfolios—largely invested in U.S. Government obligations—and, therefore, the safest fund for a serious depression. However, yields run lower than most funds.

J. P. Cabot Short Term Fund, Inc., 104 South Central Avenue, Valley Stream, N.Y. 11580, 516-561-0130, or from New York City, 212-591-2027.

There are many other money market funds available, of course, including some that specialize in tax-exempt securities. *Barron's Financial Weekly* regularly carries advertisements of such vehicles and may be consulted for further suggestions.

A Hybrid That's Definitely Worth Your Attention

The Rowe Price New Income Fund, Inc., 100 East Pratt Street, Baltimore, Md. 21202, 301-547-2136, is managed by T. Rowe Price Associates, Inc., one of the most successful of mutual fund management teams, with a superior record over many years in equity fund performance. Their income fund has its assets divided more or less evenly among long- and short-term debt instruments, and could be an excellent compromise for the investor who chooses to put all his eggs neither in the long- nor short-term basket. The fund charges no commissions. The minimum rating of its corporate instruments has been A, probably safe enough even during depression times—the portfolio heavily laden with utility, high-grade corporate, and government-agency issues.

7
GOLD: ANOTHER HEDGE AGAINST TOTAL CALAMITY?

If diamonds offer considerable appeal as a depression hedge, then certainly gold glitters in that area as well. After all, weren't the Arabs insisting upon gold recently rather than the British pound? And didn't *Barron's* report Arab buying of gold jewelry on the international auction markets? And didn't gold finish last year with a flourish, reaching new highs right at year's end—providing profit for anyone who had accumulated the metal to that point? And doesn't James Dines, not to mention other goldbugs, predict stratospheric prices in the years to come?

A convincing series of arguments? Well, yes and no. Public interest in gold certainly did reach a fever pitch in 1974, largely the result of the legalization of gold ownership in the United States effective with the beginning of 1975. And some participation in the gold markets *should* represent at least a portion of every depression strategy. However, there are pitfalls to gold speculation—serious drawbacks not generally mentioned in the ads for gold ingots and such, and you should weigh carefully both sides of the scale before you trade in your government bonds, or substitute your carats for karats.

A Five-Minute History of Gold

The roots of gold as a repository of value date back to antiquity—gold was used as the basis for monetary exchange even during the ancient Babylonian and Chinese civilizations. Moreover, the metal's beauty, malleability, permanence, and relative scarcity have maintained it as *the* medium over the many centuries since.

In the United States the federal government has made attempts now and then to print money not backed by gold. However, the attempt was laid to rest in 1900 with the passage of the Gold Standard Act, which set an official value for gold of $20.67, a value that dated to the mid-19th century. Gold coins minted in this country from 1838 to 1933 contained actual gold proportionate to the face value of the coin, based on a value of $20.67 per ounce. (A $5 coin contained roughly 1/4-ounce of gold; a $20 piece, .97 ounce.) In 1934 the dollar was devalued by increasing gold's value from $20.67 per ounce to $35 per ounce. The Gold Reserve Act of 1934 also prohibited U.S. citizens from owning gold bullion; this was the prohibition just repealed.

In 1944, at Bretton Woods, New Hampshire, a new international monetary system was established, including the International Monetary Fund, into which nations deposited an amount of their own currency, with an additional 33 percent value in actual gold. Nations could then draw loans from IMF up to double their deposit. Under Bretton Woods, too, the dollar was established as the basic exchange currency. Nations could, however, exchange dollars for gold at $35 per ounce.

In the years that followed European interests initiated raids on the dollar, converting excess reserves into gold and gradually depleting our stockpile, which fell from $22.09 billion (1953) to only $10 billion (1971). On August 15, 1971, the United States finally refused officially to guarantee gold for dollars, at the same time stating that the official exchange rate was to be raised, this time to $42.22 per ounce, a devaluation of the U.S. dollar hardly endearing to the rest of the world.

Meanwhile, back at the ranch, the U.S. Government, in March 1968, responded to speculation in the gold markets by refusing any longer to honor privately held dollars by convertibility into gold. Thenceforth, we would agree to offer convertibility of the dollar into gold only for official government transactions, at the time still at the rate of $35 per ounce. Gold in private markets was set free to find its own level.

In March 1974 a new dimension was added to the ball game. Up to then central banks valued gold reserves at the rate of $42.22 per ounce for purposes of collateral in international loans. From that point on gold could be collateralized at any price approximating the going rate on the open market. This had the effect of practically tripling the value of each nation's reserves at that point; with gold even higher by the end of the year, reserve borrowing power had risen (end of 1974) to nearly five times the amount availble before March.

The net effect of these international machinations has been the gradual debasement of currency on an international scale, which added to, rather than diminished, the significance of gold. Furthermore, with Italy and Britain on the verge of economic chaos, the thrust has been more toward a continuation rather than an alleviation of this trend. The impact upon gold prices? Consider the movement of gold. Figure 1 shows the relationship of the gold price to the value of the dollar relative to the German deutschemark, one of the stronger currencies. Which would you rather hold, paper dollars or gold bullion?

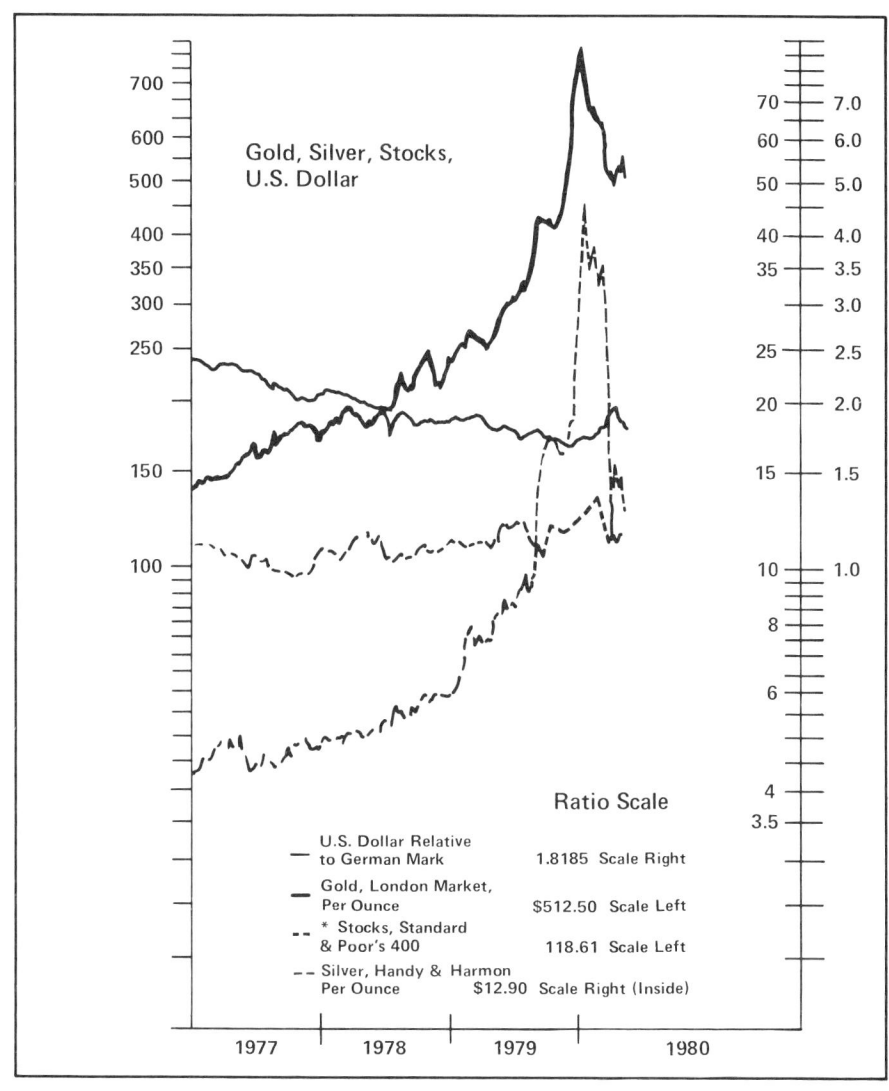

FIGURE 1
The price of gold has been rising as the dollar has weakened in recent years.
SOURCE: *The Media-General Financial Weekly*, Richmond, Va. 23261.

Gold speculation reached a then record peak during the second half of 1974 as a result of the U.S. Government's legalization of private holdings of gold bullion. Along with a proliferation of new gold mutual funds, gold bullion offerings, and the like came a sharp rise in the price of gold—gold approaching $200 per ounce as 1974 came to a close. The actual legalization, effective January 1, 1975, proved to be something of an anticlimax; the price of gold drifted down into mid-1976, falling to approximately $100 per ounce.

From that point on gold began first a slow and then an accelerating advance in price, spurred on by dislocations in the international monetary markets, worldwide inflation, the threatened refusal by the Arabs to accept depreciating American dollars, and rising oil prices. Speculative fever once again reached a peak in January 1980, this time with gold briefly climbing to as high as $800 per ounce. By that time the public press was daily headlining the price of the metal, buyers and sellers stood on line at New York jewelry shops, and gold fever spread throughout the land.

With the public so involved, only a short period was required for the price of gold—and simultaneously of silver—to break. Gold, within a few weeks, tumbled from $800 to $500 per ounce. The collapse of the Hunt's silver speculation sent brief but powerful shock waves throughout the financial community, but in the end gold firmed in price, silver firmed in price, and the Hunt brothers made arrangements to meet their silver futures margin calls, thereby bailing out the commodity exchanges, Bache (the broker involved), and very possibly Wall Street.

The Gold Markets

South Africa is the largest producer of gold today—supplying roughly 30 million ounces in 1973 of a total world new supply of 45 million ounces. The Soviet Union is second in production, with output slightly under 50 percent of South Africa's. The gold not employed in world trade is used in jewelry and art (51.6 percent), industry (38.3 percent), and dentistry (10.1 percent). However, gold fabrication has been declining in recent years, a point frequently made by bears on the metal. Should the price of gold continue to rise, we would then have to anticipate further declines in nonessential use.

The United States remains the largest holder of gold reserves in the world, with $11.7 billion worth (1973) compared with Germany's $5.0 billion, France's $4.3 billion, and Switzerland's $3.5 billion.

The price of gold is fixed daily in the London and Zurich markets; in London twice a day by a consortium of dealers. The North American price is based upon the London gold fixing, though the bulk of trading takes place in Zurich.

Gold itself is generally sold by the troy ounce, 31.1035 grams to the ounce; 32.15 troy ounces to the kilogram. The utmost in purity is 24-karat gold, 100 percent fine. Twenty-two-karat gold is 91.67 percent fine; 14 karat, 58.3 percent. Pure gold is extremely soft and is generally alloyed for coinage and jewelry to increase its hardness.

Presuming that you do wish to obtain and hoard gold (or to speculate in other ways), there are any number of avenues open to you. However, before you do so, be certain to evaluate some of the caveats mentioned as we go along.

Gold Coins

Gold coins can be roughly divided into two groups: (1) numismatic coins that have a high collector's value in addition to the intrinsic value of the actual gold contained within, and (2) coins that have no numismatic value to speak of, their price or value determined almost exclusively by the value of their gold content, a direct reflection of the price of gold on the international money markets.

FIGURE 2
Gold prices peaked early in 1980. SOURCE: Commodity Research Bureau, 1 Liberty Plaza, New York, N.Y., 10006.

Coins of high numismatic value are best left to professional dealers and experienced collectors; forgeries abound in the field, and, in purchasing such coins, you are playing more in the collector's than in the gold investor's league. We will therefore confine ourselves to coins of lower collector value, but high intrinsic gold value, as a proportion of their price.

The U.S. $20 St. Gaudens "double eagle" is the best known and the most desired, selling generally well above its intrinsic gold value. However, the majority of St. Gaudens coins are not truly rare coins—a good compromise if you prefer some numismatic play with your gold hoarding. Other coins have less historical meaning, many struck simply for the purpose of capitalizing upon the 10 percent premium over gold content generally paid for such coins.

Among the coins available purely for gold play are:

Coin	Gold Content (ounces)
$20 St. Gaudens, U.S.	.9675
$20 Liberty, U.S.	.9675
$10 Liberty, U.S.	.4837
Sovereign, Great Britain	.2354
20 Franc, Switzerland	.1865
50 Peso, Mexico	1.2056
20 Peso, Mexico	.4823
10 Peso, Mexico	.2411
100 Korona, Austria	.9802
100 Korona, Hungary	.9802
10 Guilder, Netherlands	.1947
Krugerrand, South Africa	1.000

Of the above coins, the Mexican Peso, the Austrian and Hungarian Korona, and the South African Krugerrand are the best values for pure gold content. These are mainly restrikes, coins issued purely for the gold market, and their premiums are slight. The other coins carry a greater or lesser numismatic premium.

To learn the actual premium over gold content for which a coin is selling, first find the current price of gold, say, $200 per ounce. Then take the current price of the coin and multiply it by the number of ounces of gold in the coin. For example, the Krugerrand contains one ounce of gold. With gold at $200 per ounce, each Krugerrand will contain $200 worth of gold. If it sells at $220, the Krugerrand then will be changing hands at a 10 percent premium over its gold content. You should pay no more than a 10 percent premium for any coin purchased as a pure gold play.

The Krugerrand is a particularly interesting coin. Minted in South Africa since 1969, it was not legally available to Americans under old regulations. The Krugerrand is the only gold coin in the world that is legal tender, priced daily by the Reserve Bank of South Africa. If you present it at an international bank for exchange, they will honor it at the latest quoted rate. It is an excellent alternative to diamonds if you must emigrate, or if social chaos requires your fleeing without other possessions. At recent prices ($200 per ounce), 30 ounces of Krugerrands will, in effect, be worth $6,000 on your person.

Any gold coin, of course, represents the near ultimate in doomsday insurance—should the coming depression assume a truly ugly face. Profit aside, the truly prudent will own some just in case.

Where to Buy

Right now, just about anywhere. Gold coins are sold through coin dealers, brokers, stock exchange houses, banks, and department stores. The Republic National Bank in New York has been selling coins for some time. Merrill Lynch has instituted gold purchase programs, and a number of brokerages have followed suit.

With just a little caution in making purchases from reliable sources, you'll probably secure at least the going rate on gold coins. Pay no more than a 90 percent premium over gold-content value for the St. Gaudens; 85 percent premium for the Liberty $20 piece, 50 percent premium for British Sovereigns and French Napoleons. The Krugerrand, Mexican Peso, and Austrian and Hungarian Koronas should be secured at premiums of 10 percent or less. It should be remembered that, for years, the ownership of these coins was the only legal avenue open to Americans for the physical ownership of gold. Premiums may decline in coming years now that bullion itself can be purchased. Incidentally, the greater the amount in coins you purchase at any one time, the less the premium you should pay.

Mutual Funds That Invest in Gold in Various Forms

One way to participate in potential gains in the price of gold maintaining full liquidity and avoiding the problems inherent in the purchase, insurance, and storage of gold bullion itself is the investment in shares of mutual funds that themselves invest in gold in one form or another. Such funds also afford the advantages of diversification. Many involve no commission costs of any kind, although commissions, of course, are paid indirectly via management fees and expenses paid to the managements of these funds.

Among the mutual funds that are available for this purpose are:

United Services Fund, 110 East Byrd Boulevard, Universal City, Texas, 78148. This fund is invested primarily in shares of South Africa gold stocks.

Golconda Investors, 111 Broadway, New York City, N.Y. 10006. This fund invests in gold bullion directly as well as in shares of gold stocks.

Strategic Investments, 8333 Douglas Avenue, Dallas, Texas 75225.

Research Capital, 155 Bovet Road, San Mateo, California 94402.

International Investors, 122 East 42nd Street, New York, N.Y. 10017.

These funds have all performed well during periods when gold has risen in price. The prices of United Services and Golconda appear daily in major financial newspapers in the mutual fund sections.

Shares of Golconda, incidentally, can be exchanged via telephone for shares of a money market fund or of equity funds sponsored by the same management company, The Bull & Bear Group.

Gold Bullion

Insofar as the small investor is concerned, only the most confirmed hoarder will opt for the purchase of gold bullion itself—though larger-scale gold manipulators may well prefer to. (In Switzerland, 90 percent of gold sold changes hands in bullion form; in France, only 40 percent.)

Just in case you do envision yourself a Croesus surveying your vaults, do keep these facts in mind. When you purchase gold bullion in smaller quantities, you pay anywhere from 7 percent to 20 percent above spot price (the going open market price of gold) for fabricating costs (the costs of converting raw gold into salable bars). Fabrication costs will range from 20 percent on small bars to roughly 10 percent for 20-ounce bars. Larger bars will cost less. In addition, you must lay out money for shipping, storage, insurance, and handling. And, finally, you may have to pay for assay upon sale, the verification of the size and quality of your bars. All told, these costs can add up to 15–20 percent of the spot price of gold—you won't come out even unless and until gold rises by at least 15–20 percent.

Discouraged yet? Well, consider one more thing. Gold bullion pays no dividends, so you lose the potential income that could be secured from the cash you've tied up. Let's figure another 8 percent there (easily secured recently from high-grade corporates). In short, you'll need at least a 20–30 percent rise in the price of gold just to come out even. Obviously, bullion's not for short-term trading. On a longer-term basis, you'll have to figure on at least a 15 percent annual rise in the price of gold to truly come out ahead.

Still planning to venture into bullion land? Well, figure on buying bullion in sizes ranging from ½ ounce to 400 ounces. The bullion should be at least .995 fine; .999 is better quality. Purchase bullion fabricated only by the best known of international fabricators—I recommend Engelhard Minerals, who will stamp their name on the ingot, heat-sealing the ingot in plastic to provide visual evidence that the bar has not been shaven. Engelhard will repurchase bars from you; some sources will not. Again, deal only with large, well-financed, reputable dealers. Do *not* expect fly-by-night operators to be able to guarantee repurchase. And remember, you'll get better resale from one 100-ounce ingot than from 100 one-ounce ingots. In short, if you must buy bullion, better buy big or not at all.

The Gold Futures Markets

Now, here's a speculator's delight! Came legalization, came the futures markets. In case you're new to the commodity pits, a futures contract (if long) represents your agreement to purchase a stipulated amount of a commodity at a specified date at a specified price. For example, suppose you purchase a 100-ounce gold contract on the International Monetary Market, June delivery, for $200 per ounce. Comes the last trading day in June, you are required to take possession of those hundred ounces at $200 per ounce. In the meantime, when you enter the contract, you put up minimum margin of $1,300.

Now, you do not actually have to take possession of the gold; in fact, you'll almost certainly not want to. Let's suppose that following your purchase of the contract, the price of gold rises, say, to $250 per ounce for June delivery. You can sell the contract you have purchased, profiting by $50 per ounce or by $5,000 total for the 100-ounce contract (less commissions). If the price of gold falls? Well, if you have to sell, say, at $150 per ounce, you will lose $5,000.

Gold contracts, like other futures contracts, can be sold short. Let's suppose that you believe that gold will fall in value. You can contract to sell 100 ounces of gold for $200 per ounce. Should the price fall, you can buy this contract back for $150—profiting by $5,000 on the decline. Should gold rise in price, you lose this time, since you will have to pay above $200 an ounce for gold you are obligated to sell at that level.

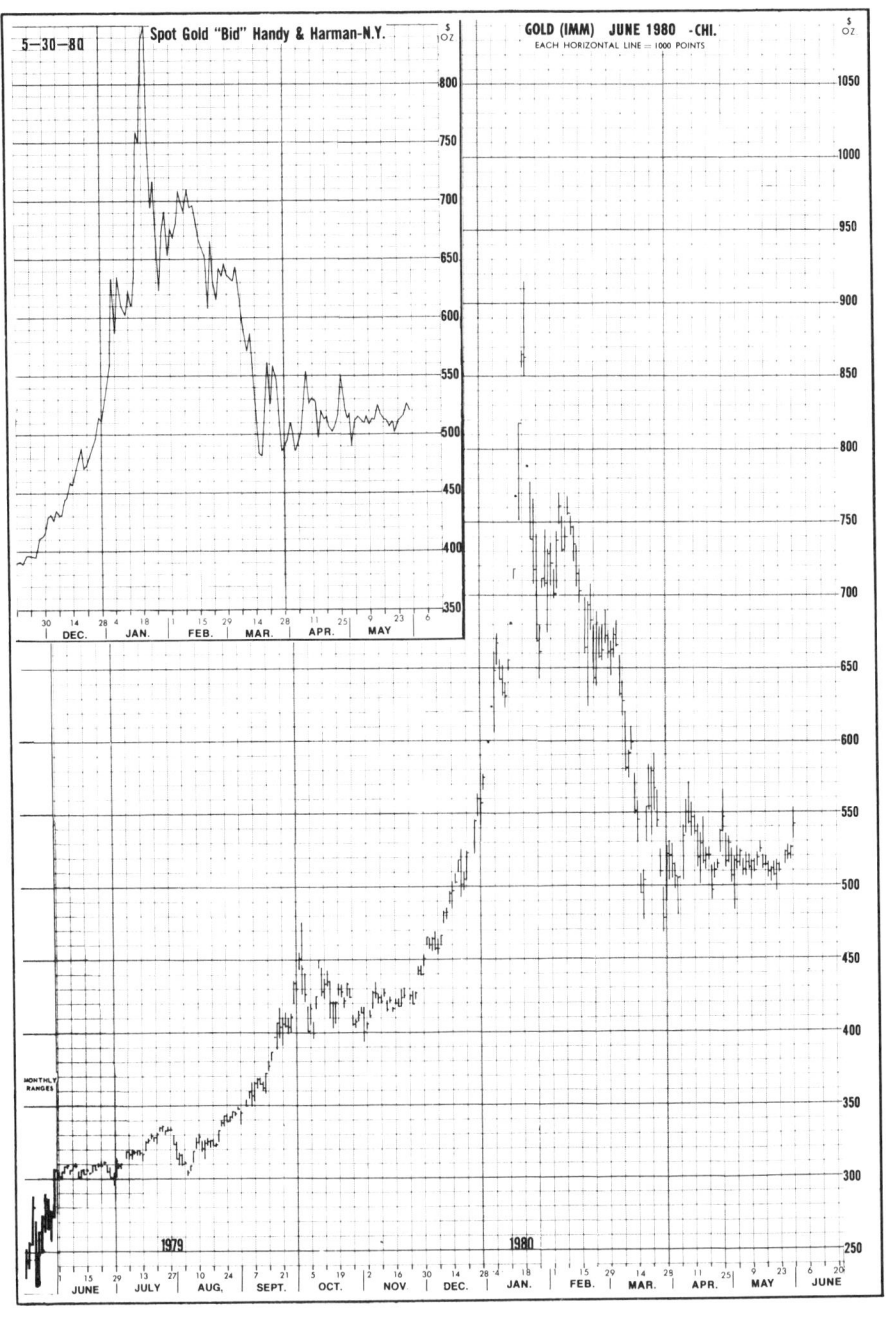

FIGURE 3
Gold futures trade on the International Monetary Market. SOURCE: Chart reprinted from *Commodity Chart Service,* a weekly publication of Commodity Research Bureau, Inc., 10006.

In the futures market, then, you incur no costs for fabrication, insurance, resale (except commissions), or delivery. If you can—or think you can—call short-term market swings, then this may just turn out to be your ball park. Fluctuations on the futures market parallel those in equities on the stock market. But on the futures market, there is one additional and major kicker....

Leverage!

At $200 per ounce, that 100-ounce contract on the IMM covers $20,000 worth of gold. You are required to deposit only $1,300 in margin. Suppose gold rises from $200 to $250 per ounce, a gain of 25 percent. Your profit? $5,000—on an investment of only $1,300. That comes to a hefty gain of 384.6 percent! On an investment that grew by only 25 percent.

But suppose that gold falls instead, say by only 6.5 percent to $187 per ounce. You've lost $1,300, your entire investment, and you're back to collecting copper pennies instead of gold sovereigns. Leverage obviously works both ways. Incidentally, you pay no interest on futures margin debits—until and unless you take actual possession of the gold, you've made no actual purchase; you're merely committed to make one.

For further information regarding gold futures contracts—regulations, margin requirements, and so forth—write to the commodity exchanges themselves. These include, among others:

Exchange	Contract Unit	Minimum Commission (round trip)	Minimum* Margin
Commodity Exchange Inc. 81 Broad Street New York, N.Y. 10004	100 troy oz.	$45.00	$1,750
International Monetary Market (Chicago Mercantile) 444 West Jackson Blvd., Chicago, Ill. 60606	100 troy oz.	$45.00	$1,300
New York Mercantile Exchange 6 Harrison Street, New York, N.Y. 10013	1 kilo (32.15 oz.)	$30.00	$ 500
Chicago Board of Trade 141 W. Jackson Blvd. Chicago, Ill. 60604	96.45 oz. (3 one-kilo bars)	$40.00	$1,500

*Minimum margin may vary according to the brokerage with which you deal and with the price of gold over the years to come.

Gold Stocks

If gold coins are for hoarding, futures for speculating, and certificates for safekeeping, then gold shares are for trading. What's more, gold securities represent the only form of gold investment that draws income while you await developments.

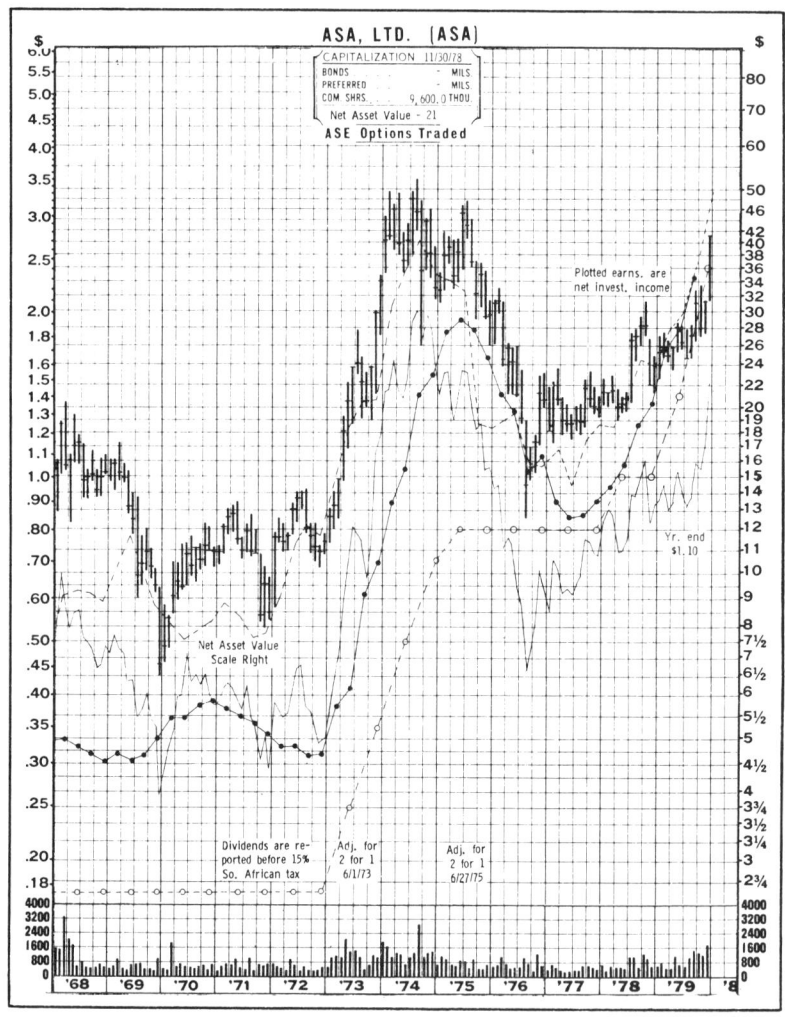

FIGURE 4
ASA is the bellwether of the gold stock group.   SOURCE: Securities Research Co., 208 Newbury Street, Boston, Mass., 02116.

The major drawbacks? Gold shares do not represent possession of the actual metal—you are purchasing gold bullion indirectly; gold shares may or may not move in tandem with the metal itself. In fact, it is more likely that gold securities will move *in advance* of the price of gold itself. The stock market tends to discount news *months in advance,* and the stock market's behavior vis-á-vis gold is no exception. Prices of gold shares tend to rise sharply at the initiation of periods of international gold fever, dropping somewhat in advance of actual peaks in the price of gold. You can use the price of gold shares to help you anticipate the moves of actual gold.

For example, ASA Ltd., the king of the gold securities moved up sharply from 1973 into early 1974, but could make little progress thereafter, weakening even prior to the peaking of gold prices at year-end. ASA, incidentally, which is a holding company of South African gold shares, has generally been a good buy when its price falls at or below its net asset value, a good sell whenever its price per share rises to 150 percent of net asset value. ASA and other listed golds—Campbell Red Lake Mines Ltd., Giant Yellowknife Mines Ltd.—pay relatively little in the way of dividends, but do tend to move contracyclically to the rest of the stock market, representative of gold's strength during periods of economic uncertainty. Gold shares remained quite firm during the thirties and far outperformed the rest of the list during the 1973–74 bear market.

South African Golds

While the New York Stock Exchange-listed golds offer relatively little in the way of income, the South African gold shares offer both substantial income and a higher proportion of mine life and earnings per share dollar. A number are traded in this country over the counter, but be sure to specify American Depository Receipts when you make your purchase. Do be aware, too, of the relatively uncertain political climate in South Africa that may, in fact, account for the lower valuation of these shares.

South African shares include, among others:

Bracken: relatively short life remaining, pays high current dividend.
Buffelsfontein: medium yield.
Doornfontein: medium yield.
Durban Roodeport Deep: medium-life, marginal mine. Needs much higher gold prices.
East Driesfontein: low dividends, but a long-life mine suitable for long-term holding.
Free State Geduld: high dividend, medium-life mine.

Harmony: long-life, low-ore-grade mine. Medium dividend.
Hartebeestfontein: medium-to-long life expectancy. Medium dividend. A good choice. Uranium too.
Kloof: long-life mine, medium dividends.
President Brand: long-life mine, good dividend. A good choice.
President Steyn: long-life mine, medium dividends.
Randfontein: gold, and uranium too. No dividends paid in 1974.
St. Helena: medium-to-long life. Fair dividend.
Vaal Reefs: good long-life mine. Dividends at low end.
Western Deep: A good quality long-term mine. Medium dividend.

High dividend payers return from 9 to 18 percent per year; medium 6 to 9 percent; low, below 6 percent. Prices are listed daily in *The Wall Street Journal* or can be secured from your stockbroker.

Pros and Cons of Gold Investment

No prudent investor should be without some form of gold in his portfolio—as a hedge against future currency debasement and inflation, for profit when gold truly glitters on the investment scene, and as pure doomsday insurance. Comes the next depression, you'll be glad you salted some away. Do be aware that gold may not fly during periods of economic prosperity—but those periods are precisely the times to accumulate gold positions. *Do* accumulate gold, and gold stocks, *when gold is out of the headlines*, and then wait patiently.

Obviously, late 1974 was *not* the time. With the impending legalization of gold, scores of scalpers, dealers, exchanges, brokerages, and just plain sharpies emerged to hawk their wares. The initial flood of advertisements, gold seminars, and speculation was matched by prophecies of doom, government warnings, and, finally, by a U.S. Treasury auction of gold shortly after legalization. Following a year-end run-up, gold declined sharply once the American public proved its disinterest; only to rally once again. In the interim France revalued its gold reserves upward to $170 per ounce. In brief, this was a chaotic period, with sharp twists and turns, definitely not the climate for careful investment.

Early 1980 gold reached an all-time high. With fears of rabid inflation, rumors that the Arab sheiks would refuse to accept American dollars in exchange for oil, and with a resurgence of speculative gold fever, the price of gold shot up almost overnight to $800 per ounce, before subsiding rapidly to the $500 region. Obviously, speculators, attracted by all the gold furor, found themselves with something less than gold nuggets on their hands.

However, by the time you read this, matters should have settled down. Again, wait until gold is out of the headlines, and accumulate during periods of quiescence, after the price of gold has leveled out for a period of time. You can limit your risk in this way, even if the aurophobes prove correct and gold simply stagnates in the months to come. It *will* have its day in the sun again some day.

Summing Up the Choices

We've already covered the pros and cons of the options open to you. Coins for liquidity. Certificates as a play on bullion with easy marketability. Futures for leveraged speculation. Mutual funds for the guy who prefers to hire help rather than do it himself. Gold shares if you're familiar with the stock market and insist upon some dividends along the way. The best choice? We prefer the Krugerrand, certificates, and gold shares ourselves. But your own taste may run in different directions.

Oh, there is one more choice, if you prefer not to hoard, polish, or trade. You *can* try digging. The U.S. Department of the Interior's Geological Survey Circular 699 mentions the strong possibility that untapped gold deposits exist in the Black Hills of South Dakota. The circular, complete with maps of potential digs can be obtained free of charge by writing to the U.S. Geological Survey, National Center, Reston, Va. 22092.

So much for values under the ground. Let's move on now to values above the ground.

8
HOW TO PRANCE THROUGH A BEAR MARKET SMILING

I know. You're supposed to stay away from bear markets. Like the plague. Didn't I say so earlier in this book? Well, let's just say "yes and no." Comes the bear, you should learn, of course, how to keep your head out of his mouth. You do *not* buy stocks (except for brief rallies, and even then you're taking a big risk), you do *not* accumulate mutual funds (except for the liquid asset funds), you avoid convertible bonds (except for deeply discounted issues when you sense the turn coming).

Common stocks should *not*—repeat—*should not* be held during bear markets. Forget your broker's pap about superhigh earnings, "imminent recovery", solid values. During bear markets they all go, or at least close enough to all to make looking for the needle in the haystack strictly a sucker play. (During 1974, for example, only 149 stocks advanced on the N.Y.S.E., while 1,320 declined. On the Amex, there were only 153 winners as opposed to 944 losers.)

Unfortunately, the public, by and large, knows only one way with common equities—buy and sell. The fact of the matter, however, is that during bear markets you can profit, and profit fast and big, by doing the reverse. Instead of buy and sell, you *sell and buy;* in other words, *sell short.*

Short Selling

Selling short is simply the reverse of the usual stock transaction. Generally, holders of securities purchase for price appreciation, taking profits (hopefully) after a price rise by selling at a price higher than they paid. When you sell short, you *first sell* the shares, delivering shares borrowed from your stockbroker. You hope for a price *decline,* so that you can then purchase the shares you sold, paying back the I.O.U. held against you by your brokerage with the shares secured by your purchase.

There are only a few requirements involved. First, the short sale must take place in a margin account. Second, the short sale must take place on an "uptick," a trading transaction at a price above the one just previous. This rule was introduced some years ago to prevent "bear raids" on particular issues, repeated short sales to drive prices sharply lower, panicking the public into selling, the short-selling group then "covering" into the panic, buying shares to repay their loan. Short sales, taxwise, are always treated as short-term capital gains and losses, regardless of how long you hold the short position.

Computing Profits and Losses

The profit or loss on a short sale is simply the difference between what you receive for the stock when you sold it and what you must ultimately pay to "cover the short" or to buy the shares to repay the loan. For example, suppose you had sold International Telephone short in October 1973 at 38, covering one year later at 14. Your profit would have amounted to 24 points, or $2,400 per hundred shares, less commissions. When you sell short you are also liable for any dividends paid by the company whose shares you are short during the period of the short sale. International Telephone paid out $1.40 per share in dividends between October 1973 and October 1974, so you would have to deduct $140 per hundred shares from your profit. Because of this provision, it is generally preferable to short stocks that offer little or no dividend payout.

If International Telephone had risen from 38 to 48, instead of declining to 14? In that case, you would have lost $1,000, plus commissions and dividend payout, instead of profiting. Short selling is, after all, a two-way street.

Profit Potential

Big! Anyone who says that large stock market profits cannot be made during bear markets simply hasn't savored the joys of short selling at the right time. Granted, a stock can rise indefinitely—doubling, tripling, or even rising by 2,000 percent, as Xerox did from 1962 to 1972. And, granted, a stock can fall by only 100 percent, never more; so the profit potential from short sales *is* limited to that extent.

But consider these facts too. Over the past century, all told, the stock market has been in declining phases one-third of the time; in fact bear markets existed for roughly half the 1966–74 period. And these were relatively prosperous times. Who knows what will happen when the next major depression strikes? Furthermore, stocks fall twice as fast as they rise! Bear market profits can be gained more rapidly than bull market windfalls. Examples? It took Avon ten years to rise from 20 to 140. It required only eighteen months for the stock to give up that entire gain. Polaroid labored up from 14 to 150 for a full decade. Within two years (1972–74) it was back to 14. SPL also gave up a full ten-year rise in less than two years.

In other words, had you shorted Avon at 140, covering at 20, you would have made 85.7 percent on your money in only eighteen months, a 57.1 percent gain annualized. Had you operated on the full 65 percent margin that pertained in 1972, you would have done even better, because your cash outlay would have been only 65 percent of the proceeds of the short sale or $9,100 (65% × $140 = 91). In that event, your profit of $12,000 per hundred shares would represent 131.9 percent of your investment. During how many bull markets have you achieved that rate of return?

Knowing When to Sell Short

Obviously the secret of profiting during depression-induced bear markets lies in picking the right time to go short and the right stocks to short. Of the two, picking the right time is the more significant—if you are correct on the market, the odds are probably in the order of ten to one that your stock selection will decline.

Here, then, are ten ways to call market tops—using information readily available in national daily and weekly newspapers.

1. Learn to Employ Contrary Opinion   I place this number 1 for an important reason: the stock market is a *lead economic indicator.* Large money interests begin their movement out of and into securities several months before the public becomes aware of basic changes in the economy. January 1973 is a prime case in point. Corporate earnings were rising to record levels, employment was high, the stock market had just crashed through Dow 1,000, *Barron's* featured an article in which experts unanimously saw higher prices—and yet the market picked that precise moment to begin the worst bear calamity since the depression. Could you have avoided the trap? Yes—if you had applied contrary opinion, acting in the direction opposite majority public pronouncements.

As a corollary, *watch the stock market's reaction to news.* Bear markets begin amidst high earnings and general optimism. *When the stock market stops reacting favorably to good news, it's time to sell.* Again, the best recent example: nearly the entire year 1973. *Conversely, when the stock market refuses to fall on bad news, it's getting time to cover those short sales and buy.* Example: The American auto stocks began to firm in early 1974, amidst lower earnings, massive layoffs, and falling sales. Implications: The 1973–74 bear market may have been drawing to an end.

The bear market of 1969–70 ended amidst shattering international developments (Cambodia), student riots, the near financial collapse of major corporations (Chrysler and Lockheed), and a major liquidity crisis. Almost certainly the next bull market will end in a spew of glad tidings.

Learn to use the stock market as a general barometer! Though its record is not infallible, the stock market does have an excellent record as a lead indicator for the general economy. For example, its crash in 1973 gave ample warning of the deep recession that followed. The market did miss the boat in 1962, the '62 decline not being accompanied by major recession. Nonetheless, better safe than sorry.

2. Watch the European Markets The American stock market does not exist in a world of its own. For better or for worse, our fortunes are inextricably tied to the general economies of the Free World— Britain, Germany, France, Italy.

Frequently these European economies, and their stock markets, turn before ours, providing advance warning of what will take place between our shores. The London market, in the past, has served as a harbinger for ours, turning down before ours did. This proved the case again in recent years, the London market beginning its decline during 1972, several months before our own.

Thorough financial newspapers frequently carry news of the foreign exchanges. *Barron's* carries the stock market averages of several foreign exchanges on a weekly basis.

3. Evaluate Dividend Yields Much as the go-go boys would like to pretend otherwise, common equities still must compete with other vehicles for the investment dollar. True, during the halcyon days of 1962–68 dividends were considered rather stodgy, and a bore at that— after all, who needed dividends when cheap Amex issues were doubling overnight?

However, sooner or later, the piper does get paid—and history has shown that the stock market is ready for a fall whenever the Dow Industrials yield, as an aggregate, approximately 3 percent, or when you have to spend near $33 to $35 in Dow stock price to secure $1 in dividend proceeds. This indicator called the turn in 1929, 1936, 1962, 1966, and 1973. Stocks, on the other hand, can be purchased when the Dow dividend rises to roughly 6 percent. We saw such levels just prior

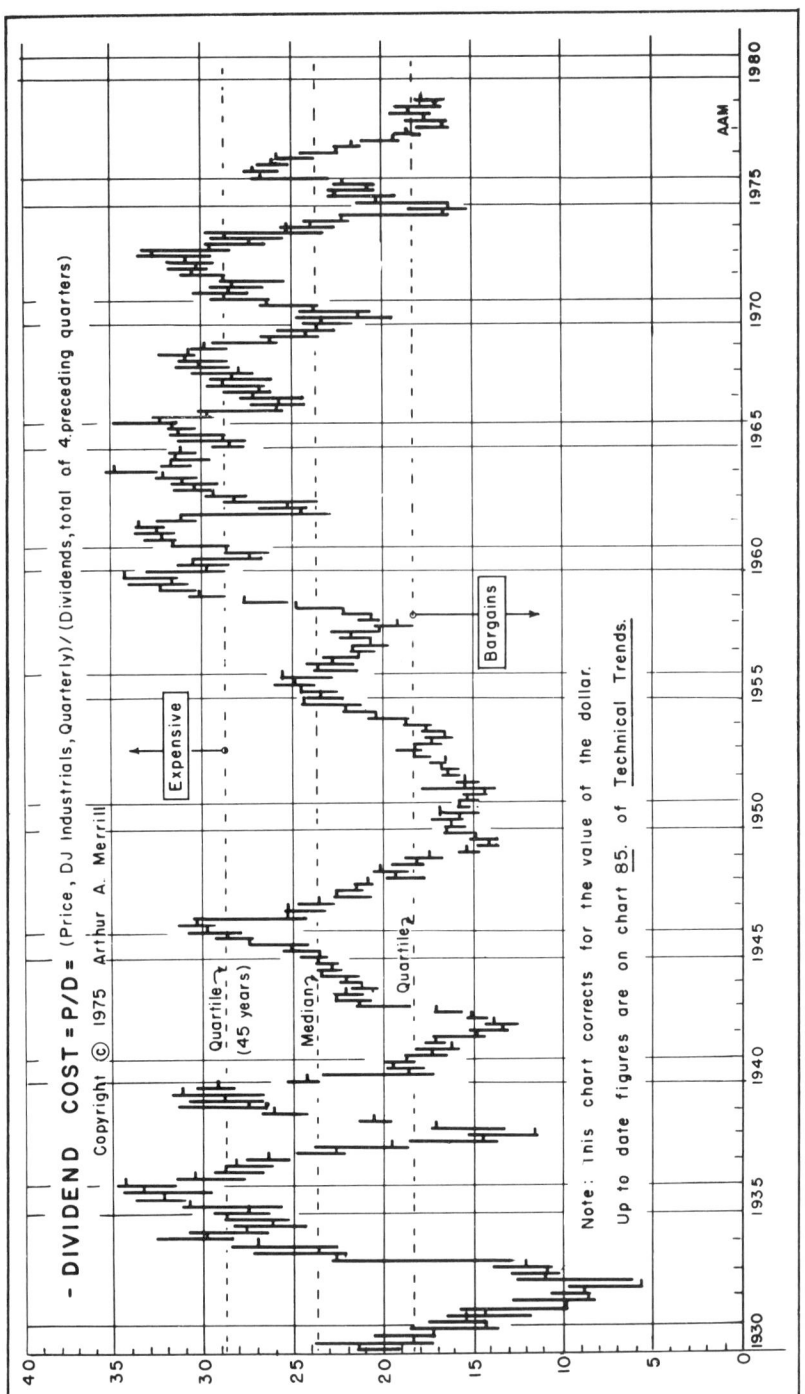

FIGURE 1

Market declines are imminent whenever the Dow Industrials, as an aggregate, yield roughly 3 percent. SOURCE: Merrill Analysis, Inc., Box 228, Chappaqua, N.Y. 10514.

to the great postwar bull market and again during 1974. *Barron's* reports this data weekly.

4. Watch the Advance-Decline Line The Advance-Decline Line is a cumulative total of the difference between the number of stocks advancing each week and the number declining. In other words, if 850 stocks advance in a given week and 550 decline, the difference amounts to +300. If 550 advance and 850 decline, then the difference is –300. Presuming that the cumulative total the prior week was +2,000, the new total would be +2,300 in the first case (2,000 + 300) or 1,700 in the second case (2,000 – 300). This data can be found weekly in *Barron's Financial Weekly* or in newspapers such as *The New York Times*.

The A-D line provides a far better indication of what the "true" stock market is doing than, say, the Dow Industrial Average, which measures only 30 issues, since it is far broader in scope, reflecting all the *roughly* 2,000 securities traded on the New York Stock Exchange.

During the early phases of bull markets the majority of issues move up broadly—the "breadth" of the market is excellent. As the bull market matures, fewer and fewer issues advance—the A-D line begins to fall away from its peak, usually even as the Dow moves on to make new highs. This disparity is referred to as a "divergence," a discord between the averages and the true market.

Generally speaking, you can expect two divergences to occur before the averages begin to collapse; but even the first divergence should serve to alert you to impending trouble, albeit several months ahead. Such divergences signaled the 1962 collapse, and certainly the 1973 cataclysm. Measured by the A-D line, the majority of shares ended their personal bull market not in late 1972 but in April 1971, when the A-D line and any number of unweighted market averages peaked. The latter half of 1971 and virtually all of 1972 were marked by a massive divergence between the A-D line and the Dow, which foretold the severe decline that followed.

Gilbert Haller, publisher of *The Strongest Stocks*, has observed that major sell signals generally develop following a decline in the cumulative total of the A-D line of roughly 3,000 units. When the A-D line drops by 3,000 units from a peak reading, anticipate further significant decline. (Conversely, when the A-D line rises by 3,000 units from a low reading, anticipate a strong market.) In both cases there is often a reaction prior to a follow-through of the indicated move. For example, if you have just received a buy signal, expect a brief sell-off first.

You can start your computations with any arbitrary number—I suggest a large number such as +20,000 to avoid having to deal with negative cumulative totals should the market decline.

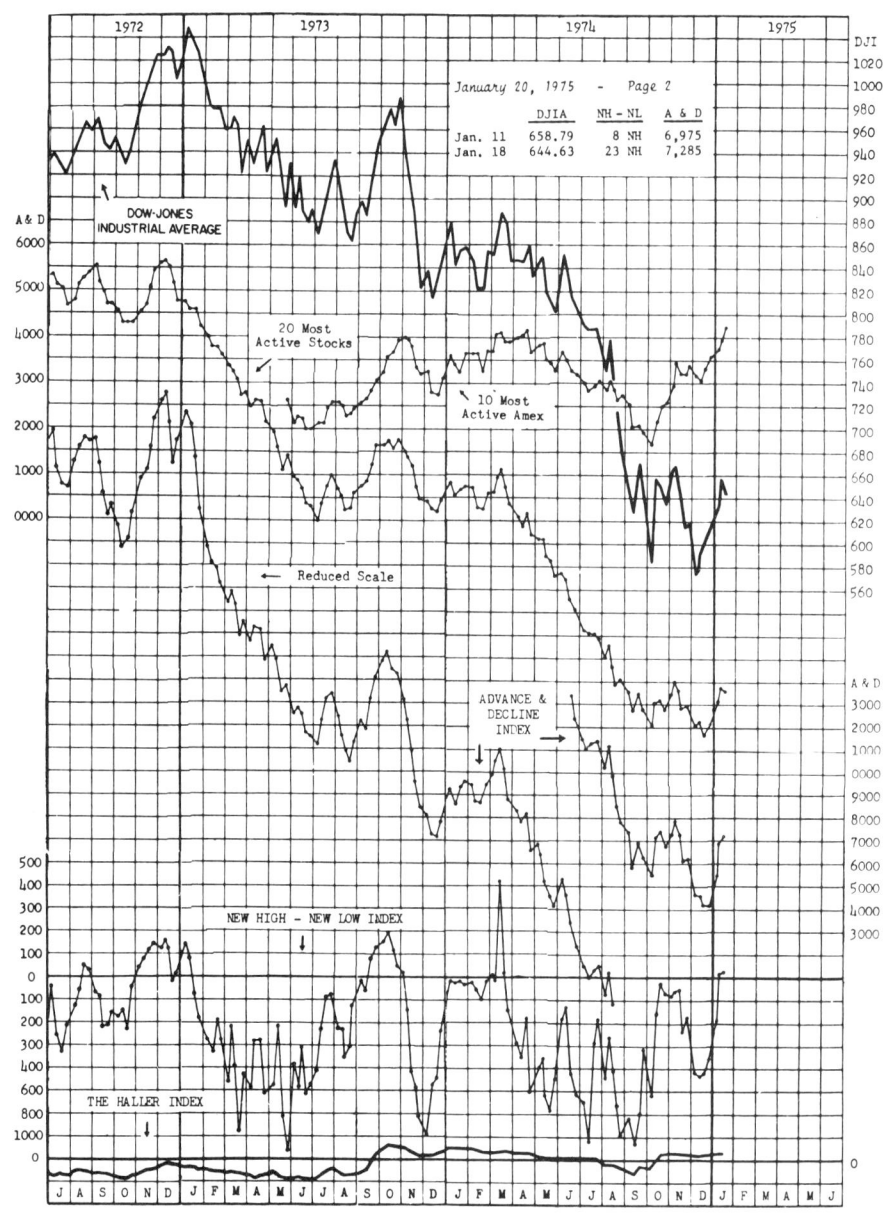

FIGURE 2
You can see that the A—D Line and the NH-NL Index both peaked several weeks before the Dow Industrial Average during the December 1972–January 1973 period. SOURCE: The Strongest Stocks, P. O. Box 2048, Stateline, Nev. 89449.

General Tips on Using the A-D Line

a) For every five-point rise in the Dow Industrials, the A-D line should advance by at least 250 units. If not, look for market weakness.

b) Peaks in the Dow and A-D line that occur simultaneously are *generally* followed by only moderate market declines.

c) However, situations where the Dow is able to advance to new highs while the A-D line is not, even if the divergence lasts for only a week or so, are usually followed by at least moderately severe market declines.

d) While divergences occur at market tops, the Dow and the A-D line tend to trough simultaneously at bear market lows.

5. Count the New Highs and New Lows Each week *Barron's* publishes on the Market Laboratory page the number of issues on the New York Stock Exchange reading a new yearly high in price and the number reaching new yearly lows during the week previous. This data can also be secured elsewhere.

Again, during the early phases of bull markets large numbers of stocks rise smoothly to new high levels. As the bull market matures and smart money begins to move out of shakier situations, fewer and fewer issues are able to break into new high ground. The ends of bull markets do not see as many issues reaching peaks as at the beginning.

To keep track, simply plot a line (not cumulative) each week of the net differences between new highs and new lows as reported in the financial press. Expect a bear market to begin within one to one-and-a-half years after the peak reading in the NH-NL Index. This indicator completed a peak formation in April 1971. The 1973 bear market began some twenty months later.

A Painless Way to Catch Major Market Turning Points

Here's a quick tool for spotting bear markets early in the game (and bull markets too).

a) A bear market is indicated when the number of new lows posted each week exceeds the number of new highs by a 9:1 ratio. For example: 54 new lows, 6 new highs; or 108 new lows, 12 new highs.

b) Conversely, a new bull market is indicated when the number of new highs in a given week exceeds the number of new lows by a 9:1 ratio.

This device would have gotten you into the 1970–73 bull market in October 1970, out of the market during the winter of 1973, total gain amounting to over 200 Dow points.

A Quick Way to Catch the End of Severe Bear Market Declines

There's no point in selling short if you do not know when to cover the positions. Generally speaking, bear market declines will come to a halt when the number of new lows over new highs exceeds 1,000–1,200. Such readings may not signal the ultimate low (two or three such panic spikes may be required), but they will usually mark interruptions in the bear market, at the least.

Check Out the Most Actives List

Is there a better way to forecast the stock market than to track and follow the operations of the large sources of market capital? Nor do you require a computer or a tape watcher to do the job. Simply track the most actively traded issues on a daily or a weekly basis. The information (weekly) is available in *Barron's*. Daily data is available in *The New York Times* or *The Wall Street Journal*.

Among the methods of interpreting the data are two that I favor. The first technique involves plotting, on a weekly basis, the net difference between the number of the 20 most actively traded issues that rise and the number that fall. For example, if 14 issues rise and six fall, the net difference is +8. If three advance and 17 decline, then the net is −14. Maintain a cumulative total, adding the results each week to the previous accumulated total. Since the most actively traded group represents areas of concentrated big money buying and selling, you can see from the direction where the market is likely to head. Look for divergences between your cumulative total plot and the Dow. For example, the Dow made a new high in January 1973. However, the Most Actives line peaked several weeks previously, in late 1972, providing excellent advance warning of the decline that followed.

A second technique, devised by *Indicator Digest*, Palisades Park, N.J. 07650, involves tracking the most active stocks on a daily basis. The task involved is a bit more cumbersome, but results have been excellent.

To plot *I.D.'s* MAS (most active stocks) indicator, simply do the following:

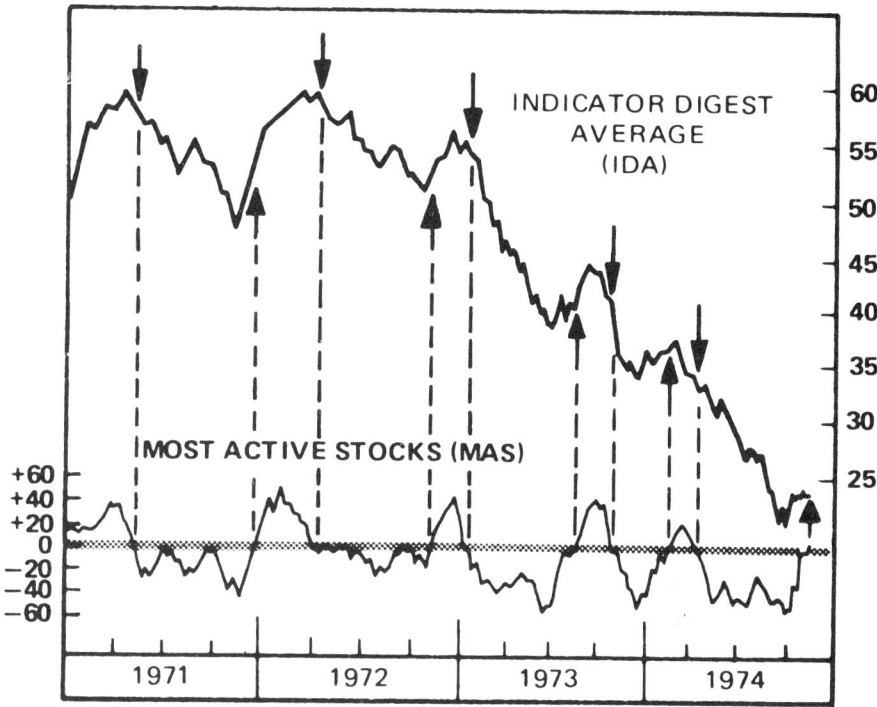

FIGURE 3
Indicator Digest's MAS Indicator gave a sell signal just prior to the 1973–1974 bear market. It gave a buy signal shortly after the 1974–? bull market began.
SOURCE: *Indicator Digest,* Palisades, Park, N.J., 07650.

a) Secure the net difference between the number of the fifteen most actively traded issues advancing each day and the number declining.
b) Add the net daily totals together for thirty days for the total thirty day results.
c) Divide by 3.
d) On the thirty-first day, add in that day's total, subtracting the data from the thirty-first day back. You should always be dealing with the last thirty days only.
e) Repeat step **c**, etc.

A buy signal is rendered when the thirty day total of the net differences in the amount of the 15 most actives rising and the number falling, that total divided by 3, exceeds +3. A sell signal is rendered when the MAS Indicator drops to −3 or below.

An excellent bear market signal was provided at the very top of the 1970–73 bull market, January 1973. This indicator would have kept you out of the market during the worst phases of the bear market that followed.

6. Plug Into the Utilities The Dow Utility Average probably represents both the most conservative and best-informed money. Conservative because utility stocks are generally employed as income havens. Well-informed because, for the most part, investors who seek income frequently already are well endowed. In any event, utility stocks are also interest sensitive—their strength tends to ebb and flow in tune to general credit conditions. How so? Well, for one, utilities are heavy borrowers of capital. The tighter credit conditions are, the more utilities have to pay to borrow—ergo, lower earnings. Secondly, utility stocks are high dividend payers, but during periods of tight money their dividend yield has difficulty competing with other yield instruments.

High interest rates bode badly for the stock market for several reasons. For one, corporations having to pay high interest costs find those costs reflected, sooner or later, in their bottom line—presuming that they can raise the cash for expansion and capital expenditure in the first place. For another, tight money and high borrowing costs mean high yields in the bond and liquid asset fund sectors. Why risk your money on Xerox when you can draw 13 percent from Reserve or 9 percent from triple A paper? In short, high debt-instrument yields suck money away from the stock market.

Utility stocks frequently anticipate trends in credit conditions by rising or falling *before* changes become generally apparent, and before the rest of the stock market. As a group, stocks comprising the Dow Utility Average tend to peak several weeks to months in advance of the rest of the list, though the Utilities and Industrials do tend to bottom together.

Be wary of any market advance that lacks participation on the part of the Utility issues; and, in particular, be aware of short-selling opportunities when the Dow Industrials advance alone. A combination platter, including an advance in the Dow Industrials (Column A), coupled with declines in the utilities, A-D line, NH-NL Index, and most active issues (together, Column B), almost always results in market indigestion; cured, in turn, by a good hefty spoonful of short selling.

7. Learn To Draw Trendlines The simplest of trading devices frequently turns out to be the most effective. Figure 5 illustrates trendlines and channels that mark the slope of market advances and declines.

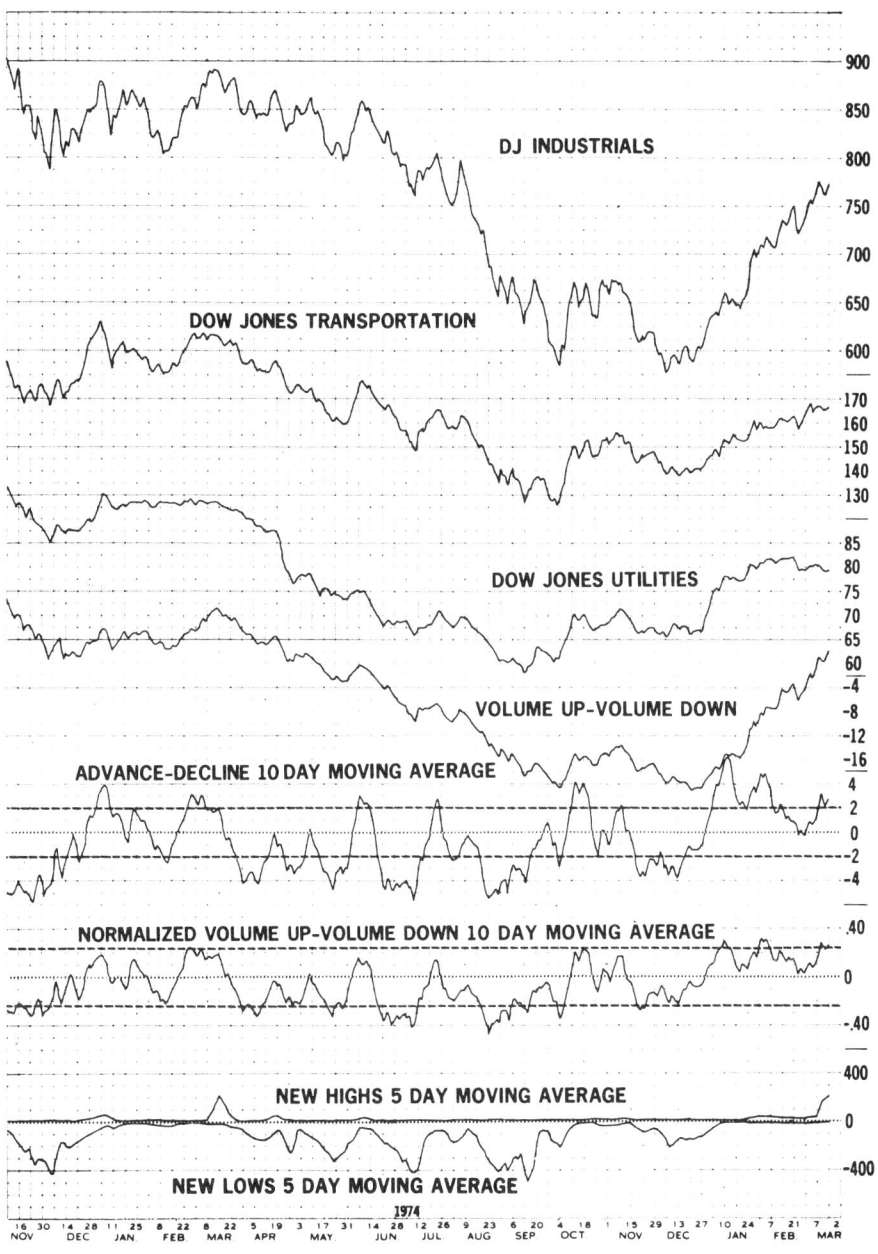

FIGURE 4
By failing to advance with the Dow Industrials during the spring of 1974, the Dow Utilities signaled the decline that followed. However, the Utilities reached bottom and turned up in late 1974, while the Industrials were making new lows. The strength, this time, in the Utilities foreshadowed the coming bull market.
SOURCE: Comparative Market Indicators, P.O. Box 1557, Bellevue, Wash. 98009.

You can see that declines in rising markets tend to halt at lines connecting previous declining lows (uptrendlines) and that advances in up markets tend to end at a line drawn parallel to that line, started at a previous high point. Prices usually oscillate between the uptrendline and the top channel line—stocks should be purchased near the bottom of the channel, sold near the tops.

Once the slope of an advance alters however (an uptrendline violated), investors must become alert to the probability of a trend reversal. If the market has been rising, look for prices to fall. For example, review Figure 5. Once the line connecting the November 1971, July and October 1972 bottoms was broken, the new bear market began. And where did the 1970–73 advance end? Why, precisely at the top of the channel, or the line drawn parallel to the uptrendline that supported the advance.

During downtrends rallies usually halt at a line connecting previous rally peaks, a violation of that line implying further upside progress. Observe the downtrendlines that operated during the 1973–74 bear market.

Even if you prefer not to sell short, be aware of the dangers of holding long positions during bear markets—and you must suspect the development of bear markets once trendlines of any significance are violated.

Incidentally, shorter-term trendlines can be employed for in-and-out trading—but short-term trading is risky at best and suicidal at worst. The majority of investors, by far, are better off investing with the major trend.

If you do sell short, you might consider covering shorts (but not buying) near the bottoms of downward-sloping channels—reshorting on advances to the top of the channel. All short positions should be covered when major bear market trends are violated.

8. Track the Federal Reserve Board As we mentioned before, the stock market is extremely sensitive to changes in general credit conditions—the lower the cost of credit, the easier loans are to obtain, the higher the stock market. Recently, two bear markets were sparked by credit crunches—the 1968–70 slide and the 1973–74 debacle. During both those periods interest rates soared, particularly during the summer of 1974.

Credit conditions are largely influenced by the Federal Reserve Board, which controls the availability of credit and the supply of money in circulation through a variety of devices. These include:

> *Margin Requirements:* The Federal Reserve Board regulates the amount of margin or down payment required by investors for the purchase of securities. The higher the initial margin requirement,

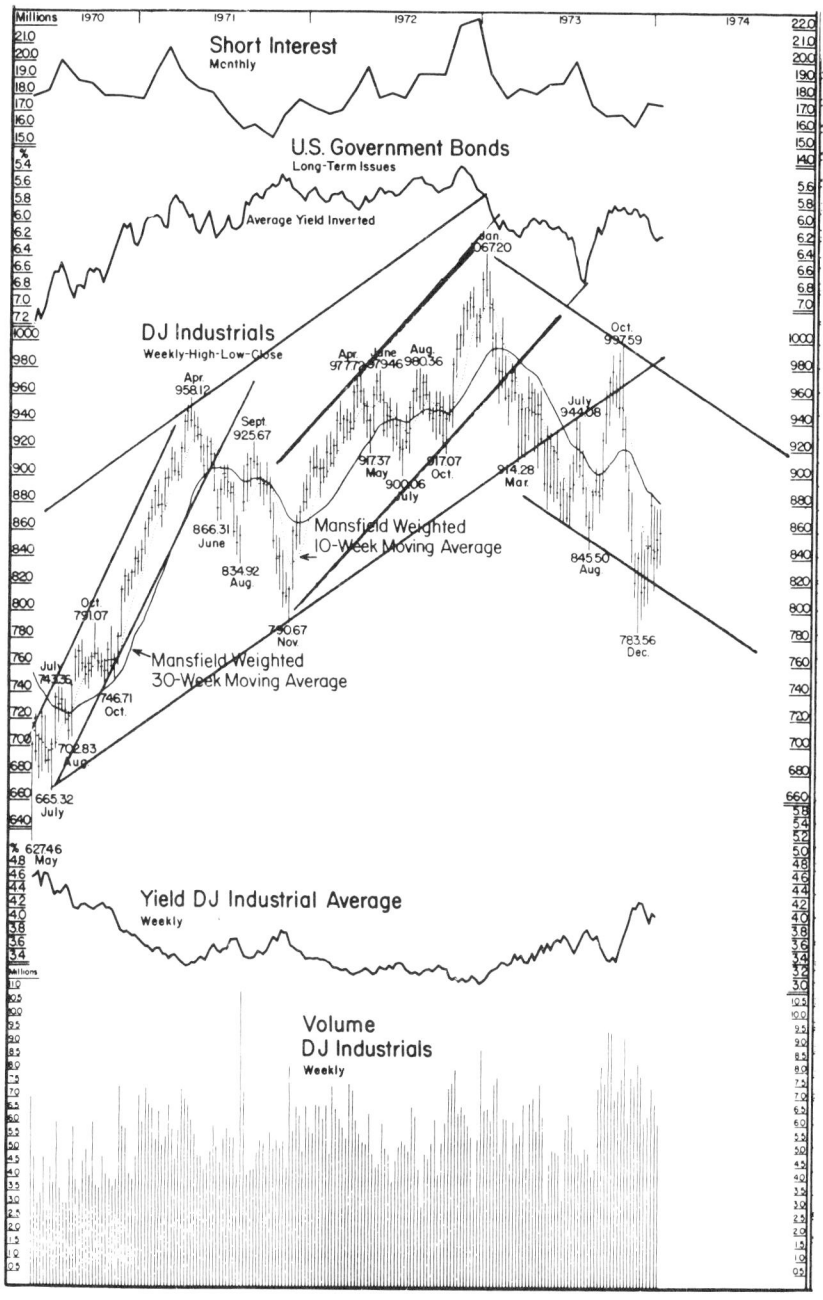

FIGURE 5
I have marked in some of the channels that supported the 1970–73 bull market. Once the uptrends were violated, a signal was given for a new bear market.
SOURCE: R. W. Mansfield, 26 Journal Square, Jersey City, N.J. 07306.

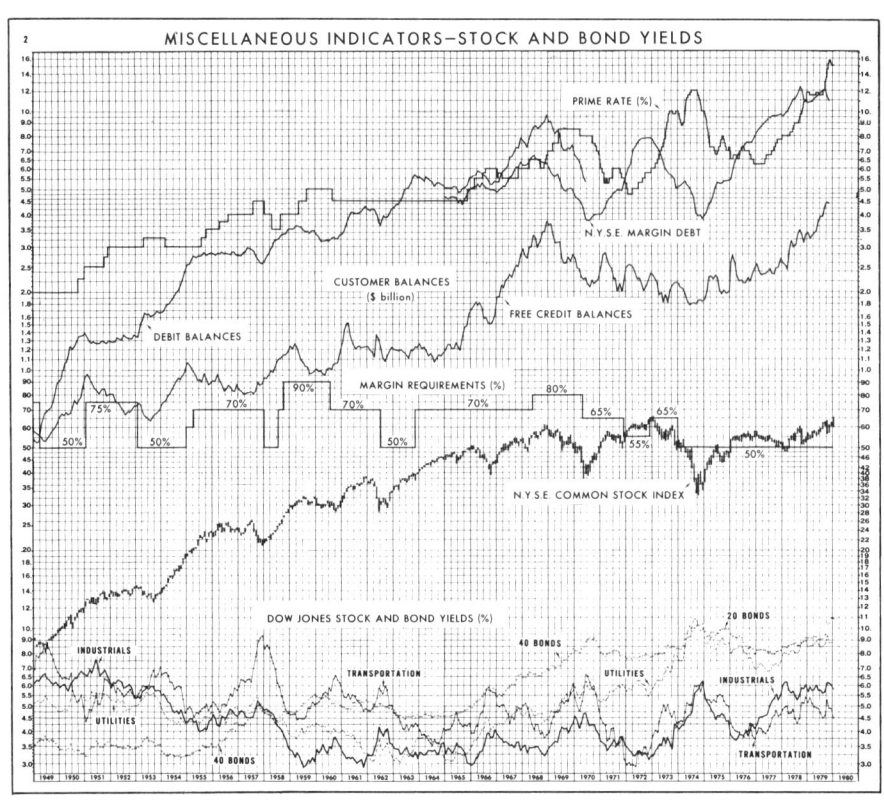

FIGURE 6
Low points in stock prices coincided with peaks in the prime and bond rates (1976, 1974). Prices of stocks began to fall as interest rates rose.
SOURCE: Securities Research Co., 208 Newbury Street, Boston, Mass. 02116.

the smaller the amount of securities the investor can purchase for a fixed cash outlay. The lower the amount of margin required, the greater the amount you can buy. In other words, if you have to put up 50 percent of a stock's cost, you can purchase shares in the amount of double your cash outlay. If you have to put up 80 percent, you can borrow only 20 percent of a stock's value.

It follows then that, by lowering margin requirements, the FRB releases considerable potential purchasing power to the stock market; therefore, a lowering of margin rates is potentially quite bullish. Conversely, by raising margin requirements, the FRB reduces potential purchasing power, which is bearish.

Changes in margin requirements are rarely followed by immediate alterations in the direction of the stock market—a lead time of several months generally prevails. However, a succession of increases in margin requirements clearly signifies the Fed's intention to curtail speculation; a succession of reductions clearly signifies the Fed's intention to aid and abet Wall Street.

The Discount Rate: By raising or lowering the discount rate, the amount banks have to pay to borrow money from the Federal Reserve System, the FRB can indirectly control the amount that banks have to charge their customers for loans. Therefore, the higher the discount rate, the more bearish for the stock market. Any change in the discount rate is significant, but two changes in the same direction generally indicate a strong statement of policy on the part of the FRB. Be aware of an impending market top whenever you read of successive upward revisions in the discount rate.

Reserve Requirements: The Fed also regulates the volume of reserves banks must maintain against bank deposits. Naturally, the greater the reserve requirements, the less banks can lend out—ergo, tighter money and more restrictive loan policies. Free bank reserves indicate latent lending power in banks. You can see from Figure 7 that

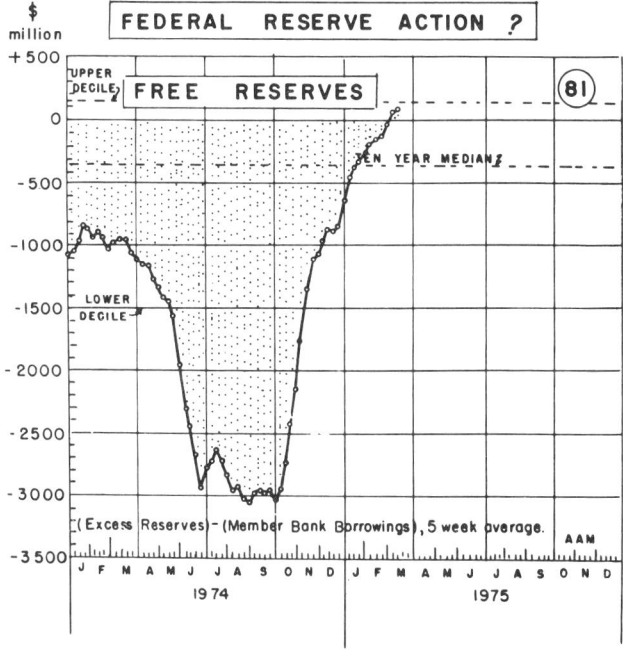

FIGURE 7
Free bank reserves hit a low just as the 1973–1974 bear market was reaching its nadir. Free reserves rose sharply in tune with the new bull market. SOURCE: Merrill Analysis, Inc., Box 228, Chappaqua, N.Y. 10514.

bank reserves hit a new low together with the stock market in the early fall of 1974.

By and large, easier credit is considered inflationary in terms of the general economy. Greater business expansion means more demand for goods and raw materials, higher employment, greater demands for labor. During 1974 the Fed, concerned mainly with inflation, tightened the screws. By early 1975, faced with recession—and possibly depression, the major fear—the FRB began to ease. Bullish for the stock market? Yes. Antirecessionary? Perhaps. Nonetheless, many economists, looking ahead, foresaw a rapid increase in inflation by 1976, followed by a major credit squeeze and economic trouble thereafter.

Other indicators of credit conditions include municipal bond yields (*Barron's* each week) and the prime rate, the rate banks charge to prime corporations for loans. You can also, of course, check out prevailing yields for commercial paper, certificates of deposit, and so forth. *Barron's* carries the data. Items of general interest on the credit front are regularly carried in the financial press such as *The Wall Street Journal*.

The yields on Treasury notes, incidentally, are a good key to future market developments. A number of stock market advisers track one particular Treasury note, the 4¼s 1987-92, trending its price. When uptrends in the note are broken, signifying investor expectation of tighter money, uptrends in the stock market may be expected to follow suit. A reversal upward in the price of this note signifies an impending end to bear markets.

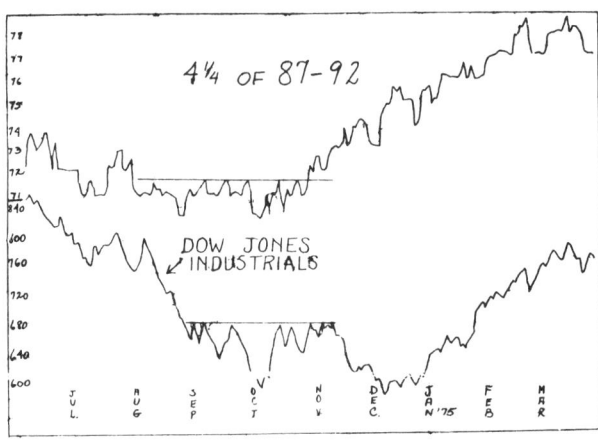

FIGURE 8
By turning up during the autumn of 1974, the Treasury Bonds, 4¼s 1987–92, indicated a forthcoming bull market.   SOURCE: *The Professional Tape Reader,* P.O. Box 96, Wall Street Station, New York, N.Y. 10005.

9. Mull Over the Mutual Funds Mutual fund management, unfortunately, even if forewarned, can really do little to protect their investors during periods of market distress. With the bulk of trading now dominated by the institutions themselves, even the astute institutional manager can find no ready customer should he wish to dispose of large blocks of shares. Therefore, funds are traditionally caught laden with shares at bull market peaks, able to unload only to a limited degree as the market declines.

Since institutions, as an aggregate, have bullishly accumulated shares by the time market peaks arrive, there is no one to whom to sell—the industry's buying power is exhausted. At stock market tops the mutual fund industry is typically loaded with securities, light on cash. The danger zone? In the past bull markets appear to have been exhausted when the mutual fund cash position as a proportion of assets has fallen to roughly 5 percent. Market bottoms have been signaled in recent years when the fund cash position has risen to roughly 12 percent. This figure has gradually been increased at recent successive bear market bottoms, and is now further distorted by the inclusion of the cash in the liquid asset funds, generally considered as a portion of the mutual fund cash position.

Whether, in fact, the cash in the money sector should be considered part of the industry's cash position is a moot question. One camp holds that assets held in cash management funds do represent potential purchasing power that will emerge during developing bull markets. The opposite view maintains that these funds probably represent pure income investments, the assets of which are unlikely to find their way into the stock market in any case. My own view is that the truth probably lies, as usual, between the two extremes. Some, but not all, of the deposits that lay in the money funds are liable to find their way to the stock markets as investors gain courage—but some will, remain happily invested for goodly short-term income returns.

In any event, Figure 9 tells the tale quite well. The mutual fund cash position is regularly cited in the financial press. However, do *not* allow yourself to be misled by glowing reports of institutional optimism. The mutuals *must* sound bullish when they are fully invested. Whoever heard of selling goods to someone while you're telling them that prices will be lower tomorrow?

10. Scrutinize the Specialists The specialists are the middlemen on the floors of the major exchanges. Exchange orders pass through their hands, bids and offerings are entered into their books. Furthermore, the specialist must supply from or purchase shares for his own account at times when an imbalance exists between purchase offerings and sales.

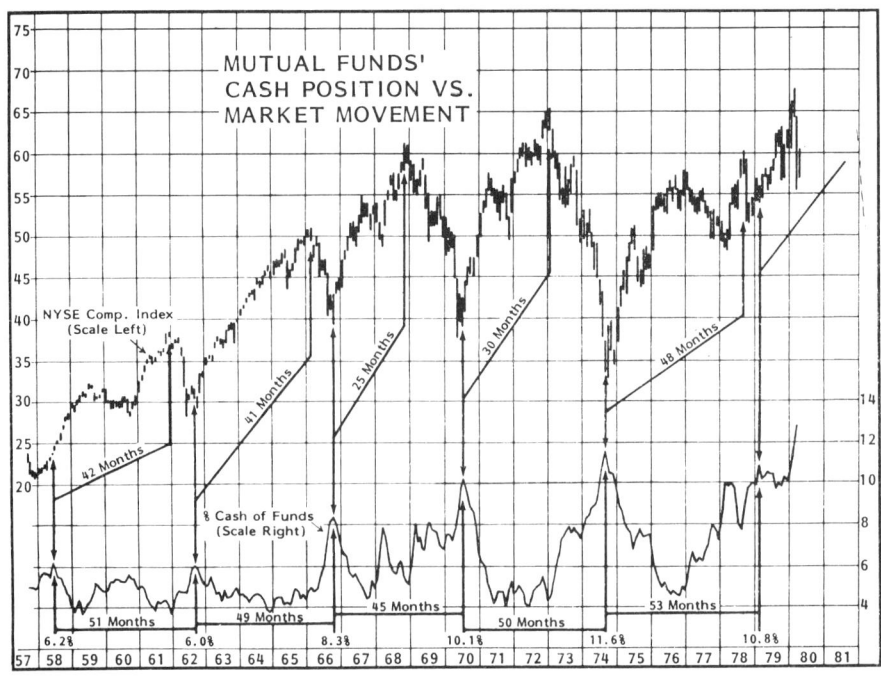

FIGURE 9
Peaks in mutual fund cash positions marks the end of the bear markets. Observe that bear market bottoms tend to space at four-year intervals. SOURCE: Growth Fund Research, Inc., Growth Fund Research Building, Yreka, California, 96097.

Whether the specialist is truly the "bogeyman" on the street, manipulating prices to his own profit; the victim himself of recent treacherous markets (specialists were said to have lost fortunes during '74); or simply the man in the middle, performing a necessary, albeit generally profitable, function—the fact remains that, as a group, specialists generally have excellent insight into the future flow of orders.

Therefore it figures to be highly bearish when this astute group shorts heavily for their own accounts, and bullish when their own short sales are relatively limited.

Historically, market declines generally take place when specialist short sales account for more than 65–67 percent of all the short sales taking place on the New York Stock Exchange. Major bull markets generally follow two or three dips of this reading to below 40 percent, and certainly to below 36 percent.

The data required appears weekly in *Barron's* and in *The Wall Street Journal,* released approximately two weeks following the actual week in question.

Altogether, it should require no more than an hour or so per week to track these indicators. The potential returns can be enormous. Again, you may not prefer to sell short; perhaps you'll want to place your money more conservatively during bear markets. In any event, knowing when to stay out of the stock market can save you untold numbers of dollars. Remember, the first rule of depression survival; preserve your capital.

On the other hand, you might just decide that you do want to sell short after all, in which case let's go on to Chapter 9.

FIGURE 10
Market peaks generally occur when the specialist's short sales ratio reaches 65–67 % of total short sales. Bear market bottoms occur following a series of readings below 40%.   SOURCE: *Indicator Digest,* Palisades Park, N.J. 07650.

9
Sifting For Short Sales

If the truth be told, this chapter is almost superfluous. Once the bear market comes, almost all stocks go, and you can probably get off a good short sale simply by selecting a group of issues at random just waiting for the ax to swing their way.

Still, there are different approaches, philosophies, and tactics to short sales, and, if you're going to play the game, a few basic rules will not hurt and may help a great deal.

Before we go much further, let's examine a particular stock, in this case Saxon Industries, and try to analyze a typical case history.

From 1962 to 1965, Saxon traded in a fairly tight range, essentially vacillating between 1½ and 2½ in price. Such a period is referred to as a base, or period of accumulation, the stage just prior to major price movement. Base building, the period during which the stock enters strong, patient hands, can continue for many months, or even years—but sometimes lasts only weeks.

The markup of Saxon began during early 1966, interrupted briefly by the 1966 bear market. However, you can see the low volume that developed as the shares retreated from 8½ to 3½; the bear market pulled the shares down but there was no aggressive selling. The resumption of the bull market in October 1966 saw an immediate spurt in SXP. Within three months, the shares had already regained their entire bear market loss—the strong markup in price carrying right into 1970.

Now an interesting phenomenon took place. Saxon's shares traded on heavy volume throughout 1970 into 1971—but could never regain their previous highs. The shares were being *distributed*, fed out to the public under cover of the 1970–71 bull market. How could you tell? By the churning, heavy trading, marked by little in the way of price progress. Furthermore, a secondary rally early in 1972 attracted no follow through. The bear market for Saxon actually began in 1972; by 1973 the panic was on in earnest. By 1974 Saxon had returned to 1964 levels.

Let's review, once again, the stages:

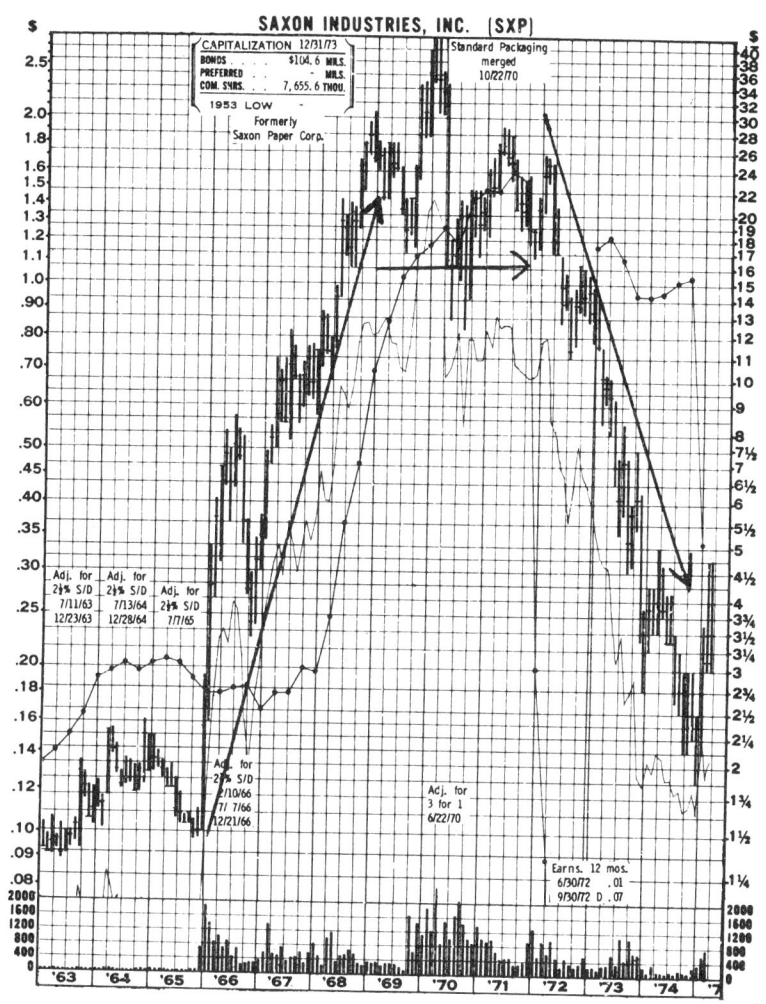

FIGURE 1
Despite heavy volume, Saxon Industries was unable to surpass its early 1970 highs—an indication that distribution was taking place. SOURCE: Securities Research Co., 208 Newbury Street, Boston, Mass. 02116.

1. 1962–65: Base building, preparatory to a markup
2. 1965–69. The markup or advance
3. 1969–72: Distribution, the passing of stock from early to late holders; churning, preparatory to price collapse
4. 1972–74: The markdown, or price collapse.

Now, where were the good points to short Saxon? Well, though the stock did decline sharply during 1966, it really wasn't a good short sale, mainly because it had not yet undergone any extensive period of distribution. But look at the chart as the bear market unfolded in 1973. We see a picture of a stock that had underperformed the market for two years, a stock in which heavy trading had taken place between the prices of 16 and 28, price areas that were crowded with losers, investors itching to get out even—if only they could. An interesting short early in 1973 at 15? What were the odds, really, that Saxon could rally through that supply overhead? And, of course, Saxon did drop drearily, losing roughly 80 percent of its value in slightly over a year.

Incidentally, take one more look at Figure 1. See how "toppy" the chart appears between 1969 and 1972, heavily weighted at the upper end, forming an "M," just ready to topple. Turn the page upside down and you will see a good base, which appears in the form of a "W"—but we'll have to leave that for when the depression's over.

There are a few basic chart formations that frequently indicate good short-sale prospects. These include Foster Wheeler and Foxboro.

Foster Wheeler shows a classic head-and-shoulders formation, the most reliable of all topping formations. This formation is marked by a rally on heavy volume to a left shoulder (S), followed by a decline. This decline is followed by a rally to a new peak, the head (H), *but on lower volume than the preceding rally*, indicating a slackening of buying interest. Another decline then follows, followed in turn by a rally that does *not* equal the rally to the head. This third rally comprises the right shoulder (S), and occurs on further diminishing volume, indicating still less buying interest. The drying up of volume from peak to peak to peak is essential to the formation's reliability, and the formation must follow a prior advance. Once the price drops below the line connecting the declines from the first shoulder and the head, a collapse is likely to begin in earnest. The *minimum* downside move you can expect is equal to the distance between the neckline (N) and the head, carried down from the point where the neckline is penetrated (arrow). Gardner-Denver shows a similar formation.

Foxboro shows another common top formation, a double top—a rally to a peak, followed by a decline, a second rally to the same peak, *on lower volume*, followed by a decline below the intervening valley. Notice the sharp decline that followed.

Let's sum up a few quick rules now for short selling:

1. Short a stock that has churned on heavy volume for a long period, following a major advance. The volume scale for these charts is on the lower scale.

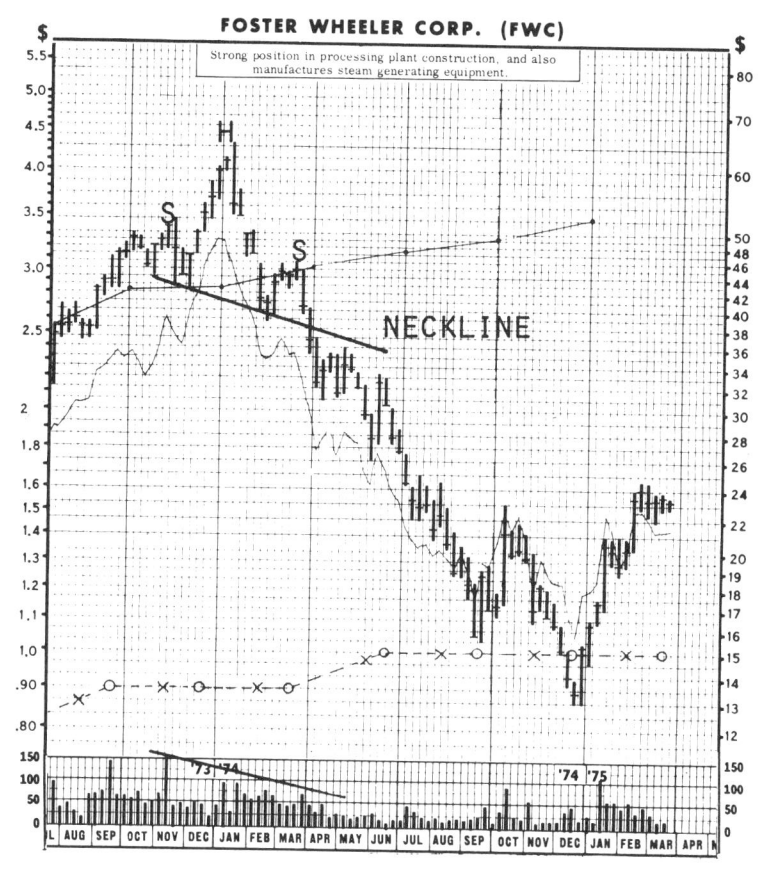

FIGURE 2
We see a classic head-and-shoulders formation that warned of the impending decline in Foster Wheeler. Observe the lessening of volume as the formation approached completion. SOURCE: Securities Research Co., 208 Newburg Street Boston, Mass. 02116

2. Sell the stock short *after* it has already demonstrated weakness by falling below an area in which heavy trading has taken place.
3. Keep riding the stock down for so long as the slope of its decline is maintained. The greatest profits during bear markets are made in the panic phase, just prior to the completion of the demise.
4. Employ trendlines. I've drawn in the pertinent trendlines for Saxon. First we see the rising trend (1966–69), then the flat trend (1969–72), and finally the descending trend (1972–74). The ideal time to sell short is when the flat trend has been broken. Do *not* try to guess peaks; wait until the stock has shown definite, unmistakable weakness.

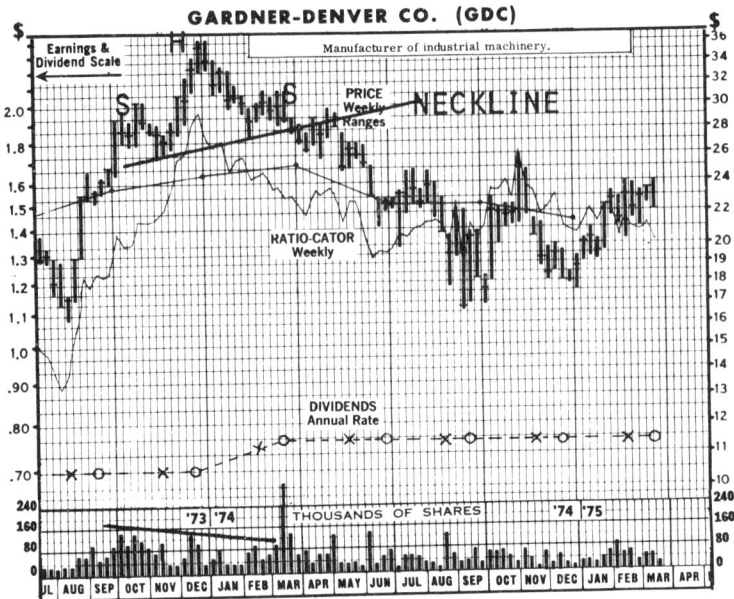

FIGURE 3
Observe the similarity between the topping formation of Gardner-Denver and the top formation of Foster Wheeler. SOURCE: Securities Research Co., 208 Newburg Street, Boston, Mass. 02116.

Fail-Safe Operations

No short sale is complete until your profit is taken—so when? There are three signs that a declining stock is ready to advance:

1. Heavy volume begins to enter the situation—heavy buying—but the shares no longer decline. (Heavy volume at the start of a downmove indicates more down to come. Heavy volume following a long downmove indicates the downmove is about to end, buyers are stepping in.) You can see that, at the very end of 1965, heavy volume stopped the decline in Saxon just prior to the 1966 advance.

2. A stock shows the ability to penetrate "resistance," an overhead area of supply. Notice how readily Saxon penetrated resistance in early 1967.

3. Downtrends are violated.

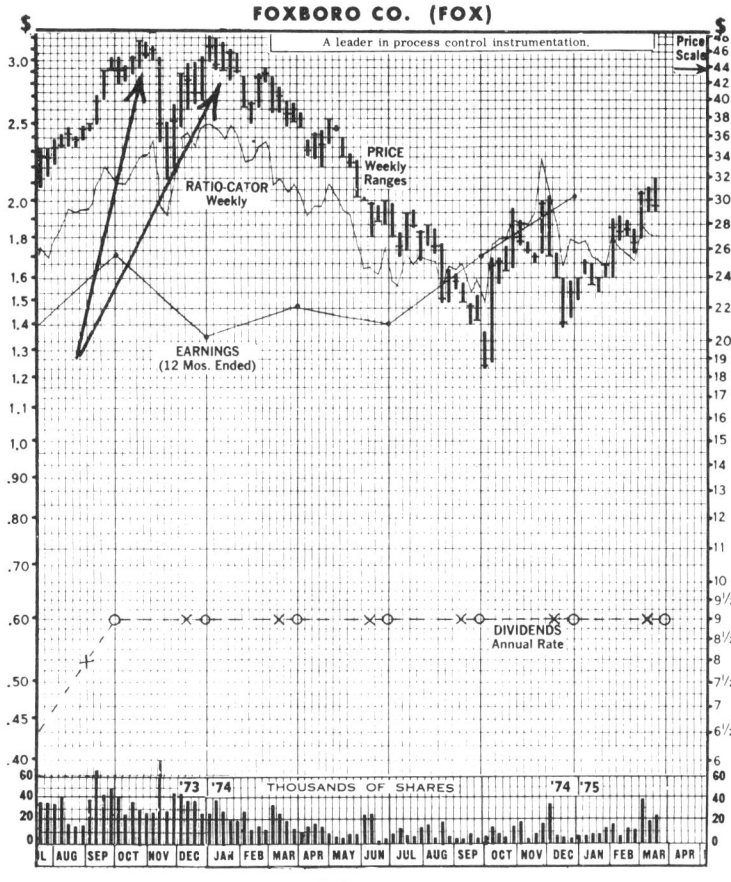

FIGURE 4
Foxboro completed a classic double-top formation between mid-1973 and early 1974. The arrows point to the peaks. SOURCE: Securities Research Co.

Further Examples

Review the charts of Santa Fe International and Sav-A-Stop. Sante Fe has gone through two complete cycles between 1962 and 1974. Sav-A-Stop, the action very similar to Saxon, has gone through one. See if you can isolate examples of the above rules on each of those charts. And finally, the chart of Ponderosa, covering the 1973–74 period, shows, on a magnified scale, what can happen to a stock once it falls beneath a trading range. Ponderosa traded between 26 and 34 for six months from the end of 1973 into the spring of 1974. Once it broke down, it ended up losing close to 90 percent of its value in *less than one*

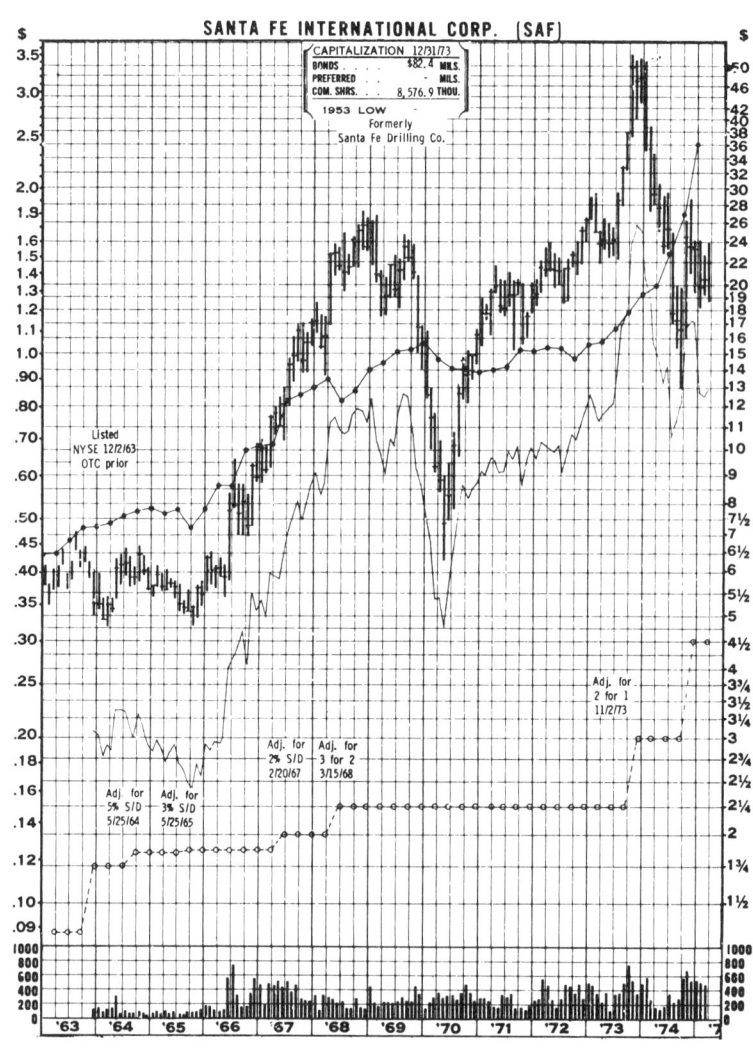

FIGURE 5
Santa Fe has gone through two complete cycles since 1964. Notice the similarity between the first cycle and the chart of Saxon. SOURCE: Securities Research Co.

year. Notice, too, how Ponderosa conformed to its declining channel all the way down. Ponderosa, incidentally, was as high as 83¾ during 1973.

The Fundamental Short

The above examples were all "technical short sales," short sales considered without any regard to corporate news, earnings, dividends,

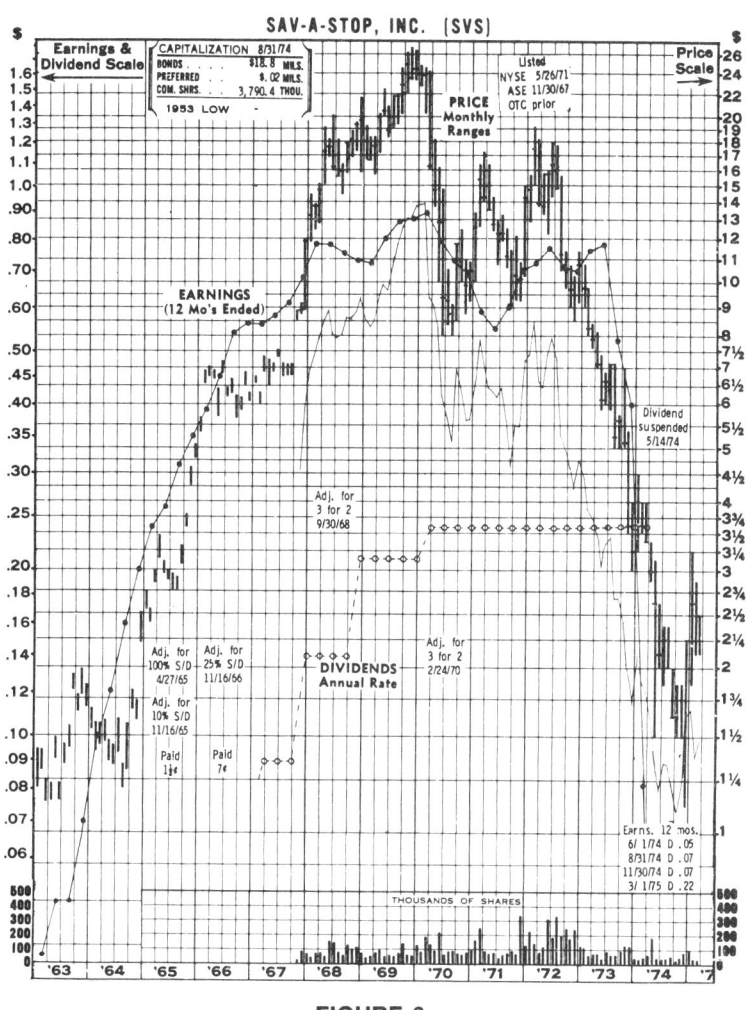

FIGURE 6
Sav-A-Stop's chart closely resembles Saxon's (Fig. 1). Despite heavy volume, it was unable to penetrate its 1969 highs in 1972. SOURCE: Securities Research Co.

and so forth—short sales entered into on the basis of stock and market performance alone.

Many professionals prefer "fundamental" short sales, short sales entered into on the basis of weakening corporate profits, industry slowdowns, labor troubles, etc. My own personal preference is for the technical short. Frequently, bad news has already been discounted by *prior* price declines, before the bad news hits.

Exceptions: unusually poor and unexpected earnings lapses. The oil embargo in 1973 caught U.S. investors by surprise in the main, leading to immediate and sharp drops in gasoline-related industries (e.g., motels,

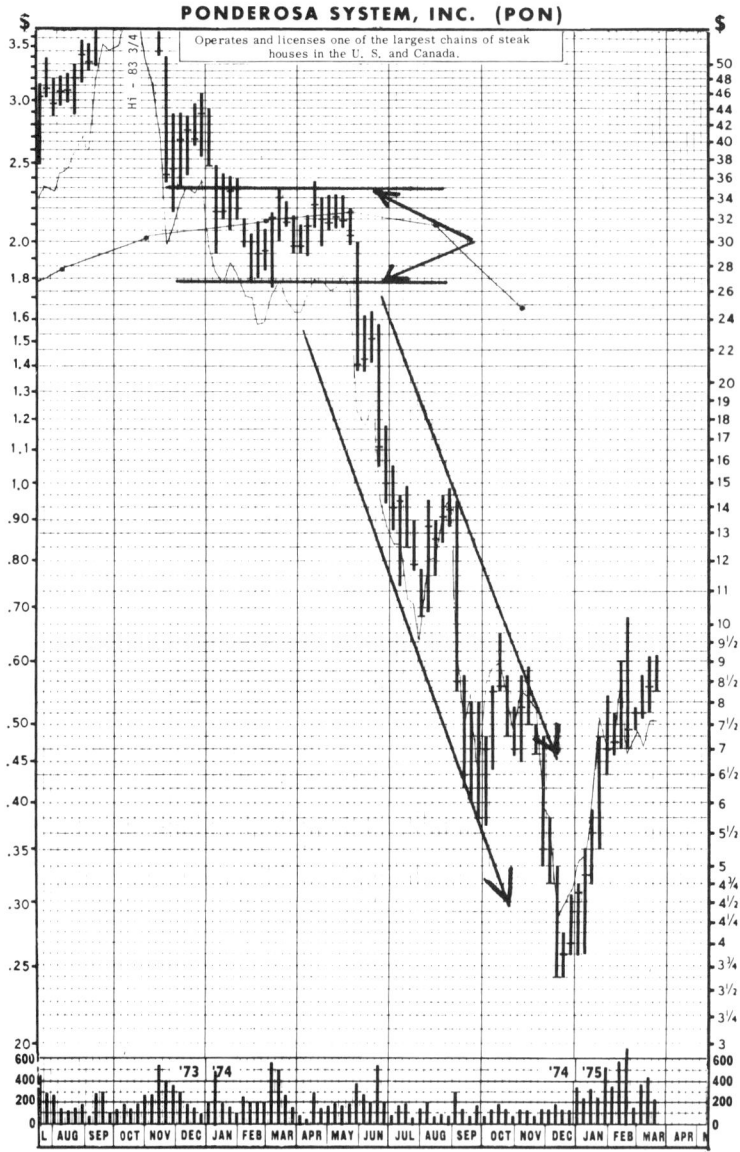

FIGURE 7
The area of resistance is marked off by the horizontal lines and arrows on the chart. Once the trading range was penetrated on the downside, Ponderosa became an excellent short sale candidate. SOURCE: Securities Research Co.

autos). Chrysler and Polaroid were believed to have basic corporate problems during 1974; Chrysler dropped to a twelve-year low during 1974, amidst sharply falling earnings. However, its decline really began in 1968, amidst record high earnings reports.

Proof: Again, the 1973–74 bear market began *before* corporate earnings began to decline. The recession did not hit full force until the bear market was already one year old.

Some General Rules Regarding Short Selling

1. Sell short on rallies, not after prolonged declines. Even the most severe bear markets are interrupted by intermediate rallies. Employ these for short selling, placing cover orders either just above down trendlines or just above areas of resistance.
2. Sell short stocks in which institutions have large holdings! Institutional selling can wreak havoc with stock prices, particularly if several decide to sell simultaneously. Institutional favorites are frequently the last to fall during bear markets, but when they fall, they fall with a thud.
3. Avoid the short selling of high-dividend stocks. You are responsible for the dividends that accrue during the life of your short sale —the dividends create a negative cash flow.
4. Short "high multiple stocks." Stocks sporting high price-earnings ratios are excellent candidates for short sales, since their price frequently derives from "hope" rather than from intrinsic value. In particular, new "glamours" are vulnerable—stocks that have no history of steady progress but rather flash periodically, like comets, across the investment scene (e.g., Four Seasons, Levitz, Ponderosa).
5. Short stocks that show no ability to rise on good news. Again, Chrysler could not advance following reports of record earnings in 1968.
6. Avoid shorting "thin" stocks. Short stocks with heavy capitalizations, large daily volume. Should the shares unexpectedly rally, the advance is more likely to be orderly, giving you the opportunity to cover at little price concession.
7. Avoid shorting stocks in which a heavy short interest already exists. Short interest figures, the number of shares already sold short in each issue, are published monthly in *The Wall Street Journal* and *Barron's*. Rallies often result in short-covering buying panics, particularly in stocks in which heavy short positions exist, driving prices sharply higher.

8. Try to determine your price objectives and your cover fail-safe points in advance of each trading day. Try not to become panicked by every minor rally.
9. Short stocks that are underperforming the market, stocks that fail to participate in any rally that does take place.
10. Short stocks that are showing long-term earnings declines or a flattening of long-term earnings growth, particularly if they are selling at above-normal price-earnings ratios.
11. Put out your shorts when others are beginning to sound hopeful. Cover during periods of intense pessimism.
12. Short stocks that are in poorly performing industry groups. By and large, industry groups tend to move up and down in tandem and, once a group develops weakness, all of its components are likely to follow suit together. The pertinent tactic: Follow the relative strength (the percentage of rise or fall of an industry group relative to the total market) of a number of industry groups. Once a group starts to weaken, look for issues showing "toppy" formations, and sell those short. There is a good possibility that these issues will be dragged down by poor group action.

For example, Milton Bradley began a serious descent during August 1973 when toy stocks, as a group, were demonstrating weakening relative strength. (The relative strength line is the solid line under the bar lines that signify price in these charts.) Mattel and Tonka began their declines only two months later, declines presaged by the collapse of Milton Bradley.

Again, observe the chart patterns that went into these topping formations in question. Tonka broke down from a minor double top, Mattel simply "spilled" down, and Milton Bradley declined from a spread double top.

The charts above are derived from an excellent, low-cost chart service, *Securities Research Co. Inc.*, 208 Newbury Street, Boston, Mass. 02116. An annual subscription includes both weekly-based charts issued each month, and monthly-based charts issued quarterly.

A Special Tool!

Many investors are not aware that stock market movements occur at regular cyclical time intervals, significant moves spaced from twenty to twenty-eight weeks apart, roughly twenty-four weeks on average. Observe the chart of Milgo, upon which I have marked off the periods between peaks (ideal points for short selling) and the periods between

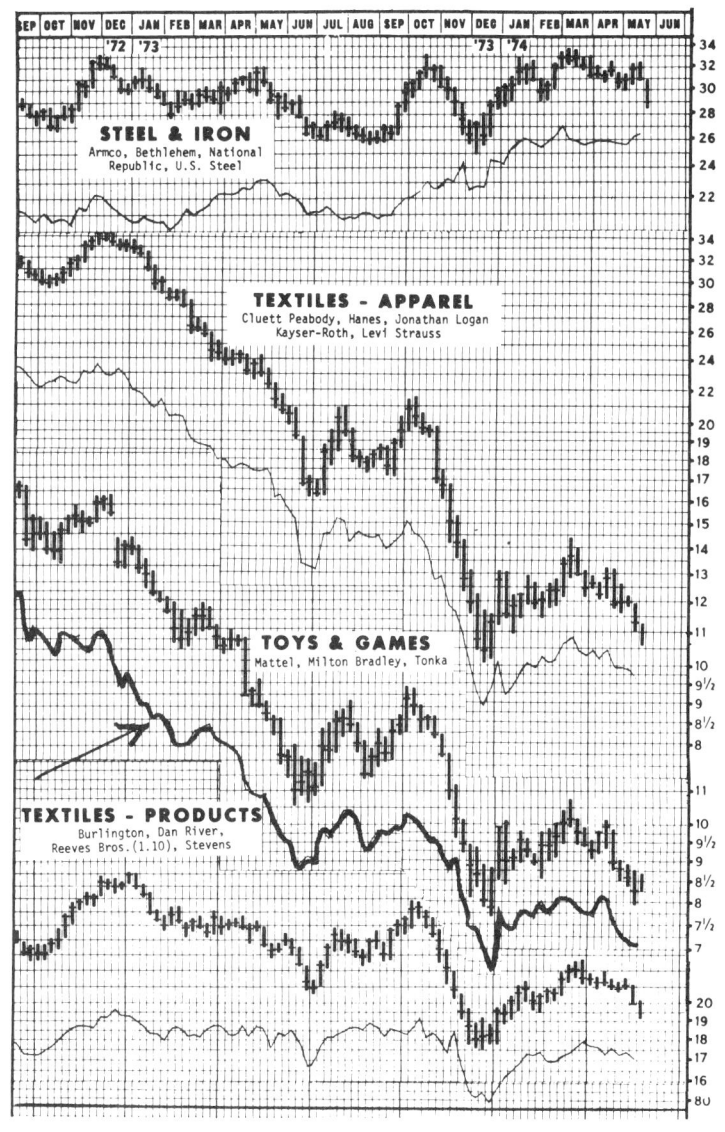

FIGURE 8
You can secure charts of industry group performance from various sources. On the charts above, it can be observed that the toy group was weaker than the overall market throughout 1972 (line beneath price bars, marked with arrow). Therefore toy stocks were ideal short sale candidates at the time. The steel group, stronger than the market, did not present a good short sale area.
SOURCE: Securities Research Co.

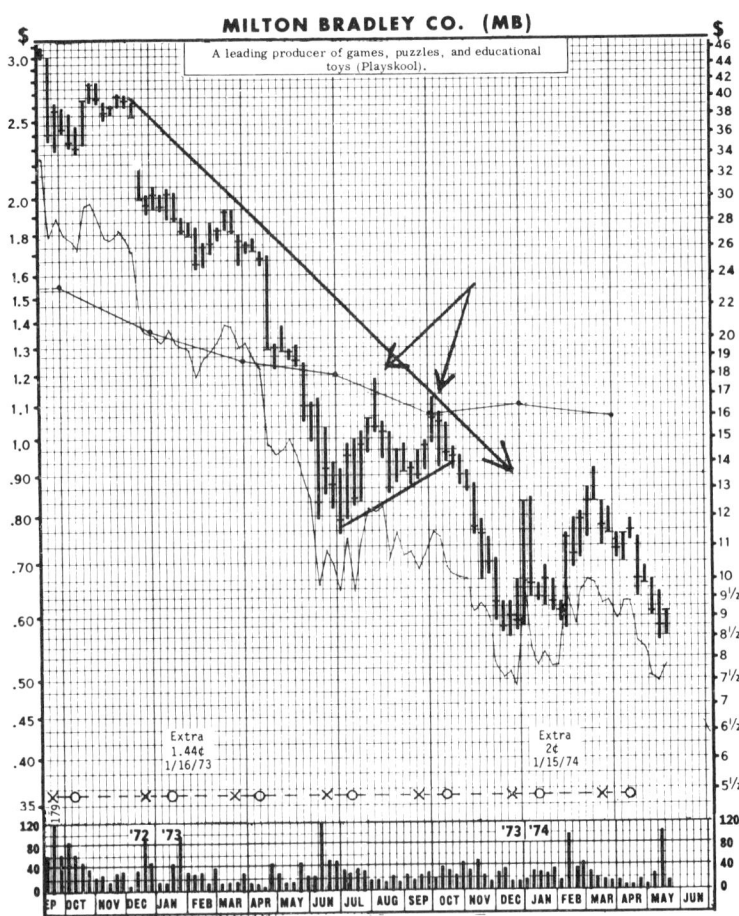

FIGURE 9
Milton Bradley was the first toy stock to begin its second-stage bear market decline, peaking in August 1973. By so doing, it warned of impending weakness in the rest of the industry group. Note the double top, and the rapid descent once the stock broke beneath its trading range. SOURCE: Securities Research Co.

troughs (ideal points for covering shorts and/or for initiating purchases). Do you think that study of such periodicity on your stocks will help your market timing?

High Beta vs. Low Beta

High "beta" (the percentage a stock will fluctuate in relation to the average security) stocks move more rapidly in relation to the total

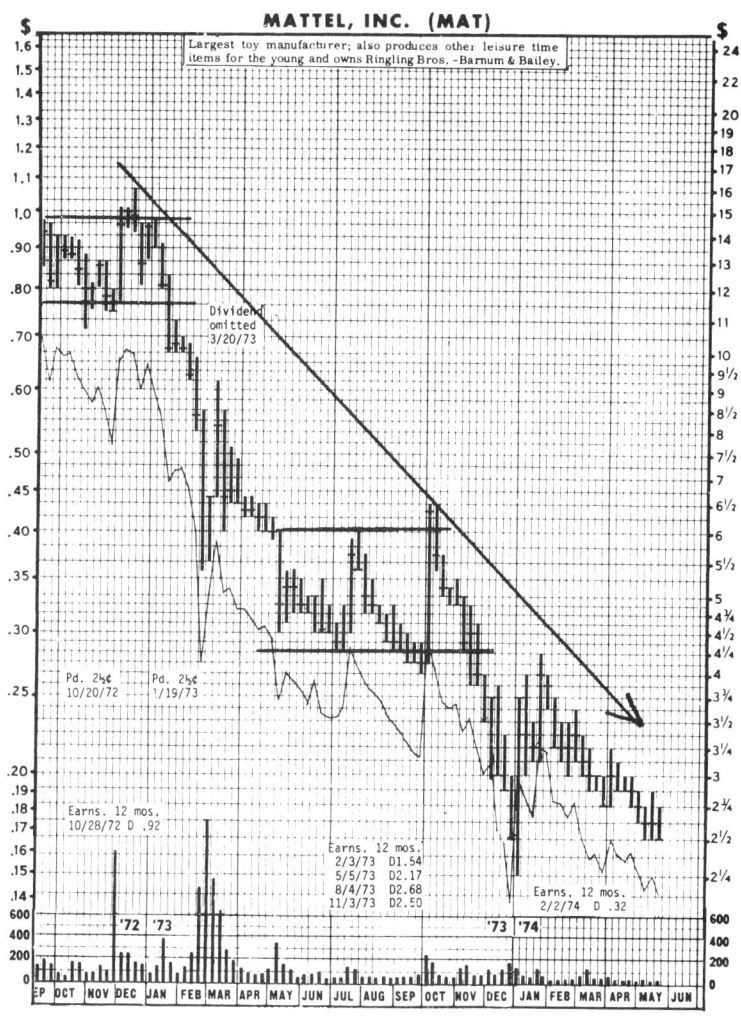

FIGURE 10
Mattel held up a bit longer than Milton Bradley, but joined in the decline in October. Again, observe how rapidly issues can fall during bear markets once they break down from a trading range. SOURCE: Securities Research Co.

marketplace than low beta securities. Therefore, when employed as vehicles for short sales, they tend to decline more rapidly during falling markets and to produce more rapid profits.

On the other hand, should a declining market rapidly reverse, these high beta issues rally sharply, wiping out accrued short sale profits almost before you can blink. Low beta stocks, on the other hand, tend both to decline and to rise more slowly, allowing more time for reflection before you must take action. Conservative investors will concentrate on lower beta issues—but investors who prefer rapid action will concentrate on higher beta issues.

A number of sources exist that provide the betas for individual issues, but you can derive your own simply by dividing the percentage a stock has gained or lost by the percentage the Dow has gained or lost during a particular span of several weeks or months. For example, suppose IBM has dropped from 300 to 200, a loss of 33 percent in six months. During the same period the Dow has dropped from 1,000 to 840, a loss of 16 percent. By dividing 33 percent by 16 percent we reach a beta of 2.06 for IBM; it moves roughly twice as fast as the market.

By and large, issues paying high dividends and having high capitalizations have lower betas than issues with small capitalizations, low

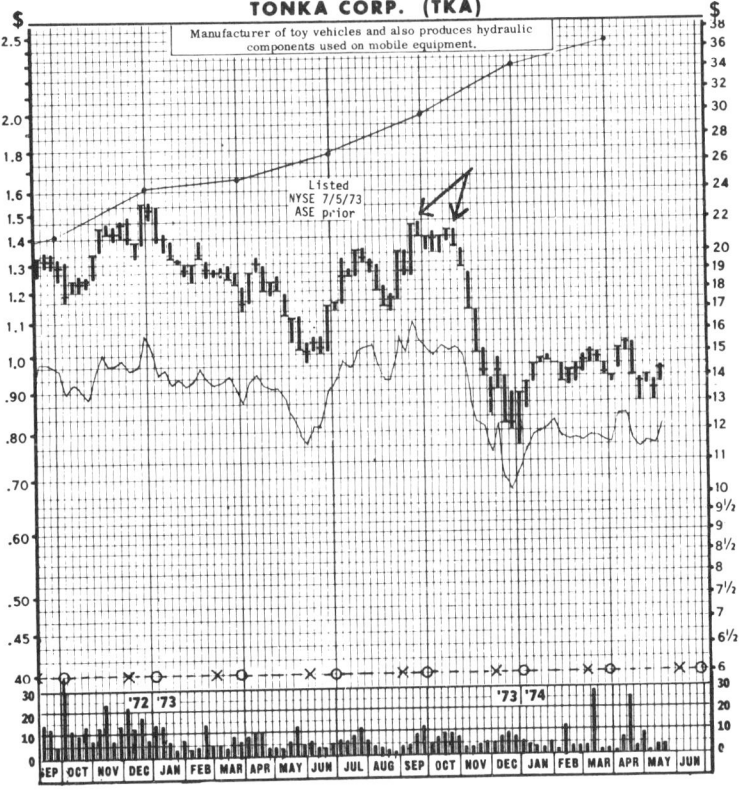

FIGURE 11
Rising earnings provided Tonka with more strength than the rest of the toy group but, nonetheless, the issue joined Milton Bradley and Mattel in their declines. The double top is shown on the chart.   SOURCE: Securities Research Co.

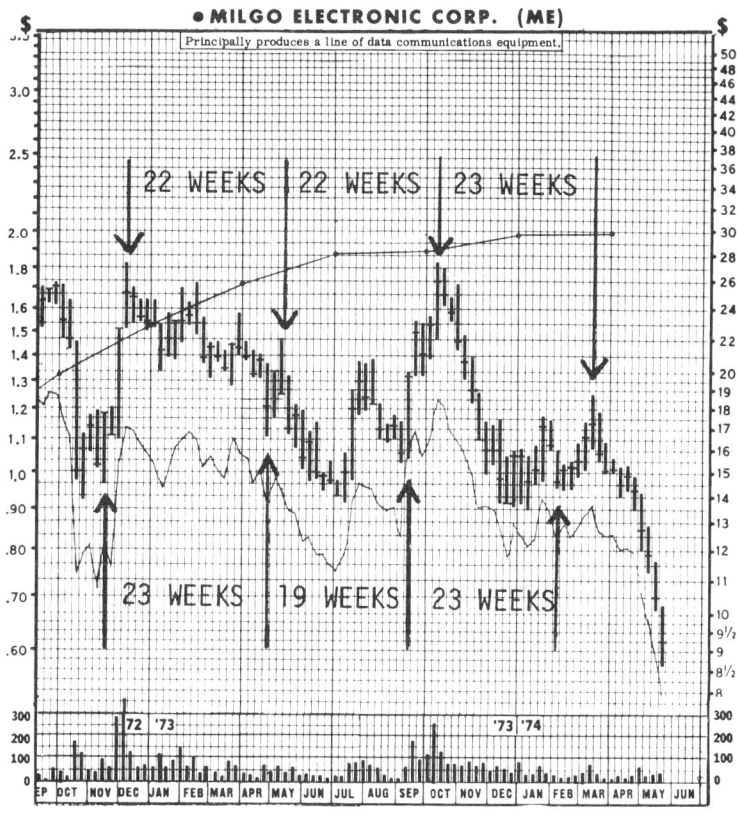

FIGURE 12
By counting weeks in the time cycle of Milgo, you could have anticipated periods when declines were likely to begin and end. SOURCE: Securities Research Co.

dividends. As a group, lower-priced stocks are more volatile, percentagewise, than higher.

The Cyclical Short

A number of issues are cyclical, stocks that rise and fall in tune with economic conditions, rather than fluctuating as growth vehicles in their own right. The drug group has been a strong growth industry over the years—earnings of many issues rising steadily, almost apart from the general economic climate. Sterling Drug is one example. You can see how earnings (the line interspersed with dots) have risen steadily through several business cycles.

On the other hand, automobile, housing, textile, and electronic stocks are generally susceptible to economic conditions. Earnings do not rise steadily, but fluctuate erratically. Cyclical stocks are *excellent* short sales just as their earnings swings begin to peak (e.g., note the chart of Chrysler, Figure 14). Generally speaking, again, cyclical stocks will

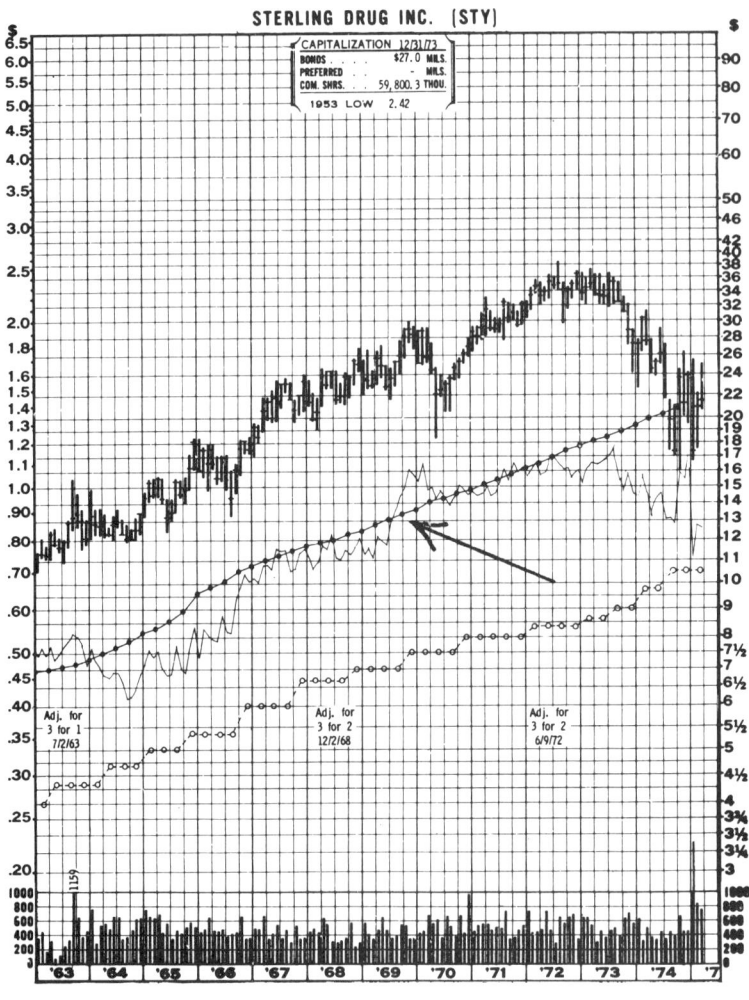

FIGURE 13
Sterling Drug is an issue that shows consistently rising earnings (line marked by arrow). Though the share prices do decline during bear markets, they will not be as susceptible to depressions as cyclical companies. SOURCE: Securities Research Co.

begin to decline *prior* to the turndown of their earnings and will begin to advance several months before earnings turn up. *Do* try to learn to recognize chart formations indicating tops and bottoms—and do remember to begin to think of short selling when the newspapers are full of reports of record earnings.

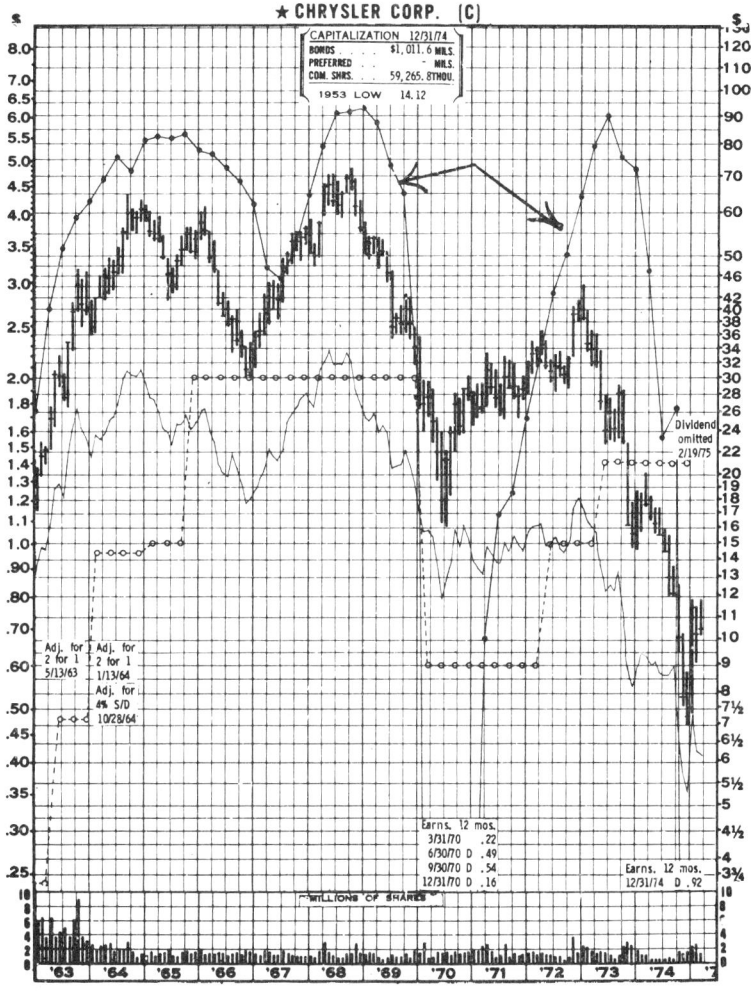

FIGURE 14
Chrysler is a cyclical company whose earnings fluctuate sharply in tune with general economic conditions. An excellent "depression short sale." SOURCE: Securities Research Co.

The Trading Range Short Sale

Certain securities seem to fluctuate over many years within well-bounded trading ranges, peaking out at certain price levels and troughing at others. They are generally safe shorts near the upper ends of their historical price ranges and safe purchases near the lower.

Bendix Corporation is such an issue—notice the regular amplitude of its price swings between 1963 and 1975. You can find numerous examples of such securities by leafing through long-term chartbooks.

The Price-Earnings Multiple Short Sale

The price-earnings ratio or multiple of a security is its most recent price divided by its past twelve-months' earnings per share. Many issues fluctuate between norms, with certain p/e multiples generally marking high points and certain lower p/e multiples marking low points. For example, Helmerich & Payne (Fig. 16) has been a good buy over the last decade whenever its price-earnings multiple has dropped to the area of

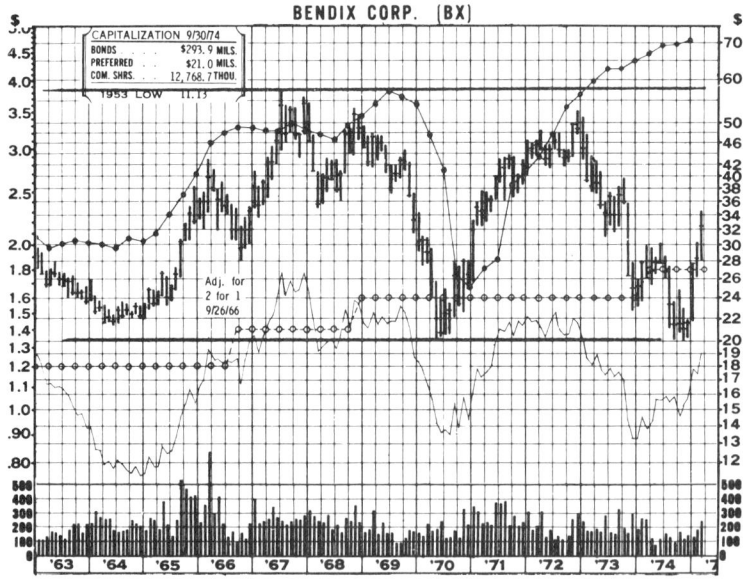

FIGURE 15
Bendix has been an excellent "lending range short sale." For the past 12 years it has declined whenever it has reached the $50–60 price area.   SOURCE: Securities Research Co.

10–11. It has been a good sale whenever its p/e ratio has risen to more than 20.

Price-earnings multiples appear weekly in *Barron's Financial Weekly*. Standard and Poor's issues security reports, generally available free of charge at brokerage houses, that carry historical price-earnings data.

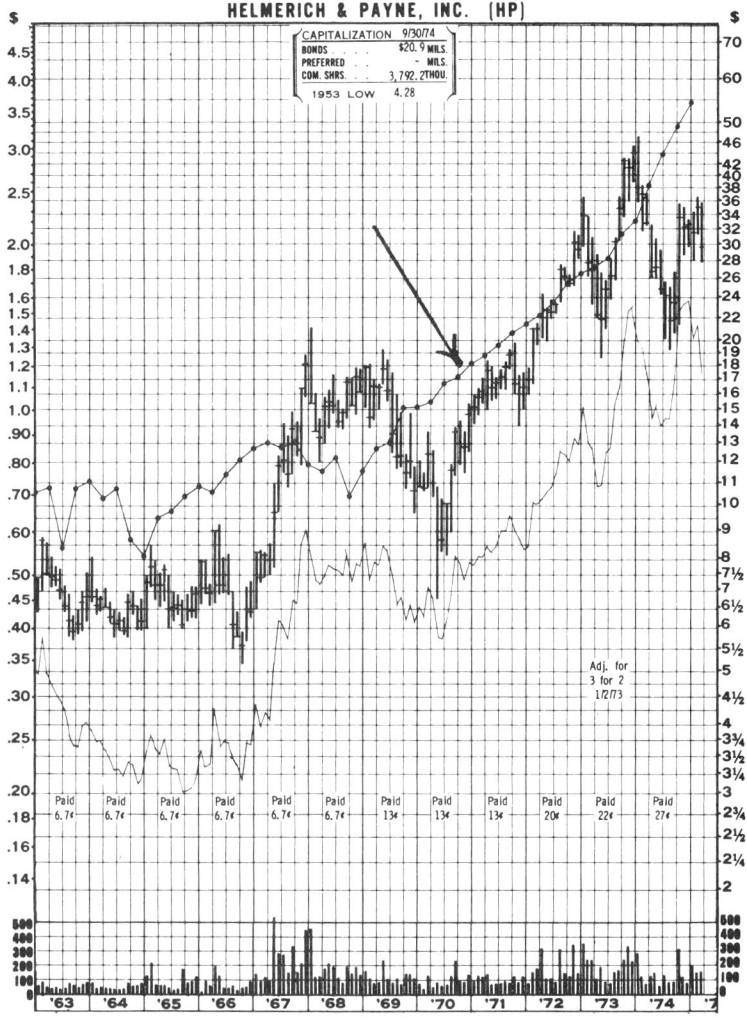

FIGURE 16
By dividing the earnings line (left scale, arrowed line) into the price line, we can see that Helmerich & Payne has been a good short sale whenever its price per share rose above 20 times earnings, and a good purchase candidate whenever its price fell to below 10 times earnings. SOURCE: Securities Research Co.

It All Depends on Your Attitude

There is a great deal of money to be made in the stock market, and during depressions. Just examine those charts and observe how quickly prices can fall—keeping in mind that, if you're on the right side, you can prosper while others falter by the wayside. Nor do you have to fear short selling. If you follow the above techniques, seeking issues that combine the characteristics of a good short sale (top formation, historically high p/e ratio, due interval between tops), while observing the fail-safe protective action, you will incur no greater risk than you incur by purchasing shares during bull markets. *However, since any security trading involves risk,* do enter the stock market, bull market and bear, only with full risk capital, setting the greater portion of your assets aside in safer income-producing situations.

10
STOCK OPTIONS: A LOW-COST MEANS OF PLAYING A DEPRESSION (AND BULL) MARKET

One Means of Securing High Return While Guaranteeing Against Loss

Let's suppose that I offered you a virtually foolproof way to have your cake and eat it too—a procedure by which you can virtually insure your emergence from the coming depression with all your investment capital intact, but a procedure that could also produce excellent profit along the way. Would you be interested? I hope so, because that is precisely what I am going to do.

From your end, you simply do the following:

1. Place *all* of your investment capital into near-maturing Treasury paper—bills, notes, and bonds. As we have seen, this is the safest form of investment that exists today; issues near maturity undergo minimal price fluctuation. Upon redemption, you will receive back *all* your starting capital, presuming that you did not pay over face value for the issues.
2. Use the income from these issues, *the income only*, for investment in stock options. Win, lose, or draw on your option maneuvers, you virtually guarantee the retention of your original capital (at least to the degree that the United States Government can man a printing press). And, as we shall see, options represent a highly leveraged, high-risk reward means of playing a depression (as well as a bull) stock market.

What Are Stock Options?

A stock option is precisely that—an option, the right either to buy (in the case of a *call option*) or to sell (*a put option*) or to buy and sell (*a straddle*) 100 shares of a particular stock at a specified price until a specified time.

For example, let's suppose that you believed early in 1974 that Polaroid was going to decline. (The stock did, in fact, drop from a 1974 high of 88½ to a low of 14⅛.) For roughly $2,000 you could have purchased a one-year *put* on the stock, at a time when Polaroid was selling at 88. This put would have entitled you to *sell* Polariod to the person from whom you purchased the put at a specified striking price (presume 88) for a period of one year from the time the option agreement was made. For this right you paid the put writer or seller $2,000.

Now, let's suppose that you did purchase that option and that in the best (or almost the best, anyway) of all possible worlds, Polaroid did decline to 14⅛. (But just to add a bit of reality to our fantasy, we'll figure you took action when the stock was 15.) You go to the market and purchase Polaroid at 15. Then, you exercise your option—selling those shares, purchased at 15, for *88*, the agreed-upon (striking) price. Your profit amounts to $5,300 (73 points X 100 shares, less the $2,000 you paid for the put option). Commission cost and dividend payments are excluded. Since you put up only $2,000 for the option (the rest of the transaction is simultaneous), your profit of $5,300 amounts to a return of *265 percent* on your money.

And suppose that Polaroid had risen from 88 to 200, instead of declining? In that case, you simply would not have exercised your option, which would have become worthless upon expiration, resulting in a total loss of your $2,000. However, you could never have lost more than $2,000, and, in this regard, selling short via the put option is less risky than outright short selling. The purchase of any stock option is highly speculative and should be entered into only with full risk capital. But let's see now how our game plan works out, presuming that you exercised the option on its last day of life, and presuming that you employed one-year Treasury notes, purchased at par to yield 8 percent.

You would have required $27,000 for starters. Of that $25,000 would go into the purchase of the notes. The additional $2,000 is earmarked for the purchase of the option.

1. If the option expired worthless, you would have lost $2,000 on the option, gained $2,000 in interest, for a break-even.
2. In the example given, you would have made $2,000 in interest on your $27,000 invested, plus a $5,300 profit on the option maneuver. Total gain, $7,300 or a *27 percent* return on your money.
3. If you had simply placed all the money into Treasury notes, you would have earned a virtually guaranteed 8 percent on the $27,000, or $2,160.

There are intermediate possibilities as well. For example, let's suppose that Polaroid had declined only to 55, and you exercised your option at that point for a $1,300 profit (88—55 X 100 shares, less the $2,000 option cost). Your total return on the $27,000 you put up would have come to $3,300 or 12.2 percent. Or let's suppose that Polaroid had declined, say, only to 75, you exercising your option and selling at 88. You would have netted $1,300 on that part of the transaction, partially offsetting the $2,000 cost of the option—net loss $700 on the whole option gambit. Your net yield in that instance, from your $27,000, would have amounted to $1,300 ($2,000 interest minus $700) or 4.8 percent. Remember, in no instance can you do worse with your money by this overall strategy than to recover your original capital.

Is the total tactic worthwhile? Only you can decide that for yourself. I personally do believe that the approach, at the very least, merits consideration.

Back To Options

O.K., so much for the total game plan. We've already gone through a typical put maneuver, an excellent strategy in bear markets. When do you buy puts? Well, just review the section on short selling. By and large, any stock that is a good short sale probably represents a good put buy. The advantages? Less capital required, limited risk. The disadvantages? The premium you pay for the put (or any other option) starts you off with a loss. Remember, a simple decline in Polaroid was not sufficient to produce a profit on the put; a drop of *at least* 20 points was required. It should be pointed out that, in the main, option buyers do lose money on balance because of the initial handicap and/or faulty timing. But then, again, so do the majority of commodity speculators and, in recent years, the majority of stock market investors, even the most conservative. Which is, again, why I emphasize option investment as a tactic for risk money only.

A Tax Strategy

There is one major tax break available with puts which is not available to outright short sellers. Successful short sales are always treated, taxwise, as short-term capital gains, no matter how long the short sale is maintained. You can convert a put into a long-term capital gain (taxed at half the rate) in this manner. When it comes time to close out the position, do *not* exercise the put. If you do, your purchase and sale of the underlying shares, unless the shares are held for at least six months, will be treated as a short-term gain. Instead, sell the *put itself*. Put-and-call dealers will repurchase options that contain a built-in profit, exercising them themselves. You will receive the total profit represented by the put option, less a small discount to the dealer. If the put was held for six months or longer, your profit, represented by the purchase and sale of the put itself, will be treated as a long-term capital gain.

And, of course, the possibility of long-term capital-gain taxation provides another reason for sacrificing those sure Treasury issue yields (always fully taxable) for a play in options.

Using Puts As Insurance

Let's suppose this time that you've come through the last bull market or intermediate rally quite nicely, thank you, that you *believe* a serious decline may be coming, but you are, however, not certain. Instead of selling those securities that you own, you might consider *buying* puts on those securities. Should the decline come, you'll be fully protected, less the cost of the option premium. Should your holdings continue to advance, you'll have the opportunity to add to your profits.

How To Buy Your Favorite Stock 20% Below The Market Or Make A Nice Profit If You Don't

Every depression does come to an end sooner or later (a point we have and will be making repeatedly) and every bear market, likewise, eventually comes to rest. Fortunately for put players, puts become quite popular, relatively speaking, *near the ends* of bear markets—which fact could provide you with an excellent opportunity.

Let's suppose that you discern the signs of a bottom close at hand but, this time, you do believe the possibility exists for some, but not great, further decline. *Why not sell some puts at the market on shares you'd otherwise consider purchasing outright?* You will receive from 15 to 20 percent of the share price for the options you sell. True, you are now obligated to purchase those shares if the put is exercised. But what if you are? After all, you were considering the purchase of those shares in any case, but this way your cost is reduced by 15 to 20 percent of the market price at the time you sold those options, this 15 to 20 percent of the market price at the time you sold those options, this 15 to 20 percent represented by the option money or premium you received from the sale.

And what if the shares rise instead and the put is *not* exercised? Just as well. The option money you received will become yours free and clear once the option expires—income to you deriving from a rise in price of shares you never owned.

The Call Option

A *call* is just the opposite of a put, representing the right to *purchase* 100 shares of a specified issue at a specified price until a specified time. While puts are purchased by bears, calls are purchased (generally) by bulls. One example should suffice. Suppose you believed in April 1974 that LTV, then about 10, was going to advance strongly in the year to come. For roughly $200 you could have purchased a one-year call on LTV, striking price 10, expiration in April 1975. Remember, no matter how low LTV dropped, you could never lose more than your $200 option premium. As it turned out, LTV did advance within the next year, reaching 19 by the end of April 1975. Had you exercised at that time, you could have purchased the shares as per your option at 10, selling on the open market at 19, for a profit, before commissions, of $900 per hundred. Your investment, originally, was only $200 for the call option, so the net $700 profit (after we deduct the $200 you paid for the option) represents a percentage gain of 350 percent, derived from a security that advanced by only 90 percent. Obviously, call option purchases can prove excellent tactics during the early phases of bull markets—but since this is a book dealing with depressions, bear markets, and the like, let's see how the call can come in handy in those dreary climates.

Use a Call as Insurance Against Short Sales Going Wrong

We've already seen how you can use a put as an alternative to putting out a short sale. But suppose that there are no put sellers for the puts you want to buy? (The over-the-counter option market doesn't always offer the wares you'd like to secure.) You can put out that short sale after all, buying a call at the market this time as insurance. Should the short sale go awry, you simply exercise your call to purchase shares at the striking price, using those shares to cover the short sale. Your total risk is limited to the cost of the call option, but again, as in the case of the purchase of the put, the stock must decline by at least an amount equivalent to the option premium for you to profit.

Over-the-counter calls are not always available, but at the time of this writing hundreds of listed put and call options are available on

Amex, CBOE, and other exchanges that are actively traded and are readily available.

Sell Naked Calls As an Alternative to Selling Stock Short

For every call buyer there must be a call seller who agrees to deliver shares to the buyer at a specified price. Generally the seller or writer of calls already holds those shares, willing to part with them for the profit represented by the call premium and willing to risk holding the shares, drawing extra income from the sale of the option to cushion any decline. This is probably an excellent, conservative market tactic for rising or neutral markets, not, however, for severe bear markets.

The sale of a call against shares already owned is referred to as the writing of a *covered call*. The sale of a call option against which no shares are held is referred to as a *naked call*.

What do you gain potentially by writing a naked call? First, you incur little or no commission for the short sale and repurchase of the common shares. The commissions charged on CBOE and the Amex for the sale of call options are far below the commission costs for dealing in the underlying common. Second, in selling the naked call, you tie up less cash than if you sell the underlying common short. And third, you can profit from the sale of a naked call *even if the underlying security does not decline at all.*

How You Can Make 116.9% a Year Selling Short a Stock That Actually Rises In Price

The purchaser of a call option pays his premium for leverage and hopes that the underlying issue rises sufficiently to offset the cost of the option premium. Listed options can be traded back and forth in their secondary markets, even after issue, and a study of one of them should illustrate the point.

In February 1975 the Atlantic Richfield April-90 call option was trading on the CBOE at a price of 4, the Atlantic Richfield common trading at the time at 86. The designation "April-90" means that the call expires on the last Monday in April, and that the striking price is 90. The price, 4, means that a call on 100 shares of Atlantic Richfield trades at $400 per call.

Let's suppose you were bearish in February and sold that call "naked" for $400. The call is trading "out-of-the-money," that is, its striking price (90) is above the current market price (86) of its underlying common. Does the call at this point have any tangible value? No, not at all. Atlantic Richfield would have to rise by at least 4 points for an option to buy it at 90 to have any value at all—and remember, the stock was selling at 86. In fact, the call buyer must see Atlantic Richfield at 94 at the call's expiration for the call to be worth more than 4 at the time. (A call's value at expiration equals the difference between the market price of the shares and the striking price, except of course, that the option can never have a negative value. For example, if Atlantic Richfield is selling at 100 on the last Monday in April, an April option to buy the shares at 90 should be worth roughly $1,000.)

Now, obviously, the $400 value of the call on the open market shrinks as expiration approaches—the less the life remaining to a call, the less its value, all else equal, since there is less time opportunity for the underlying common to rise in price. Suppose that Atlantic Richfield were to have remained at 86 from February through April 1975. The call option would have expired worthless, bringing a $400 profit to the naked seller. Suppose Atlantic Richfield rose by 4 points to 90. The call would still have expired worthless. In fact, the seller of that naked call would have made money, the call remaining below 4, unless the common rose from 86 to 94, a gain of 9.3 percent in roughly ten weeks. This comes out to an annualized rate of increase of 48.4 percent. Since Atlantic Richfield, on average, does not gain in price at that rate, the odds clearly favored the seller of the naked option. (Exception: new bull market.)

Sellers of naked options generally make their short sales with some head start in hand, represented by the amount of intangible value in the price of the call. (In the above case, the option price was 100 percent intangible value.) However, potential profit is limited to the price received for the call option. No matter how low Atlantic Richfield dropped, you could never make more than $400 on the premium received for the short sale of the option.

Despite your head start, you should consider the sale of naked options quite speculative. Employ risk capital only and do place protective stop orders in the position, limiting your losses should the short sale develop against you.

Also keep in mind that margin requirements for naked short sales of call options involve more than the cost of the option itself. Exchange margin regulations for such transactions have been in a state of flux, varying, in addition, from brokerage to brokerage. Do check out current exchange and house regulations with your broker. As of this writing, minimum margin requirements would have called for you to put up $1,780 in margin for the short sale of the Atlantic Richfield April-90 call option. Had the common remained at or below 90, your $400 profit would have represented a percentage gain of 22.5 percent for a ten-week period—or 116.9 percent on an annualized basis!

Write Covered Call Options

This, of course, represents another departure from the game plan of guaranteeing your preservation of capital, but still, at the right time, does represent a conservative means of entering a new bull market, or of putting your feet in the water of a market in transition.

If you observe the following precautions, you should come out intact enough in all but the very worst situations.

1. Write calls only on high-dividend-paying stocks. On the CBOE and Amex the seller of the options gets to keep all dividends, even if the call is exercised. On over-the-counter calls, the buyer of the call gets the dividends accruing during the life of the call, if he exercises.
2. Write calls only on stocks trading in the lowest 20 percent of their last twelve-month trading range. This rule will keep you from entering positions prior to major declines, or at least not until a considerable portion of the decline is past.
3. Do *not* write covered calls if you suspect that a bear market is about to begin.

An Example

In late 1974 Loews common was trading at 13¾. Its April-15 call option was trading on the CBOE at 1¾, or $175 per option. The common paid $1.20 in dividends at the time, a yield of 8.7 percent. For a six-month holding period a holder of Loews would have stood to receive $60 in dividends, plus the $175 option premium, had he sold the covered call—a total income from his holdings, then, of $235 or 17.1 percent of the value of his shares. Unless Loews dropped by 17.1 percent by April 1975, he would not lose any money.

On the other hand, the striking price of the option was 15, so if the common rose he would have made an additional $125 per hundred shares, selling common then worth 13¾ for 15. Totaling this up, we find that the covered writer could have made $60 (dividends), $175 (option premium), and $125 (difference between the striking price and the price of the shares when the option was sold)—total, $360 or 26.2 percent of the value of the shares when the option was sold. The seller could never make more; no matter how high Loews rose, he was committed by the terms of the option to deliver the shares at 15. However, a 26.2 percent return in six months does annualize out to 52.4 percent. (All commissions excluded.)

How To Figure Potential Payouts

Actually, I have understated the potential returns from such operations. Let's assume that this transaction had been entered into six months prior to the option's expiration and that you had purchased the common at full 50 percent margin. We will presume further that Loews did trade at 15 or better in April 1975 and that the option was exercised.

Initially, option sellers receive their premium money immediately, and the proceeds so derived can be employed to meet margin requirements for the purchase of the common shares. At 50 percent margin, your deposit for a $1,375 stock purchase, plus commissions, would amount to roughly $725.00. We subtract from this the $150 net option premium (after CBOE commissions), leaving you with an approximate net cash outlay of $575.00 to initiate the position.

Expenses

Cost of shares	$1,375.00
Round-trip stock commissions	75.00 (approximate)
CBOE commissions on option sale	25.00 (approximate)
Cost of margin loan at 11% for 6 months	40.00 (approximate)
Total Expenses	$1,515.00

Income

Proceeds from exercise of option at 15	$1,500.
Option premium	150.
Dividends over six months	60.
Total Income	$1,710

Your net ($1,710 minus $1,515) comes to $195 per hundred shares. Since your cash outlay per position amounted to only $575, your *rate of return, after all expenses, would come to 33.9 percent for a six-month period*, or to 67.8 percent on an annualized basis!

This presumes, again, that Loews rises to 15. If it stays at 13¾? Well, you simply pocket the premium you received and sell another option for added income. You incur no loss, even considering all expenses, until and unless Loews drops by at least one full point, or 7.3 percent, and even then you incur loss only if you close out the position at that juncture. Do keep in mind that Loews, at a price of 12¾, figures to yield 9.4 percent, and could be held for further dividends and further option writing. (Loews, in fact, did drop to as low as 10⅞ during the bear market, but by February 1975 had recovered to over 18, well above the striking price of the option. As of this writing, the odds favored the exercise of the call—a 33.9 percent gain to the option writer.)

However, do remember again that such an option-writing program should be undertaken only either late in bear markets or early in bull markets, and preferably on high-dividend-paying issues.

Straddles

A *straddle* is a combination put and call, its premium price generally somewhat less than the cost of the put *and* the call purchased separately. The buyer of the straddle is betting that a significant move in the underlying common will take place whatever its direction. So long as the move is sufficient, he may be able to exercise either the put *or* the call with sufficient profit to offset the larger straddle premium. In fact, while our fantasies are running rampant, we should at least acknowledge the possibility that the straddle may be exercised in *both* directions.

For example, suppose you had purchased a straddle on Loews in late 1974, the price then 13¾. You might have paid, say, $475 for a one-year straddle, striking price 13¾. As we have seen, Loews dipped to 10⅞— let's figure that you exercised the put side at 11, purchasing the shares at that level and selling at 13¾ as per the put side of the straddle option. Profit on that end, $275. By mid-February 1975 the shares had run to as high as 18¾. Suppose you exercised the call at that level, buying at 13¾, selling at 18¾. Additional profit, $500—total profit, $775. Since the straddle cost you $475, your net would have amounted to $300, or to a 63.2 percent gain (before commissions).

Generally speaking, both sides of straddles are not exercised, but at least one side generally is. The seller of a straddle will receive a larger premium than for the sale of a put or a call alone, but he too must be prepared to have at least one side of the option exercised.

The sale of straddles is best ventured into late in bear markets or early in bull markets, and the call side should not be carried naked. You have to plan, again, either on delivering shares (if the market rises and the call is exercised) or accumulating shares (if the put is exercised).

The Shopping Centers

In the past option trading was restricted—in fact, not in principle —to the more sophisticated market traders. Puts, calls, and straddles had to be purchased via put-and-call dealers, or sometimes through exchange brokerages that had in-house option departments. To purchase an option, you had to call the dealer, enter a bid, and wait while he "showed the bid around." If a seller was available, odds are that the dealer would come back to you with an offer, which might differ from your bid either in premium price or in stipulated striking price. A bit of negotiation usually followed, the dealer sometimes offering to settle the matter by reducing his profit, which accrues from the difference between what you pay for the call and what the seller actually receives. Each option, therefore, represented an individual transaction, individually arrived at. Periods of life generally ranged from 90 days to one year—six months, ten days, the most popular length. Puts and straddles, as well as unlisted call options, are still transacted in this manner. If you have interest in this area, put-and-call dealers regularly advertise in *Barron's, The Wall Street Journal,* and *The New York Times.*

Listed Options

Option trading really hit the big time in April 1973 when the Chicago Board Options Exchange (CBOE) opened its doors for business, sporting an entirely new concept in option trading.

Borrowing from the commodity markets, CBOE standardized option contracts. All options originally listed expired in one of four months—January, April, July, and October—options brought out for trading nine months prior to expiration. Striking prices are standardized too, at intervals of 5, 10, or 20, depending upon the price range of the stock. For example, should Loews be trading at 14 at the time a new maturity option is introduced (new options are introduced as old ones expire), the striking price of the option would be set at 15, the "5" closest to 14.

Once an option is introduced for trading, it continues to trade, no matter how its underlying shares fluctuate in price. Since the options are both listed and standardized, active trading takes place in the options themselves. For example, suppose you had purchased that Loews April-15 call for $175, when the common was trading at 13¾. You would not actually have to exercise the option to profit; you could simply sell it at 3¾ in the CBOE listed secondary market, near expiration, if the common had risen to 18¾.

The ease of purchasing and selling the options themselves, the ready availability of pricing, plus the leverage possibilities, rendered CBOE an instant success. Virtually every brokerage instituted facilities for trading CBOE options, and the original CBOE roster grew within two years from 16 to 40 listed stocks. In addition, the American Stock Exchange joined the act, listing, early in 1975, 20 issues of its own. Other exchanges plan to join in as well, and plans have been announced for the listing of put options.

Your brokerage can supply you with a prospectus detailing the mechanics of option trading on the Amex and CBOE, and a number of excellent books have already appeared relating to spreads and hedges possible via listed options. Quotations for listed CBOE and Amex options are carried daily in *The Wall Street Journal*.

You'll Probably Be in Good Company

Ever since the CBOE began operations, the Securities and Exchange Commission has been voicing concern over the possible impact of active option dealing on the stock market, on speculative fever, and on low-priced stocks (the natural alternative to options for many investors). Indeed, my own observation is that since listed option trading has come into being, warrants have lost some popularity. (A warrant is a long-term option to buy shares of stock at a specified price until a specified time. However, in this case the seller is usually the corporation itself.) This loss in popularity is readily explainable. The bear markets of 1968-70 and 1973-74 drove many issues down so low in price that the exercise price of related warrants seemed so high as to appear quite remote. The availability of similarly leveraged instruments, the listed option, attracted speculative buyers instead.

In response to SEC prodding, the CBOE has repeatedly issued studies showing that its operations have had minimal, if any, effect upon trading in its underlying issues. One such study was released on February 13, 1975. During 1974, volume on CBOE amounted to 5.6 million options contracts. Roughly 100,000 investors participated in CBOE options trading, generally among the more affluent of our citizens. Buyer income tended to range in the $15,000-$50,000 area, while sellers tended to earn between $25,000 and $100,000. It would appear that the more speculative buyers drew from the ranks of the somewhat smaller investor. Option selling, generally a more certain road to profit, attracted the more income-minded, the less speculative segment of the investing community.

Bull market or bear, options do seem here to stay, and you might as well learn to turn them to your advantage.

11
REAL ESTATE: DURING THE COMING DEPRESSION? NO! NO! A THOUSAND TIMES, NO! BUT AFTER—? NOW, THAT'S A DIFFERENT STORY ALTOGETHER

O.K. We're on the verge of or into a major depression. You've left the stock market (good for you), but you have neither a yen for Yen nor a yen for short selling. Still, you don't trust the banks, and you do want your money placed into something of true tangible value. Gold? Maybe —but you're afraid that even gold may be too speculative. Land? Property? Now that grabs you. Isn't land a fixed commodity—after all, the world can't get any larger, can it? And don't people have to maintain a roof over their heads, whether or not they do go out to buy that new car?

True, all the above does seem logical enough; but, sorry, it just doesn't quite work out that way. The inflation-deflation-depression cycle wreaks havoc on real estate in any number of ways. And if you don't believe that, just witness the recent plight of the hapless real estate investment trusts (REITs) in recent years. Authorized by an act of Congress in the early 1960s, the REITs apparently had a good thing going—borrowing funds from banks and lending out the money to builders and developers for higher rates of return. A good thing, that is, until, first, inflation and then depression came along.

It began to cost the REITs dearly to borrow; they couldn't get the spread they needed between the cost to them of the funds they lent out and what they could secure. Even worse, with mortgage rates sky high during the inflationary period (1973–74), the developers couldn't find buyers. Ergo, a number of developers went under, defaulting on their loans to the REITs. The REITs, in turn, couldn't pay their own bills, a number of them filing for bankruptcy, or else passing up dividends and bond-interest payments. Nor did the buck stop there. Failures in the

REITs, resulting in defaults on bank loans made to them, bit into bank earnings. And, of course, we haven't even touched on the myriad of individual investors who put hard-earned dollars into REIT stock issues in search of the high dividend yield promised therein. In short, if the developers, real estate trusts, banks, and other investors all got stung playing with real estate at the wrong time, what chance do you have?

How Inflation Strikes the Property Owner

You'll concede that depressions hurt builders, lenders, and stock investors. But why should the actual property owner get hurt? Well, he does—take it from an actual owner of apartment dwellings, yours truly. Let's take inflation first. While certain costs of income-property ownership remain fixed (mortgage payments and interest), others do rise steadily with inflation—oil, electricity, repairs, taxes. To some extent these costs can be passed along to tenants in the form of increased rentals; to some extent, particularly in areas of rent control, they cannot. As a result, the gap between expenditures on the property and the income derived therefrom does narrow—you can usually get only so much from a tenant, after all. (All, as we shall see below, while the value of property does rise during inflationary periods, tight mortgage money greatly limits your ability to sell your holdings.)

And depression? Here we have another problem—the limited ability of tenants to meet rents, rent increases, and such. As an owner of income realty, you'll find it increasingly difficult to fill vacancies at increasing rentals. In addition, peripheral sources of tenants begin to dry up. For example, a major source of tenants for nonluxury housing includes welfare recipients. During prosperous times, local communities tend to respond more generously to welfare needs. Until recently, for instance, Nassau and Suffolk counties in New York State paid not only the rents for welfare clients but also real estate brokerage fees if these apartments were obtained through real estate agents. As recession hit these areas, claims for welfare mounted, and services were reduced wherever possible. An example? No longer would the departments of social service in these areas pay brokerage fees. This meant that property owners were forced either to absorb advertising costs themselves (an added expense), show the apartments themselves (additional time), or absorb the realtor's fees. Problems mount with rent delinquencies. The risks of increasing taxation mount as well as local communities require cash to meet rising welfare costs.

Compounding the problems of operation are increasing difficulties in marketing properties. During periods of intense inflation, high mortgage costs discourage would-be purchasers. During periods of depression, general pessimism and fearfulness deter buyers. Result: you may become stuck with property against your will. Real estate is not as liquid an investment as equity securities—make no mistake about that.

Are syndicates the answer? (A syndicate is generally a limited partnership that invests in properties that would be too large for the single investor to handle alone.) We'll return to the concept a bit further on, but, for the present, keep in mind that syndicate-owned properties are generally subject to the same risks and pit-falls as individually owned properties. Some will continue to thrive during depressions; many marginal syndicates will fall by the wayside.

Raw land? Perhaps the worst. Raw land prices tend to decline during depressions. Farmers, hard pressed to meet expenses, withdraw bids for added acreage. Investors, in general, shy away from committing capital into difficult-to-liquidate situations. Moreover, raw land pays no interest, no dividends—but does draw mounting capital from you in the form of mortgage interest and realty taxes.

I think you have the idea by now. Depression spells disaster for real estate, and spells it with a capital "D."

But When the Depression's Coming to an End....

Then, indeed, is the time when the man with cash becomes king! Fortunes—fabulous fortunes—have been accumulated by investors foresighted enough to secure real estate at the truly distressed prices that pertain as depressions draw to a close. At such times you can virtually steal (legally, of course) realty property from overly leveraged, underfinanced owners, holding it yourself for income, appreciation, and resale during the next business upturn.

Sources? Plenty. Try foreclosure auctions (check realty agents and banks) and real estate ads. Look into areas heavily hit by the depression, areas in which single-family dwellings are, in the mass, in danger of foreclosure. These families will be forced to sell—in a buyer's market —at almost any price to salvage something before the bank takes over. Commercial property? Often available for a song, though the techniques of property selection are more complex. Simpler to purchase and maintain are smaller apartment houses—excellent for starters—and raw land. Or else, see if you can obtain syndicate shares from eager-to-sell owners. (Stock-minded investors might look, too, into housing and housing-related equity issues, generally cyclical in nature, that frequently rebound sharply as the business cycle turns.)

Potential Returns

The long-lived 1973–74 bear market, following closely upon the bear market of 1968–70, led to considerable reappraisal on the part of pension funds and other institutions regarding the viability of continued concentration of funds in the equity markets. Many institutional investors have already begun to diversify into real estate—citing steady returns, tangible value, and lower risks involved when real estate is compared to the equity markets. In this regard, *Institutional Investor* magazine, November 1974, reported that roughly 50 percent of pension funds surveyed plan to invest funds in real estate or to increase current commitments. Their favorite vehicles? Income-producing properties and land sale/leaseback deals. Anticipated rates of return? Forty-one percent of the respondents to a survey anticipated returns in the area of 11–16 percent annually.

Stephen Roulac, writing in the same magazine (September 1974), estimated that real estate investments on a long-term basis have yielded *after-tax* returns, over the years, of roughly 8 percent, compared to roughly 6 percent for the stock market. He presumes that one-third of capital gain and dividend returns from securities are paid in taxes.

In my own estimation these are *conservative* expectations, including a goodly number of realty investments entered into for tax shelter rather than capital gain and income considerations. I believe that *you* can do much better with the right approach—*achieving gains of from 20–30 percent annually, pretax.*

And just in case you aren't aware of what a 25 percent annual compounded rate of return can mean—$10,000 compounded at 25 percent for 20 years amounts to $867,000 plus! At 15 percent, $10,000 will grow in 20 years to $163,665.35—still a tidy little sum at that.

The Profit Magic of Real Estate Leverage

For the majority of investors the choices in realty lie among raw land, income property, syndicates, or real estate securities. Income property, the ownership of multifamily (or even single-family) dwellings, primarily for the rental income involved, may be the best bet for neophytes in the game. The imponderables are more readily calculated than are the imponderables in securing commercial property for rental income; management is simpler and financing less complicated. Returns can be excellent, particularly when leverage possibilities are considered.

Here's how it works. Let's presume the purchase of a $60,000 five-family dwelling; total rental-income-roll, $12,000. (A good rule of thumb is to try to pay no more than five times annual rental for the property. During a depression you should readily be able to secure such deals.)

A typical annual balance sheet for such a property might appear as follows, presuming a 33 percent down payment on a twenty-five-year mortgage at 8 percent.

Income: . . . . $12,00 (rental)

Expenses: Mortgage Interest $1,860*
(a rough average over the 25 years; more initially, less later)

Taxes	$1,600
Heating	1,000
Repairs	750
Water	150
Insurance	400
Electricity	150
Miscellaneous	500
Total Operating Expenses	$4,550
Total Expenses	$6,410.00
Net Profit	$5,590.00

Based on the dwelling's price of $60,000, this comes to a rate of return of approximately 9.3 percent per year. Roughly equivalent, this rate of return is huge. However, you have not put $60,000 of your capital into the deal; you have put in only $20,000, your down payment on the property.

Based upon the down payment, your actual cash out-of-pocket outlay, your true return on your investment comes not to 9.3 percent, but to 28 percent! By using leverage, in this case the bank's money working for you, you have tripled your rate of return!

Now, before we wander too far off into outer space, we do have to add in a few caveats. For one, we've based our calculations upon a rental

---

*We are estimating that the total mortgage payment will average approximately 50% for repayment of principal and 50% for repayment of interest. The total mortgage payment, each month then, will come to $372.00. Half of that amount represents the amortization or repayment of your bank loan, and represents a portion of your net profit.

income total of $12,000. We haven't discounted for potential vacancies. Nor have we allowed for the fact that in the beginning of your ownership mortgage interest carrying charges will be greater (they diminish as the mortgage is paid off). And finally, we have not considered true cash flow, the cash that comes in to you *after* repayment of the mortgage. In this case we are presuming that roughly $1,860 of your income goes to the bank for mortgage repayment (see footnote). This adds to the value of your equity in the property, but is not cash in your hand. The actual net cash to you will amount to roughly $3,730 annually, or to 18.7 percent of your investment.

Are such deals possible? Yes! As an owner myself of realty property, I can attest to fairly regular returns in the order of 20-30 percent on property that I was able to purchase at 25 percent down—and in a seller's market at that. If you employ your cash during periods of economic distress, you should do even better.

Tax Considerations

Income tax laws work both to your advantage and to your disadvantage, but mainly to your advantage. Let's get the disadvantage out of the way first. The income tax you pay on your profit must include as its basis your total return, including the amortization of your loan to the bank. For example, if you are in the 50 percent tax bracket, you will have to pay income taxes in the amount of 50 percent of $5,590 or an amount of $2,795. Considering your cash flow of $3,730, your net cash flow—after this form of taxation alone—would come to only $935, hardly inspiring, considering an investment of $20,000 cold, hard cash. (However, your equity in the property has increased, as above.)

That's the bad news. Now, here's the good news, and why real estate has long been a haven for truly big money.

Depreciation!

Obviously, the income dwelling you purchased will not last forever; its usable life is finite after all. The reduction in value of the property as a result of wear, aging, and damage is referred to as depreciation. This depreciation is carried on your balance sheet as an expense, even though it represents no cash whatsoever out of your pocket. And since it is an expense, your reportable profits are reduced by the extent of depreciation that you can legitimately claim. Land is *not* depreciable, only the house itself. So let's presume that, of your $60,000 payment for the property, you estimate that $55,000 went for the dwelling, $5,000 for the land. Presuming a usable life of 25 years, you might depreciate the property at $2,200 per year. This represents a potential tax savings to you, since the $2,200 can be used to offset the profits otherwise in the deal, or if there are none, *can be used to offset other ordinary income you may have.* Let's figure this time that, in all other regards, your property breaks more or less even. The depreciation you can claim will, in itself, save you $1,100 in taxes or 5.5 percent of your cash investment.

That's the good news. Now back to the bad news. When you sell the property, you must deduct the total of depreciation claimed over the years from your cost price in computing your capital gains and losses. For example, suppose you ultimately sell your property for $60,-000, say, after ten years and $22,000 worth of depreciation claims. For income tax purposes, you subtract the $22,000 from your cost basis, $60,000, leaving you with a cost of $38,000 and a reportable long-term capital gain of $22,000. So you do have to give back some of those tax savings in the end.

Now, one more time, back to the good news. The long-term capital gain is taxed at only half your normal tax rate, in other words, at 25 percent (if you're in the 50 percent bracket), so you end up being taxed on only one-half that $22,000 depreciation you deducted from ordinary income over the years. Various forms of accelerated depreciation have been possible, which allow for greater depreciation deductions during the early years. However, these are fraught with other tax consequences; should you so opt—better discuss the matter with your accountant.

The usual practice is to roll over or trade in your income property once the depreciation runs out and/or when the amortization portion of your mortgage payments becomes so large as to generate a minimal or negative after-tax cash flow. (Remember, you pay income taxes on amortization.)

General Operating Principles

The time-honored means of investing in smaller income properties has been to pick up a fairly run-down property in *a good location*, upgrade the property via some relatively inexpensive cosmetic operations, raise the rents, and then ultimately sell the property at a handsome profit.

Here's how the technique works—and again I can personally attest to its feasibility. Suppose you buy a rather neglected two- or three-family property—we'll figure a cost of roughly $39,000 for a three-family property. Figuring that you can purchase at five times rental, your initial rent roll should come to $7,800.

Now, what will it take to build up that rent roll, apart from usual rent increases accruing from inflation, tenant turnover, and such? (I hardly need tell you that rents have not been falling over the years.)

I'll have to relate to my own locality, the Long Island area in New York State. Let's figure that the $7,800 rent roll divides among the three units in this way: two apartments rent at $220, the third at $210. These are moderate rentals, assuming ample-sized three- or four-room apartments, but left unpainted by the previous owner, outdated fixtures, and so forth.

We will now suppose that you invest some $2,000 in general face-lifting—nothing major—some paint, a few modern but inexpensive lighting fixtures, perhaps some moderately priced paneling. If you're handy and have the time, your costs will be reduced greatly if you do the work yourself. Otherwise, you'll have to figure in labor costs.

Once the work is done, you should be able to raise your rentals readily by 25–30 percent, if not immediately, certainly as tenants vacate. Let's presume this time that you do secure an increase of 25 percent in your rent rolls. Instead of drawing $7,800 in annual rentals, you draw $9,750, a rise of $1,950. The cost of your home improvements has been returned to you increased rentals within a single year!

And what has happened, as a result, to the value of your property? Still basing price on the five-times rent formula, we find that with a rent roll of $9,750 the value of the property has risen by $9,750, or 25 percent! In other words, your $2,000 investment has been multiplied five times in property value, not to mention the increasing rental proceeds generated therefrom.

Just one more piece of arithmetic. Let's suppose that you put 33⅓ percent, or one-third, down on the property ($13,000) at the time you made your purchase. By increasing the value of the property by $9,750, you can, should you decide to sell, achieve a rather rapid return on your cash outlay of 75 percent, not including the income that you took in while the property was held.

Sounds unbelievable? Well, it is not. Thousands of small-scale realty entrepreneurs are operating in just this manner right now throughout the country, reaping the rewards involved. And you can do the same; you do not have to start off as any sort of expert. You need only the courage to take the step. (Incidentally, in case you're wondering about the odds—99 percent of real estate mortgages are paid off on schedule.)

One more question. Why, if the process of purchase and rent roll increase is easy, don't all owners do it? Why are such potential money-makers available at all? The fact, again, is that the majority of property operators do precisely that; the majority of properties up for sale have already been upgraded, are fully priced in terms of potential rental, and are not necessarily worth purchasing at all. On the other hand, properties do exist that offer excellent upgrading potential—but you have to search for them actively. Following extended periods of depression these properties should become more readily available. During periods of general pessimism owners are loath to invest money in capital improvements. Furthermore, depressions are likely to lead to an increase in the number of single-family dwellings coming up for foreclosure. Normally, single-family homes do not offer sufficient returns for income investment—but if you can obtain them dirt cheap. . . .

How to Buy

The key to any real estate purchase—land, income property, or syndicate deals—is location. No other factor is as significant to the ultimate success of your investment. Look for property preferably located in a stable residential neighborhood; hopefully your purchase will be the *worst* building on the block, with the potential of being upgraded to the neighborhood norm. In many areas your tenants will lie economically somewhat below the level of private homeowners surrounding your small apartment house. For them the move to such an area may represent a "step up," a move greatly desired. Properties so located are relatively easy to rent, always in good demand.

In evaluating the neighborhood, be certain to drive around yourself, exploring the vicinity from all sides. Realty agents are prone to take the most "scenic" route in showing a property. Look for deterioration encroaching from any corner. A positive sign: new residential construction in the immediate vicinity, indications that professional developers are willing to take a position in the area.

Pricing

The basic rule is to shoot for five times rental. However, you can figure your permissible purchase price in other ways as well. Total up all estimated operating expenses, *feeling free to ask the seller to show you his actual books* along the way. Add in payments for mortgages and taxes, but exclude repair estimates. Your cash flow, money received over and above mortgage payments, should run from 10 to 15 percent of your down payment or cash outlay. This should leave you sufficient cushion for repair expenses and vacancies.

Another way to proceed is to compute the total operating expenses of the property, including taxes, but excluding mortgage interest and payments. Deduct this amount from your rental income. You can pay roughly six to seven times the difference. For example:

Income: $7,800 (rent)

Expenses: $1,200 taxes
　　　　　　150 water
　　　　　　150 electricity
　　　　　　400 repairs
　　　　　　150 insurance
　　　　　　400 heat
　　　　　　350 miscellaneous
Total Expenses: $2,800

The difference comes to $5,000. Multiply that by, say, 6 or 7, and you secure a price range for the property of between $30,000 and $35,000. During a buyer's market you should be able to come close to the lower figure, which, again, is why you should be entering real estate *near depression bottoms* when cheap buys are available, not near the peaks of economic booms when you'll have to pay top dollar.

Incidentally, take nothing for granted in calculating expenses. Ask to see the owner's books, check out the local taxes at the county clerk's office, call the oil supplier to ask what actually was paid for oil last year, and so forth. Secure written representations regarding all occupancy permits, the absence of any violations, and so forth. Also, verify all existing leases and ask for a record of the vacancy rate over previous years. Anticipate rental losses of roughly twice the vacancy rate, to allow for tenants who are physically present, but who do not meet rent payments. You may find it profitable to take a second mortgage from the seller, to supplement existing bank mortgages, in case you cannot secure a new bank mortgage. You will require a book of mortgage tables, which can be obtained from your realty broker or from Realforms, P.O. Box 1, Brookline, Mass. 02146. This firm also offers lease forms and other printed forms pertinent to your operation. Mortgage tables are essential if you are to accurately compute your cash flow and actual net amortization each year.

A Checklist for Apartment House Hunting

The following checklist should be of some help in the final determination of your purchase. Skip no steps! Once in, you cannot dispose of real property as easily as you can dispose of your General Motors holdings. One of the disadvantages of realty investment is that the investment is relatively illiquid. It can frequently take months to sell at *your* price, once it's time to roll over the property.

1. Asking price
2. Schedule of current rents (verify all leases personally)
3. Side income from property (e.g., garage rental, laundry machines)
4. Concessions that exist in current leases
5. Amounts of rent security held by previous owner (these revert to the buyer)
6. Existing mortgages
7. Taxes (verify personally)
8. Utility and water costs (check with the companies themselves)
9. Existing insurance (is it sufficient?)
10. Labor costs (if the property involves a superintendent, gardener, or manager)
11. Needed repairs (have a professional inspector examine the premises)
12. Termites
13. Appliances (who provides—condition—replacement costs?)
14. Cesspool or sewer?
15. Garbage collection (who provides?)

Buildings that offer tenants a driveway, a garage, or a yard to relax in are more desirable than buildings that offer none of these. Do *not*, incidentally, think in terms of your own standard of dwelling when you are contemplating an investment in apartment income property. Think in terms of whether the apartments in the property are desirable in terms of the rental charged, the class of tenant you expect, and the general area.

Caveats

Real estate management is not for everybody. Although you can hire management agents (at about a 50 percent reduction in your total profit), you will probably prefer to manage your initial properties yourself. In so doing, you must be prepared to deal with people and you *will* encounter tenant problems, rent arrears, complaints from neighbors, the need to evict deadbeats, and so forth. The majority of tenants are steady, reliable, and, believe it or not, more than ready to cooperate with a landlord who gives them a fair shake. (I have always found it worthwhile to make promised repairs promptly, and to maintain the premises we rent.) However, there *are* occasions when you will have to appear in court or otherwise deal with personal unpleasantness. It is best to let a recalcitrant tenant move—vacancies are not generally that difficult to fill. Eventually, you will have a roster of tenants with whom you can live comfortably.

Again—just to sum up—for diversification and profit that has, over the years, exceeded investment in common-share equities, do obtain some income properties, particulary during periods of economic distress. Who knows, you may end up owning half your state some day.

12
SOME SUNDRY REALTY INVESTMENTS...

Residential income property aside, entrepreneurs in realty do have various avenues of approach open to them.

Participation in a Real Estate Syndicate

A syndicate is a group of investors joined together to enter into a realty deal too large for any of them to handle alone with the amount of funds individually available for that particular investment. Syndicates exist for investment in income property (residential and commercial), raw land investment, new construction, motels—you name it.

As a general rule, syndicates require a high ante for starters—figure $25,000 as a bare minimum for most deals, $50,000–$100,000 a more likely range, based upon my discussions with a broad spectrum of syndicate managers. You cannot start small, as you can with apartment dwellings, self run, where you can pick up a two-family for as little as $5,000 or so down.

On the other hand, for the most part there is little to do in a syndicate aside from investigation of the deal and placing your bets. The syndicate management does it all for you, from selecting the property to collecting rents to seeing to repairs. Prospective returns? Probably in the area of 10 to 12 percent in a successful operation, on average, but this depends very much upon the type of syndicate you enter.

Some syndicates are set up to provide a reasonable rate of cash flow to investors: again, perhaps, on the order of 10 to 12 percent. Others are so structured that you may receive no profit at all for many years, if ever! In that case, why would you enter such a deal? For the hefty tax shelters involved, of course.

For example, suppose you are in the 70 percent tax bracket and put up $100,000 in a highly leveraged commercial property—in other words, the syndicate can purchase the property for, say, 10 percent down. Your $100,000, in effect, buys you $1 million worth of property.

And suppose, further, that that property can be depreciated over twenty-five years, resulting in a $40,000-per-year depreciation credit for you against your ordinary income. In the 70 percent tax bracket, this means that you will receive a reduction in your taxes of $28,000 per year, based upon your original investment of $100,000.

Even if the property goes bankrupt in ten years, you've received a return of 28 percent a year in the interim (based upon income taxes saved), or $280,000 in total for the $100,000 you laid out. Which is why many investors in the upper strata cheerfully put their money into syndicate deals, knowing in advance that the property will do little better than break even.

Structures of Syndicates

Syndicates are generally structured along the lines of *limited or general partnerships* rather than as corporations, since depreciation tax shelters cannot be passed along from a corporation directly to its shareholders, and the tax shelters involved are generally the frosting on the cake that makes the whole syndicate concept palatable.

Limited partnerships involve two classes of partners: the general partners, who control the management of the syndicate, and the limited partners, who share in the profits but who have no say in the operations. While you do give up decision-making authority in accepting a limited partnership, you receive a major benefit. Like corporation stockholders, limited partners cannot be held personally liable for the operations of the partnership except to the extent of their original investment. That means that if your property folds (your syndicate owing millions out), your own assets cannot be attached for nonpayment.

Should you join a general partnership, receiving full say in the operation, you do not receive this protection.

The Syndicate Manager

And what does the syndicate manager or organizer receive for his trouble? That depends. In some deals he receives a free share in the partnership, perhaps up to 20 percent of total assets. Such arrangements obviously represent a disadvantage to the investor, and in no case should you enter into such an agreement unless your contract, at the least, prevents the organizer from liquidating and collecting his share until you can receive back your original investment in full as a minimum.

Usually the syndicate organizer will package the project for a management fee, if he is acting as a money manager, or for the typical realty management fee, once the property is in operation—usually about 5 to

6 percent of total rental. These charges are not unreasonable so long as the deal meets your needs.

Do check out the local reputation of the syndicate organizer, and have your tax lawyer and accountant thoroughly study the pospectus of the offering, carefully examining all present and prospective statements of income, expenses, and tax shelters involved. The majority of realty syndicates operate intrastate to avoid federal regulatory obligations. You can probably locate local syndicates within your state by consulting real estate attorneys or brokers. Look for a firm that has a lengthy background of activity in the area, a proven track record, and, if possible, a deal that does not provide the syndicate manager a free piece of the pie. Incidentally, tried-and-true investments, such as standard income properties, probably have a better chance of success than some of the more exotic condominiums, ski lodges, and motels sometimes offered to investors.

Syndicates are, of course, as adversely affected by depressions as any other realty play, and are best avoided during the early part of economic down cycles. Moreover, shares in syndicates can be extremely difficult to liquidate, even presuming that your partnership agreement provides the free right to liquidation at all. However, there is one type of syndicate deal that does offer at least fair prospects during a depression.

On occasion a syndicate is formed that purchases a prime commercial property, carrying within it a long-term net lease to a prime tenant, say, a major corporation. On the strength of this lease the syndicate can often secure favorable terms from a bank to finance the purchase, the long-term lease virtually guaranteeing syndicate income from the property. In a net lease the tenant covers all operating expenses. Such leases are nearly as secure as corporate bonds, and, if the corporation is A-rated, you can be at least fairly certain of weathering any but the most calamitous depression.

Tax Dangers

Do be aware that the IRS has been tightening up on tax regulations affecting syndicates and that Congress may soon pass tax-reform legislation adversely affecting such investments. Verify tax consequences carefully before investing.

Raw Land

Another classic inflation hedge, the purchase of raw land, is about as safe a way to invest, during depression periods, as a day at the races.

Of course, during boom periods the reverse is true. From 1958 to 1972 the average price of land in the United States rose by roughly 7 percent per year, or nearly triple the average annual rise in the cost of living. In fact, the trend further accelerated during 1972-73, farmland values up by roughly 13 percent during 1972 alone. According to the *Warren, Gorham & Lamont Real Estate Investors Report,* Wisconsin was a particular strong state; California, Utah, Arizona, and Louisiana among the weakest.

Farmland really took off in 1973, values rising by more than 20 percent, according to the U.S. Department of Agriculture. Colorado, Pennsylvania, South Carolina, Alabama, and Iowa led the parade (values rising by more than 30 percent), Louisiana again trailing the pack. Why the surge? It happened that commodity prices rose during 1973, leading to the promise of high profits to farmers and rising demand for farmland.

All told, the boom in land prices ran from 1933 to 1974, a record forty-year period. However, by mid-1974 falling commodity prices and rural financial troubles led to a paucity of bids, and land values appeared on the verge of a crest. Though popular theory holds that land values must rise, since land is a fixed commodity, longer-term studies show that land values, as all other investments, undergo cyclical fluctuations.

How can you tell when the end of a boom is at hand? The usual techniques—apply contrary opinion and avoid the crowd. Be particularly cautious when the popular media spew forth tales of fantastic land profits recently made by investors and when unsophisticated acquaintances propose the formation of partnerships for land speculation. Remember, investment in raw land pays no dividendds and usually draws no income, whereas you must pay out money each year in note payments and interest until the land is sold. And just try selling during a vicious depression. You'll be lucky if you can manage the mortgage.

But in Better Times . . .

The usual story. If you've conserved your capital during the economic holocaust, you should be able to pick up some earth dirt cheap and profit handsomely as the economic cycle reverses direction once again.

Regarding the purchase of Florida Fiefs, Pocono Paradise, and Arizona Acres—either forget it or check not twice but ten times. Some developer has already done what you should be doing, purchasing large tracts of land, subdividing, selling slices of the pizza for far more than the total cost of the whole—the whole package neatly tied up with free dinners, weekend trips, and entertainment for prospective investors. *Do not fall for fancy, high-pressure promotions.* True, the land may appreciate in value in due course, but you will be paying retail dollar, even presuming that the developer does indeed develop that golf course after all.

There has, incidentally, been a shift in population movement since 1970—more families are now moving into than leaving rural areas. The implications for investment should be obvious.

Subdivide for Superprofit

Your best bet is to purchase a large tract of land yourself, the largest you can swing, and subdivide on your own. Subdivided land can be sold during favorable periods at markups of from 200 to 500 percent over the cost of the same land purchased in a block! The closer to a major metropolitan area the better, particularly if the land is in the path of industrial and residential progress. Waterfront land, water-access land, or even water-view land is always desirable, particularly if it lies near natural scenic or developed tourist attractions. Very desirable in recent years has been vacation property that can double as a summer playground and winter resort, with proximity to ski slopes.

Do, however, familiarize yourself with local zoning regulations and secure a study of the terrain to establish potential problems with water supply, foundation digging, and road laying.

Shopping Tips For Raw Land

Never, but never, purchase land sight unseen. Do *not* rely on fancy brochures, color slides, or movies—see for yourself not only the land but the surroundings as well. We happened to be in Florida during early 1974, just as a land glut was developing. Wherever you drove—land and condominiums for sale. What are the odds of a quick resale in those circumstances?

Your best approach is to establish a good contact with a local real estate agent. Discuss your needs with him, requesting a pricing history of actual transactions that have taken place in his area. Do *not* buy into any area in which the land has not risen by at least 15 percent per year in recent years. You should also verify that land in the area, subdivided, sells for at least twice the price of similar land undivided. Again, the larger your initial tract, the greater your own price discount when you buy, the greater your potential profit.

One more thing, and it is significant. Financing for speculation in raw land has become increasingly difficult to secure, particularly during periods of tight money. Your odds of securing a loan will be better if you purchase farmland on which a farm actually exists, thereby qualifying you for a residential mortgage.

Some Tips For Generating Income from Raw Land

1. See if it can be employed as a campsite while you are awaiting its appreciation. If a road, a lake, drinking water, and electricity can be inexpensively provided, you might be able to generate some generous side income. Camping has become increasingly popular.
2. Convert the land into timberland. Christmas tree varieties grow rapidly, crops developing in from eight to twelve years. You can figure on roughly 120 trees to a good usable acre. Your initial costs will run about $100 per acre for seedlings and other expenses, about $30–$40 per year per acre for maintenance. However, you will be able to secure up to $1,000 per acre from your first crop. Check with your local forester or state conservation department for details and assistance.
3. Rent out gardening tracts. Natural food gardening is becoming very popular in certain areas of the country. If your land is suitable, you can subdivide the land into gardening sections, drawing extra income.
4. Rent out the farmhouse for vacationers or for ski weekends. Should your property include a dwelling, consider the extra income you can derive from renting the premises during periods when you, yourself, do not occupy it.
5. Rent out land as grazing land. Nearby farmers may require grazing land for their livestock.

General Tips

Raw land slated for use as vacation property should lie no farther than a four-hour drive from the nearest metropolitan center.

If you can, try to purchase along the path of new major highway construction. Prices in the Pennsylvania Poconos, for example, skyrocketed after the completion of a major highway to the area.

In subdividing, waterfront property can be packaged in smaller parcels. Land farthest from the water can be cut up into larger slices at similar prices.

You can establish a long-term tax deduction on your summer home by establishing that you purchased it primarily for investment rather than for personal use. Once this is established, you can deduct expenses on the property, even if they exceed income. The usual rule of thumb is that you must show a profit in at least two of five consecutive years. If you can do this, renting the premises fully during the early years of ownership, you may be able to establish a permanent deduction. Check with your accountant.

Miscellaneous Notes on Real Estate

Stocks that may rise and fall in tune to the housing industry include:

Johns-Manville
Boise Cascade
City Investing
Georgia Pacific
Armstrong Cork Co.

Evans Products
Emhart Corp.
Kaufman & Broad Inc.
National Gypsum
Sunbeam Corp.

These are all cyclical securities that will tend to start to rise several months before the turn in the housing industry, and that will start their cyclical declines several months in advance of a downturn in housing activity.

Realty Values Rise As Interest Rates Fall

Try to time your offerings of income property to troughs in the interest-rate cycle, when mortgage money can be obtained more cheaply. Your buyer will include interest payments when he computes his bottom line net, and he will make his offer based upon his projected net return. The lower his interest costs, the higher his potential profit, the more he will be willing to pay for the property. However, if possible, avoid giving a second morgage at such times—you will be locking in a low return for yourself.

Raw Land Includes Small Suburban Plots, Often an Excellent Investment

Urban and suburban homes have generally proven to be excellent investments. First, the cost of replacing homes has risen with the rising costs of labor and materials. Second, land values have risen sharply in suburban areas near major cities. Land cost, as a proportion of the cost of new homes, has nearly doubled over the past thirty years, now representing roughly 25 percent of the cost of the total property. You may find excellent opportunities in isolated suburban building plots in developed areas, plots too small for large-scale developers to employ.

Protect Your Interest Deductions
If you own tax-exempt securities, such as municipal bonds, the IRS may disallow interest deductions on other investments on the grounds that you are borrowing indirectly to purchase the tax-exempts. However, the rule is not likely to apply if the tax-exempts comprise less than 2 percent of your total investment portfolio.

Take Full Credit for Operating Expenses
Itemize all operating expenses in the running of a realty venture. This includes telephone calls, travel, and the purchase of pertinent investment literature—including this book.

It Usually Pays to Raise Rents
By and large, rent increases will prove profitable, rarely resulting in a loss of tenants large enough to offset the profits derived from the rent increase. You can figure that a 10 percent rent increase should net you an additional 2 percent net income immediately, based upon usual notice-to-move rates following such rises.

You May Be Better Off Offering Short-Term Leases
With inflation probably here to stay, you may not want to lock yourself into long-term commercial and apartment rental leases, which will fix your income while maintenance costs and taxes rise. Many savvy property owners will now accept only short-term leases, including tax escalation clauses that pass tax increases along to the tenant.

Pyramid for Real Profit
Major real estate fortunes are built through the pyramiding of profits. For example, let's suppose you own an apartment house that cost you $10,000 down and whose total price is amortized at $2,000 per year. Although your equity builds up, the money you earn via amortizaion is not working for you.

Solution: Either refinance as soon as you have developed sufficient excess equity to provide a down payment on a second unit or else sell, using the cash proceeds to purchase extra units. You multiply returns greatly by pyramiding your returns in this manner.

If You Have Children of Working Age, Put Them on the Payroll
This tax tactic can work for you no matter what business operation you maintain. The rationale? Simple enough. Your children will be in a much lower tax bracket than you, and you save on the income tax differential involved.

Looking for a Vacation Spot? Consider a Time-Shared Condominium

One way to secure access to Florida or to some other vacation spot is to purchase a share in a time-sharing condominium.

Here is how it works. You purchase the rights to use your vacation apartment for periods of, say, one or two weeks per year. Your costs include the one-time purchase charge (roughly about $3,000 for a two-bedroom Florida apartment for one winter week of use), plus a maintenance charge for the week you use the premises. Theoretically, you *own* this share of the apartment, which you can rent, sell, or whatever. Over the long pull, you should be able to save considerably on hotel bills. The major disadvantage is your reliance upon the developer, a breed that (or at least some of which) is known for its propensity either to jack up maintenance prices after the initial offering or else not to deliver promised services.

Your best bet is to deal only with large, well-established developers whose earlier developments are open to inspection.

Purchase a Vacationland Condominium that You Can Rent Out for Extra Income

Developers in Florida, Puerto Rico, Spain, and Costa Rica, among other places, are promoting the sales of income condominiums. You purchase the condominium at full price, use it whenever you please, renting it out via the managing agent at other times. Hopefully, your rental income will completely offset your costs, bringing you what is, in effect, a free or even profit-producing vacation apartment.

This, however, is positively *not* a depression gambit, since travel declines considerably during difficult times. Also, since many of these offerings are for foreign investments, you are subject to the vagaries of foreign legislation and social developments. For example, condominium owners in the Virgin Islands have been running into serious trouble because of the islands' racial difficulties, which have led to a sharp decline in tourism in the area.

For further information regarding either of the above two maneuvers, contact the consulates of countries in which you might have interest for information regarding the addresses of realty developers in major areas where you might wish to locate.

Secure Free Nationwide Listings of Raw Land and Farmland

For free catalogues of land available for sale throughout the country, write to Strout Realty, 60 East 42d Street, New York City, N.Y. 10017 or to United Farm Agency, 612 West 47th Street, Kansas City, Mo. 64112. Each catalogue contains hundreds of listings, descriptions, and photographs.

Do consider some avenue of real estate to diversify your investment portfolio—but once again, do *not* move in early in a depression. Real estate is strictly a play for better economic climates.

13
HOW TO PROFIT FROM INTERNATIONAL MISFORTUNE: TRADING IN CURRENCY FUTURES

Were you perchance abroad during the summer of 1971? If you were, you'll know at once what we mean by trading or investing in currency. Why? Because if you happened to be journeying in Zurich or Paris or Vienna at that time, you really took a bath—providing that you could find a hotel to let you in with your American dollars, that is. (It was in August 1971 that President Nixon announced his new international monetary game plan. For a period of time Europeans refused to exchange local currency for dollars at all except at a ridiculous discount.)

My own family happened to be in Switzerland during the summer of 1973—once again a period when the dollar was suffering severe international pressure. Americans lined up in New York to exchange dollars for Swiss francs *before* they went, in anticipation of further declines in the dollar's purchasing power abroad. We ourselves exchanged roughly 10 percent of our currency before we departed, watching our own dollars' purchasing power shrink even as we made our way from Geneva to Wengen to Zermatt.

Needless to say, contrary opinion won out once again—you can almost always bet your shirt on it. No sooner were Americans lining up to secure francs for dollars than the dollar rallied (just as we were leaving Switzerland as it turned out). To repeat object lesson number one: buck the crowd.

The dollar, once firm as the Rock of Gibraltar, sank by roughly 30 percent between December 1971 and mid-1973. In other words, had you owned Swiss francs, German marks, or Japanese yen during that period, you would have ended up roughly 30 percent richer, at least in terms of overseas buying power. American citizens, international travelers supreme, have faced these hard facts annually. Each year, it seems, travel abroad becomes more costly, partly because of international inflation, of course—but also partly because the dollar, becoming progressively weaker against many currencies, draws fewer and fewer francs or marks when you drop in to that friendly Swiss bank to exchange your traveler's checks. This is something American Express may not warn you about. (The dollar did strengthen during mid-1975, however.)

Defensive Action

Many Americans—legally and otherwise—have sought to protect themselves against the dollar's debasement by opening Swiss bank accounts, converting dollars into Swiss francs for such deposit. In fact, this practice (including deposits from other nations as well) reached such proportions that by early 1975 the Swiss government was imposing *negative* interest returns on foreign money deposited in Switzerland, virtually guaranteeing a loss to foreign depositors.

Or, as an alternative, you can purchase amounts of many different world currencies, holding those currencies as a hedge against weakness in the dollar. Act when you sense a major financial crisis here, compared to, say, Switzerland or Germany. If you want to play it more aggressively, you can borrow money for such speculation, playing the currency game with your bank's cash. But remember that, in that event, you are liable for carrying costs of the loan in addition to the currency dealer's markup—in the meantime, drawing little or no return from the currency you have purchased. The smaller your ante, the higher your operating costs, the greater your handicap. (Besides, international banks and dealers don't generally allow a small fry to play on their turf.) Or, as an alternative, you can turn to the currency futures markets.

The International Monetary Market

Although the small investor could play at international moneyship via foreign bank accounts—and, theoretically at least, via dealers and certain banks—they were essentially locked out of large-scale speculation until May 16, 1972, the day the International Monetary Market (IMM) of the Chicago Mercantile Exchange opened its table for the little guy.

Currency, on the IMM, is treated just like any other commodity—only instead of playing with porkbellies, you play with pesos. In other words, let's suppose that you believe the pound will rise in value vis-à-vis the dollar six months hence. You simply buy pounds on the IMM for future delivery for dollars, depositing minimum margin for the contract. (IMM's minimum margins run to about $4,000 per contract, roughly 1½–5½ percent of the contract's value, depending upon the volatility of the specific contract—the greater the potential fluctuation, the greater the margin. However, many brokerage houses enforce higher minimums. The Swiss franc and German mark have required the highest margin percentages; the Mexican peso and Canadian dollar the least.)

Now, suppose the pound does rise in value, as predicted, say, by roughly 4 percent against the dollar. (Remember, you have contracted in effect to buy pounds for dollars.) Operating on an approximate cash outlay of 4 percent of the value of the contract, you have doubled your capital as the total contract has gained 4 percent. Ninety-nine percent of currency futures players do not take delivery—they simply close out their contracts prior to the delivery dates, which are set on the IMM at quarterly intervals. (Of course, $60,000 worth of British pounds deposited on your doorstep isn't quite as bad as 18 tons of frozen eggs.) By closing out your contract you lock in the profit (less brokerage commissions, which are minor).

It goes without saying—but we're saying it anyway—that the currency game is not quite a one-way street. A 4 percent drop in the pound would wipe you out entirely, maybe even more if you can't get your trade off in time. (There is no guarantee that you cannot lose more than your initial margin requirement.) It also goes without saying that you do not have to go for broke. The commodities markets are actually no more volatile than the stock markets; it's the leverage possibilities via lower margin requirements that make or break the plungers. Were you to deposit the full cost of the pound contract, you'd find that you were getting a far slower ride on the British pound, say, than on Polaroid. However, since no interest is charged on commodity margin debits, you're better off putting up minimum margin and keeping the reserve in some income-producing vehicle such as the money funds.

Which Currencies Are Traded

Currencies traded on the IMM include the following:

Equals Per Currency Contract	Amount	Minimum Fluctuation
British pound	25,000	$.0005
French franc	250,000	$.00005
Mexican peso	1,000,000	$.00001
Canadian dollar	100,000	$.0001
Deutsche mark	125,000	$.0001
Dutch guilder	125,000	$.0001
Swiss franc	250,000	$.0001
Japanese yen	12,500,000	$.0000010

Foreign exchange quotes are generally stated in terms of the cost of that currency expressed in U.S. dollars. For example, if the pound is quoted at $2.18, it means that you can purchase one pound for $2.18. (Sometimes you'll encounter a spread quote like 2.1795–2.1800. This means that if you're a seller, you can receive 2.1795 per pound; if you're a buyer, you have to pay at the rate of 2.18. This is similar to the familiar stock market quote of, say, 16 bid, 16¼ offered.)

Given an initial value of one pound per $2.1800, we can figure that a rise in the pound to a cost of $2.1805, its minimum fluctuation on the IMM, results in a minimum increase per contract of $12.50 (gain of $.0005 per pound x 25,000 pounds = $12.50). Should the pound rise so that it would cost $2.25 to purchase a pound, the 25,000-pound contract would gain $1,750 ($.07 x 25,000 pounds).

Publications such as the *New York Journal of Commerce* (99 Wall Street, New York, N. Y. 10005) and *The Wall Street Journal* carry quotations of foreign currency, both spot (immediate delivery) and futures. A lower futures than spot price indicates that speculators are betting on a decline in the currency vis-à-vis the dollar in the months to come; a higher futures versus spot price indicates that speculators are betting on a rise in the currency.

Liquidity

You should be aware that although the IMM lists nine currencies, fluid and active trading has been, by and large, confined to the German mark, the British pound, the yen, the Swiss franc, and the Mexican peso. Minimal trading takes place in the Dutch guilder, which means large spreads between bid and asked prices, definitely a problem in moving into and out of that currency. No guarantee that this situation will pertain forever, of course, but do check the open interest in any contract before you enter the arena.

A Brief History of Currency Fluctuation

In the nineteenth century virtually all currencies were backed by gold or silver or both, recognized storehouses of value. Such backing lent stability to currencies, which were convertible into precious metals that were themselves considered worldwide to have intrinsic value. The gold standard, pertaining throughout the world, suddenly collapsed with the start of World War I, nations embargoing gold. The inflation of the twenties and the depression of the thirties further undermined what currency stability was left. We ourselves contributed to the flood of worldwide devaluations when President Roosevelt devalued the dollar—increasing gold value from $20 per ounce to $35. (Devaluations—the reduction of a currency value in relation to others—are generally undertaken to render local products more competitive in price to foreign products. While devaluations do not affect prices of local goods to their own nationals, they do cheapen the cost abroad, since less foreign currency is required to match the devalued currency. Consequently, a devaluation, say, of the dollar renders foreign goods more expensive here, since more dollars are required to match the foreign cost. The hoped-for effect is to strengthen exports, weaken the volume of imports.)

In 1944 the international agreement at Bretton Woods, New Hampshire, established a monetary system based upon the dollar. The exchange rates of other nations were pegged to the dollar, which, in turn, was guaranteed by us to be convertible into gold at $35 per ounce. The agreement further called for central banks to support exchange rates by buying and selling currencies—limiting fluctuations to 1 percent on either side of the central rate.

The Bretton Woods agreement lasted for some twenty-seven years, but finally collapsed as a result of continuing runs on the U.S. dollar, a continuing balance of payments deficit here (more cash going out than coming in), a diminution in our gold reserves, and the specter of U.S. inflation. Subsequent agreements likewise broke down, spurred in fact, again, by another dollar devaluation (February 1973). The upshot was the development of a floating dollar, pound, and lira, other European nations maintaining rates in relation, the one to the other.

What Makes Currencies Run?
Currency values, naturally, rise and fall in tune to a myriad of factors: the political stability of nations, respective rates of inflation, balance of payments relationships, interest yields, and the general strength of each economy.

Balance of Payments
It follows that if a nation continuously spends more abroad than it takes in, that nation as a whole becomes a world borrower or debtor, its ability to repay, in the long run, subject to question. The United States has been in such a position for years. However, Italy and Britain have been in even worse shape, and price rises in oil have actually helped us because of our superior position in terms of oil reserves as contrasted with most of Europe. (The U.S. position did improve during 1975.)

Balance of payments includes every kind of transfer of capital from country to country: all expenditures, dividend and interest payments, travelers' money spent abroad, etc. *Balance of trade* reflects only the issue of whether a country sells more of its goods overseas than it imports. The United States has seen balance of payments deficits since 1950 (exception, 1958), but until recently our trade balance has been favorable. The difference is accounted for by our citizens' overseas travel and our expenditures abroad for military bases.

A favorable balance of payments tends-to strengthen a nation's currency; a weak balance of payments tends to undermine it. (Data available in many financial newspapers.)

Political Stability

It also follows, of course, that the more politically stable a nation, the more its currency is likely to be respected, since the more likely that nation will be to meet its obligations, internal and external. (Anyone for some czarist bonds?) A major contribution to recent weakness in the lira has been the danger of Italy's political situation mixed with labor unrest and strikes by civil servants.

Monetary Policy and Interest Returns

Fiscal authorities can and do attempt to attract foreign capital (improving balance of payments) by taking steps to increase interest returns within their country. This often serves to slow inflation internally by slowing business expansion (loans for expansion become too costly). A slowdown of a domestic economy generally results in some deflation (price cutting), rendering that nation's goods more competitively priced in world markets, another boon to trade balances. Our own Federal Reserve Board controls yields here by its ability to control bank reserve requirements and the discount rate.

Interest Arbitrage

One favorite game among currency cognoscenti involves interest-rate arbitrage, the playing of inequalities in interest yields among nations. For example, yields in Mexico have traditionally remained higher than in the United States—the result of a shakier economy and social order there, and Mexican interest in attracting foreign capital. Suppose you were tempted by those higher returns to place money in Mexican banks or to lend money abroad there. A good idea, perhaps, but your potential profit is always subject to the risk that Mexico might devalue its peso and that your repayment in pesos will be worth less in dollars than you started with.

Well, suppose you did send that money abroad, say, for a 4 percent yield advantage over money similarly invested within our borders. And let's suppose further that you simultaneously sell pesos short in the futures market in the amount that you lent and for an equivalent period of time. By selling pesos now for future delivery, you might receive, say, 2 percent less than their current spot price, but you will be guaranteed a fixed amount of dollars for your pesos. If you gain 4 percent by investing in Mexico, but lose 2 percent on your futures contract, you're still 2 percent ahead—the profit locked in by the arbitrage. A game for the little fellow? Not really. But certainly a game to consider if you do plan sizable overseas investment, and when arbitrage relationships prove favorable.

International corporations, incidentally, regularly hedge against foreign devaluations by selling foreign currencies short to ensure that the payments they receive will be worth their anticipated value in dollars. When the currency does arrive in payment, they can simply use it to deliver against the short sale.

Rates of Inflation

Countries undergoing high rates of inflation have generally been more likely to devalue their currencies than countries with lower rates of inflation. In addition, high national rates of inflation mean that if you hold such currency for ultimate expenditure within that nation, you will, in the future, be able to purchase less goods with that currency. Ergo, speculators or holders of a currency issued by a nation with a high rate of inflation tend to want to dump that currency before it loses too much value. This results in an oversupply of that currency on the world market, dropping prices. Small wonder, in view of worldwide inflation, that the Arabs are said to be demanding payments from some nations in gold.

Incidentally, the skyrocketing price of oil has suddenly added impetus to the inflationary spiral taking place in the free world in recent years—a spiral that was already underway *before* the OPEC cartel really got moving. In the Arabs' defense, it must be noted that prior to the oil-price surge they were giving away a limited quantity of a natural resource (oil) in exchange for rapidly depreciating assets (unbacked paper currency). All else aside, for how long could they do it?

Rising price levels tend, too, to disturb national balances of payments by gradually pricing goods out of international competition.

Wages are usually a major factor. Japan was able to capture the world photographic market from Germany after World War II, not only because of Japanese innovations in optical instruments, but because lower labor costs in Japan rendered their cameras highly competitive in price to equivalent German and American products. We, ourselves, have been priced out of many markets by our own high labor costs, but the availability of cheaper foreign goods has been diminishing as well, as wages throughout the world have been rising to match our own. Wages, of course, are not the only determinant of price—worker productivity must be considered too. In an efficient economy worker productivity is high; even if worker wages rise, the cost can be offset if each worker can be made more productive. However, when wage increases exceed increases in productivity, the result is inflation.

Our own rate of inflation is, of course, widely publicized. In addition, financial newspapers regularly report on the rates of inflation throughout the world.

Down to Specifics

Make no mistake about it—currency speculation is *not* for the faint of heart. On a short-term basis it's strictly for the professional commodity trader, adept at catching short-term market swings. On a longer-term basis, if you leave yourself with plenty of backup money beyond your original margin deposit, you should have a good chance—providing you keep in touch with international financial developments and exercise at least some discretion in not following already overextended price trends. (Whether the vehicle be stocks, bonds, oats, or deutsche marks, almost every extended price movement in one direction is followed by some profit-taking or price reversal, at least on a short-term basis.)

Short-term, leveraged speculation *is* speculation and has already resulted in the collapse of several banks throughout the world. In short, caveat emptor! Still, and with all cautions duly in mind, let's examine the currencies traded on the IMM.

The U.S. Dollar

Favorable factors: the international oil situation, decreasing international travel, early signs of an abatement in inflation, our financial markets and political stability that invite Arab investment, our relative abundance of natural resources.

Unfavorable factors: our global military commitments, high labor costs, trade deficits, falling interest returns, and the possible hoarding of gold by U.S. citizens, gold that comes from abroad. Our products are becoming more competitively priced as time passes and European labor costs rise.

The U.S. dollar has been in a basic downtrend against other currencies since mid-1971, on the average, but has risen above mid-1973 levels, aided and abetted again by the oil crisis.

Britain has been attempting for years to overcome the shock waves caused by the dissolution of the British Empire, its dependence upon other countries for raw materials, labor unrest, and high inflation. For periods during 1974 rates of inflation in Britain reached 18 percent, and the British have been heavy borrowers of capital.

Britain was an early victim of OPEC price increases, which led to considerable weakness in the British pound for a while, but the development of North Sea oil resources has been of considerable help to the country. The pound, weak during the mid-1970s, seems to have re-

FIGURE 1
SOURCE: Chart reprinted from *Commodity Chart Service,* a weekly publication of Commodity Research Bureau, Inc., 1 Liberty Plaza, New York N.Y., 10006.

gained a good deal of strength vis-à-vis the American dollar and has proven to be an excellent trading currency in recent years.

Arab money has always been attracted to Britain because of high interest yields available in that country and because of the sophistication of the British financial markets, not to mention the relative stability of the British society. On balance, however, Britain's dependency on outside resources for its raw materials may prove negative, particularly as the undeveloped countries become more militant.

The German Mark

Germany has, indeed, demonstrated one of the world's stronger economies—a moderate rate of inflation, consistently favorable balance of payments surpluses, extremely high monetary reserves, and, until recently, competitive interest yields for foreign investment. The mark has risen sharply against the dollar since 1971, though the currencies have more or less retained parity since late 1973.

Fundamentally, the deutsche mark appears in a strong position—so strong, in fact, that international pressure has been brought to bear against Germany to revalue the mark upward (the opposite of devaluation). Although several revaluations have already occurred, further similar moves would reduce Germany's ability to compete internationally. Rumors of revaluation have served to create a jittery up-and-down market in the mark in recent years, price fluctuations more reflective of rumor than of the economy itself.

The German monetary authorities, more than most, appear capable of making the right moves at the right time, and have managed to stabilize prices even in the face of prosperity and rising national demand for goods and overseas travel.

On the unfavorable side: recent problems with auto exports, the potential drying up of international markets for German goods, and a lowering of local interest rates.

The Dutch Guilder

As I mentioned before, trading in the Dutch guilder is very slight on the futures market, although the guilder has been among the strongest of currencies relative to the dollar in recent years. Some volatility in the currency has developed as a result of rumored revaluations upward, the guilder rising in price as these rumors circulated.

The Netherlands has developed into a highly commercial and industrial nation—visions of "Little Hans" and picturesque dikes to the contrary. Fully 40 percent of their national income derives from

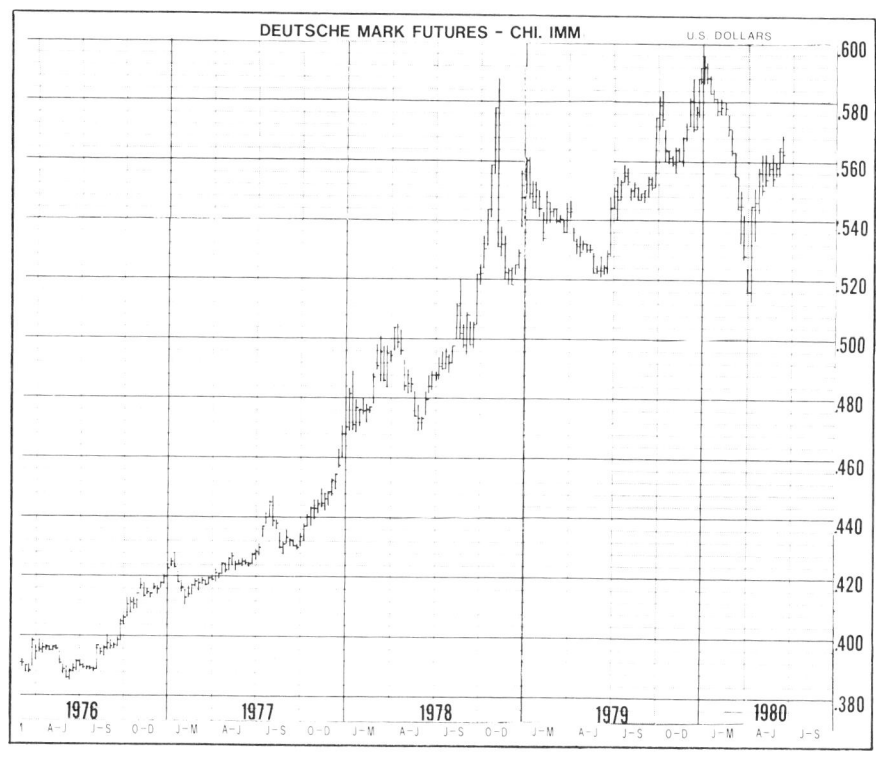

FIGURE 2
SOURCE: Chart reprinted from *Commodity Chart Service* a weekly publication of Commodity Research Bureau, Inc., 1 Liberty Plaza, New York, N.Y. 10006.

manufacturing, the closest trade ties lying with Germany, which takes 33 percent of Dutch exports. Balance of trade has remained strong.

As a result, the performance of the guilder should remain closely tied to the performance of the deutsche mark. The major drawback: Dutch dependence on foreign oil.

The French Franc

A newcomer to IMM's trading roster, the franc declined precipitously in relation to the dollar following the rise in the price of oil, the rise threatening to create massive inflation within France, as well as a sharply deteriorating balance of payments picture. Inflation is already high in France; however, rising interest yields do offer the promise of attracting foreign capital. The major question: Will the French government be successful in its programs to cut oil consumption? Can inflation be reduced? And can recent balance of trade deficits be reversed?

The French franc has been slowly creeping up in value against the dollar since the initial oil shock wave, but French dependence upon foreign petroleum remains a long-term debit. Trading in the franc on the IMM is relatively new, and volume is expected to remain light.

The Swiss Franc

The Swiss franc is possibly the most volatile and actively traded of IMM's currency contracts—more, if the truth be told, for psychologi-

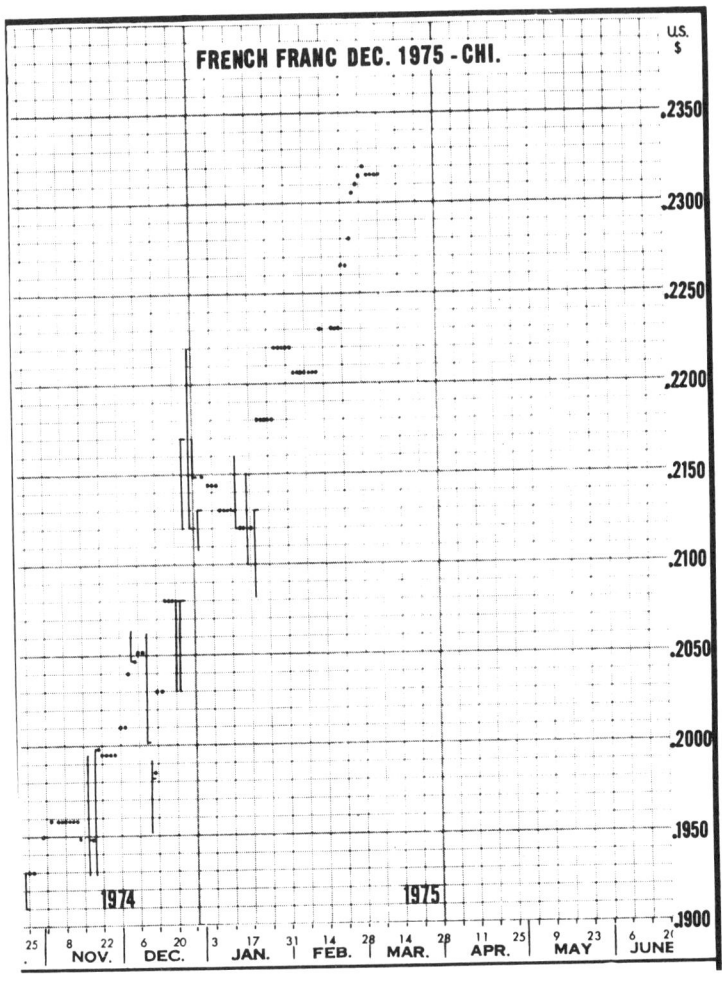

FIGURE 3
SOURCE: Commodity Research Bureau

cal and emotional reasons than for fundamental. True, Switzerland, politically, is as stable a nation as you can find, and, true, the country, with its history of neutrality in war and sound financial management, has been a haven for international investors. In fact, Swiss banks have been so in demand that Switzerland has had to take action to keep foreign capital *out* (by actually setting up negative interest rates for foreign deposits, among other measures). As a result, the Swiss franc was the strongest of currencies in relation to the dollar (1971–74), despite some profit-taking in the franc beginning in mid-1973.

Before you plan to climb the Alps, however, you should keep in mind that the rate of inflation has been climbing in Switzerland (oil again) and that worldwide depression could cut into the tourism that at least partially offsets Switzerland's balance of trade deficits. (Switzerland does maintain regular balance of payments surpluses, however.)

The franc, as a result of Switzerland's renowned financial stability, comes most into demand when other currencies, for one reason or another, become suspect. With the dollar in question because of Watergate, gold drainage, recession, and general pessimism—not to mention the high rates of inflation in the United States during 1974—considerable amounts of security-prone money went into the Swiss franc. Whether the franc will continue to rise if and when confidence in the dollar is restored must be considered a moot question.

From the mid-1970s into 1978 the Swiss franc enjoyed a strictly one-way ride to the top of the Alps, as it were. Since late 1978, however, the franc has leveled off against other currencies, taking a back seat to currencies such as the British pound and the German mark in terms of

FIGURE 4
SOURCE: Reprinted from *Commodity Chart Service,* a weekly publication of Commodity Research Bureau Inc., 1 Liberty Plaza, New York, N.Y. 10006.

appreciation against the dollar. Which proves, I suppose, that even the Alps, do not, after all, quite touch the sky.

The Canadian Dollar

Canada is in the eviable position of holding sufficient oil reserves for complete self-sufficiency, in addition to other largely untapped natural resources. A major exporter of raw materials, the country should benefit from the increasing power that is being secured by commodity-producing nations as opposed to commodity-consuming nations.

Despite the advantages accruing to Canada by virtue of its oil resources, the Canadian dollar fell sharply during the 1976–78 period, to a large extent perhaps because of the French separatist movement, which has embroiled that country in internal controversy. The matter seems to have been at least temporarily settled by a vote in 1980, and it is very possible that Canada will stage a major turnaround.

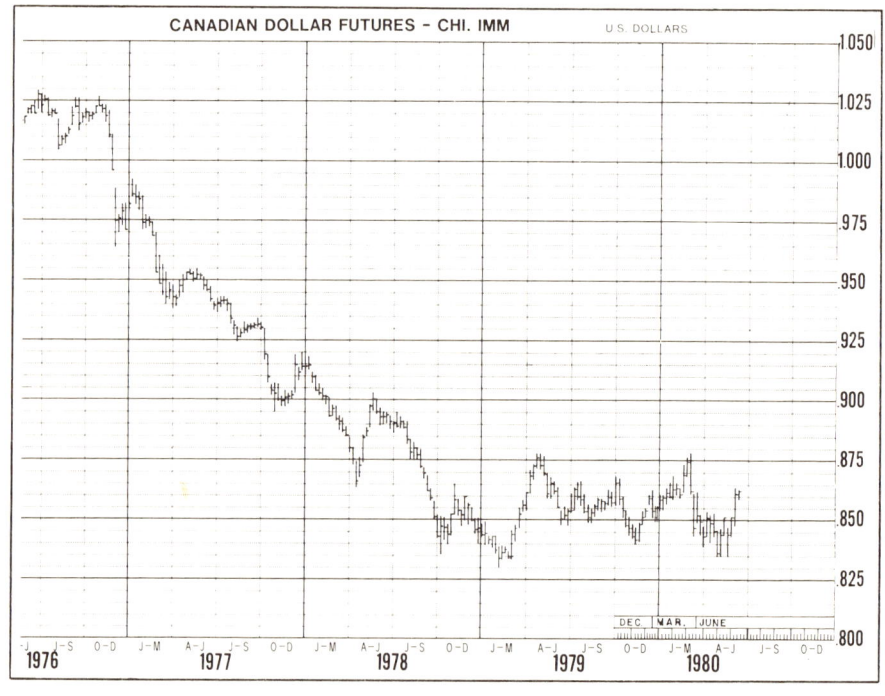

FIGURE 5
SOURCE: Chart reprinted from *Commodity Chart Service* a weekly publication of Commodity Research Bureau, Inc., 1 Liberty Plaza, New York, N.Y., 10006.

The Canadian dollar has stabilized in recent months, and with Canada's natural resources and generally stable political climate (I am presuming), the area seems to offer a great deal of long-term potential. I consider the Canadian currency one of the best buys as a long-term sleeper for ultimate economic growth in that country. Considerable capital fled from Quebec during the period of uncertainty regarding the outcome of the separatist movement. Should the issue be finally resolved, a strong net inflow may take place that could strengthen the currency considerably.

And, after all, there is always all that oil.

The Japanese Yen

With a rapidly burgeoning postwar economy, excellent manufacturing resources and technology, a growing export market for its autos, electronics, and optical production, Japan thrived until recently as few other countries have.

However, by early 1973 the rise in the yen compared with the dollar began to falter, the yen trading almost flat against the dollar during the subsequent months. The oil crises finally highlighted Japan's basic economic vulnerabilities—her shortage of raw materials and her dependence upon favorable international commerce for survival. In addition, rising wages in Japan, one of the highest rates of inflation among industrialized nations, labor unrest, and the need for heavy international borrowing, all contributed to a perceptible weakening in the yen throughout the bulk of 1974.

Recently the yen has been supported by the Bank of Japan, and Japan, by early 1975, seemed possibly on its way to increase exports sufficiently at least to offset a good part of the $13-billion rise in its oil bill. If the nation can succeed in this regard, the yen might regain its former strength.

However, basic questions regarding Japan's ability to sustain its economic growth do exist for the long pull, problems possibly mitigated by Japan's growing commerce with China. Pessimists regarding the yen compare Japan's basic position to Britain's—both are island nations, both lacking in their own raw materials, both facing labor crises, and both highly susceptible to shortages and increases in the prices of basic commodities. Optimists on the yen point to Japan's technological resourcefulness, her success in capturing world markets in many areas of advanced technology, and the consistent and remarkable growth of her gross national product.

I personally consider the matter touch and go, since Japan's ability to compete pricewise will decline in time *unless* the rate of inflation

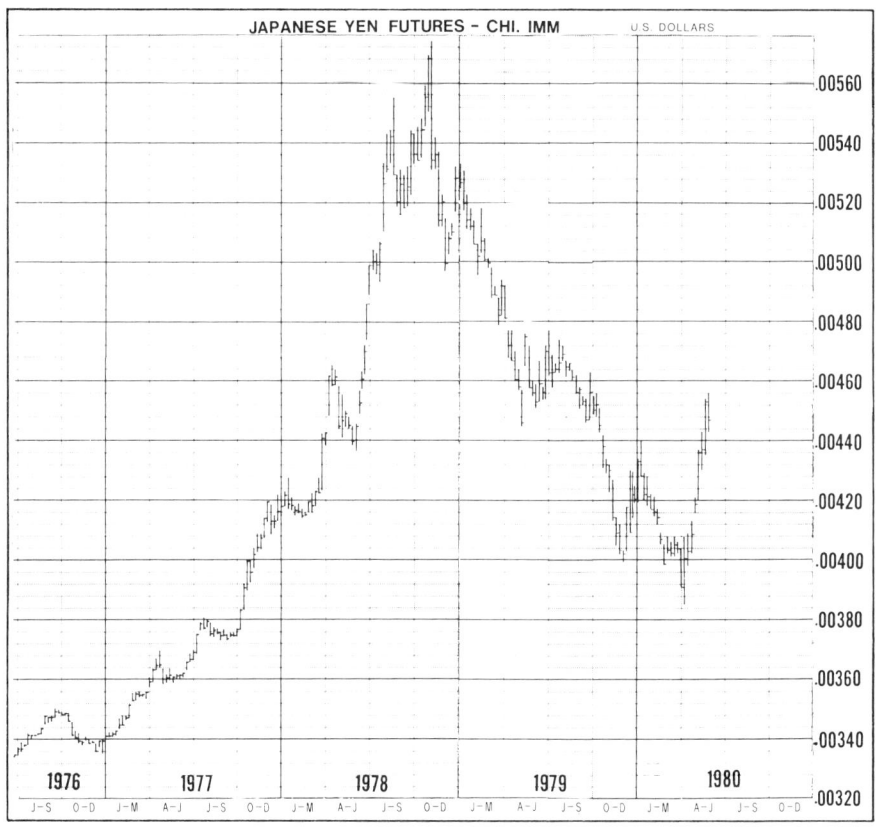

FIGURE 6
SOURCE: Chart reprinted from *Commodity Chart Service* a weekly publication of Commodity Research Bureau, Inc., 1 Liberty Plaza, New York, N.Y. 10006.

within the country can be reduced, and wage hikes brought under control.

The Mexican Peso

Mexico has been gradually strengthening economically, shifting to increasing export of manufactured goods during the mid-1970s. Previously, Mexico's exports had been confined to argicultural, food, and textile products as well as silver, of which Mexico had been the world's third largest supplier.

By the late 1970s Mexico had become a major factor in world oil production, and their oil was in heavy demand. This has led to increasing strength in the Mexican peso, which rose steadily during the first half of 1980.

The prospects for Mexico and for the Mexican peso remain bright as the country is steadily gaining in economic solvency and significance. Certainly, the balance of power between Mexico and the United States has shifted dramatically in Mexico's favor.

The major question: Will the political unrest that has been sweeping South and Central America reach Mexico and disrupt what has been a fairly stable political and economic environment?

The Italian Lira

What can we say? *The Godfather* may have been a big hit over here but, unfortunately for the Italians, the picture was produced by an American and not an Italian company.

Italy *is* in trouble, deep trouble, possibly on the verge of total bankruptcy. Even before the oil crisis, the country was suffering heavy trade deficits. Dependent upon imported oil for 80 percent of its energy needs, Italy found itself, after the oil price rise, facing an additional $5

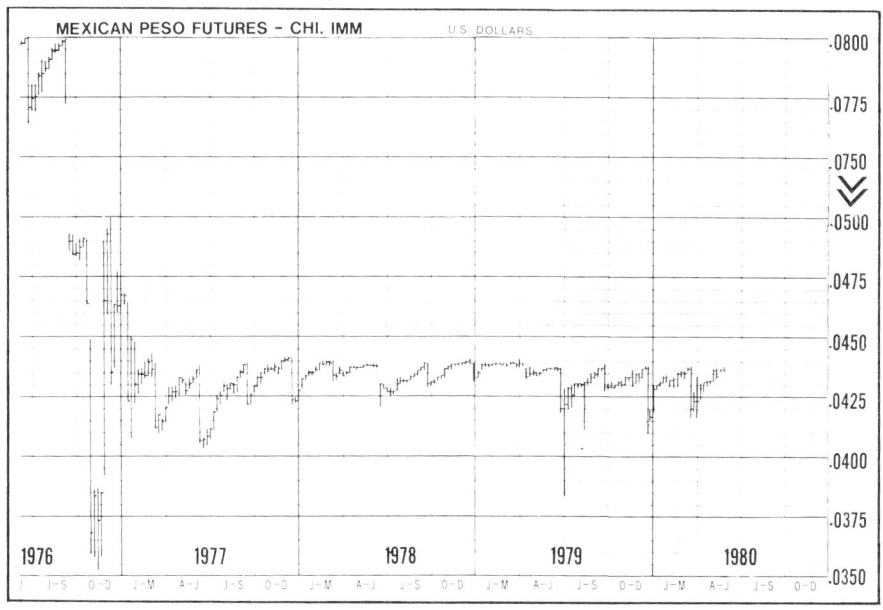

FIGURE 7
SOURCE: Chart reprinted from *Commodity Chart Service* a weekly publication of Commodity Research Bureau, Inc., 1 Liberty Plaza, New York, N.Y. 10006.

billion in annual trade deficit. To boot, the country seems in almost continual social crisis, a movement to the left a distinct possibility. Add to that a civil service noted for inefficiency (Italians were said to be crossing the Swiss border to mail letters), and we do, indeed, find a nation in turmoil.

It figured then that the lira would underperform virutally all other world currencies, and, indeed, it has, weakening instantly as the Arabs became more aggressive in their demands, staging only brief recoveries since.

Will they be able to salvage the Roman ruins after all? Frankly, I wouldn't bet too much on it myself.

Will Recent Currency Fluctuations Continue?

For the time being, at least, it would seem so. Reuters announced on February 10, 1975, that Western banks had reaffirmed the policy of smoothing out exaggerated exchange-rate fluctuations, but said also that the Bank for International Settlements had arrived at no new major decisions regarding support for the dollar, which resumed its decline against many European currencies. Nor is it likely that any decisions reached could have a more lasting impact than recent agreements. Only worldwide economic stability can, in the end, hold currencies in line and, let's face it, the shadow of depression hangs over the entire free world.

It should be clear enough that profit in currency trading depends, in the end, upon your ability to assess where depression will strike the hardest. This is *not* a game to enter with any but absolute risk money. It *is* a game, perhaps, for aggressive investors who seek an avenue of possible enormous profit, providing that you exercise the fundamental rule with the bulk of your resources—preserve your capital.

But just in case you do have faith in your ability to read the signs, and just in the event that you do have risk capital available, keep in mind that a 2 percent margin, you double your money if the Canadian dollar rises by only 2-percent.

For More Information

Brokerage houses such as Merrill Lynch issue regular opinions on the futures markets, including the IMM. The International Monetary Market itself (444 West Jackson Boulevard, Chicago, Ill. 60606) issues free literature on trading currency futures. For eight dollars they will send you a home-study course (recommended). You will, of course, want to keep track of major international developments by way of *The*

Wall Street Journal, Barron's, and other financial newspapers. And you might want to peruse some of the books regarding commodity speculation available from financial publishing houses.

In the meantime, here are two international gambits you might want to try right now.

How to Profit North of the Border

From time to time Canada offers higher interest rates to bank depositors than can be secured in the United States. For example, as I write this, Canadian banks are offering 10 percent on regular savings accounts, depending on the length of the deposit—fully insured by the Canadian Deposit Insurance Corporation up to $20,000 per account. You can safely deposit larger amounts by spreading them among different banks.

Funds can be deposited by mail; postage to Canada is the same as in the United States, although American dollars do have to be converted into Canadian dollars for the purpose of deposit in a Canadian bank. The bank will make the exchange for you; your cost on the exchange for, say, an amount of $24,000, will come to roughly 1/16 of 1 percent. In addition, while your money is in Canadian dollars, you run the possible risk (or reward) of exchange fluctuations should the Canadian dollar vary in relationship to our own. By and large, in recent years variation has been slight. Canada, as we've memtioned, is rich in natural resources and self-sufficient in regard to oil. Some Canadian dollars may prove to be an excellent hedge against weakness in the U.S. dollar.

Like American banks, Canada's fluctuate from time to time in the interest they pay to ordinary depositors. And fluctuations are more frequent than in the United States. However, at times when Canada offers higher interest rates, you can lock in the yield by making *term deposits,* deposits made for fixed periods of time—roughly equivalent to American certificates of deposit.

In March 1975 Canadian banks were offering 6¼ percent for 30-to-89-day deposits, 6½ percent for 90–179 days, 6¾ percent for 180–269 days, and 7 percent for 270 days to two years. These rates were roughly one-quarter of 1 percent above U.S. CD yields in most of the above categories, below long-term deposit rates available from American banks, however. On the other hand, in comparing the placement of money in Canada to accounts here, you do have greater flexibility regarding time duration there.

In measuring Canadian yields against U.S., you should also be aware that you can make term deposits in amounts as small as $5,000 if the term is under one year, for only $1,000 if the term is for more than one year.

The minimum transaction in American CDs is $100,000. The primary alternative here is the money fund, where you can secure CD rates of yield via small, fully liquid investments, so you will want to go north only if (1) you're worried about the stability of the U.S. dollar, and/or (2) Canadian yields clearly surpass our own. Again, this procedure can represent a worthwhile hedge and a low-risk way to play the currency game.

Investors seeking further information may write to the *Toronto-Dominion Bank,* 55 King Street West, Toronto, Ontario, or to the *Canadian Imperial Bank of Commerce,* Commerce Court, Toronto, Ontario. The Canadian Imperial Bank also maintains an office at 22 William Street, New York, N.Y. 10005. They will send you all necessary papers and forms, and respond to any questions you might have.

Should you do it? You can see that decision depends upon a variety of factors. I, myself, always did prefer the Canadian side of Niagara.

How to Speculate in the Swiss Franc Without Losing Too Much Sleep

The Swiss franc has, of course, been among the strongest of the world's currencies, and holders of the franc have fared very well indeed compared with holders of the American dollar. You can speculate in the Swiss franc via the futures market, if you like, and if you can tolerate the risks involved. You can also simply purchase some francs and put them away. There is, however, a better way—a means of investing in the Swiss franc that is superior to opening a franc-denominated account at a Swiss bank, such accounts paying minimal if any interest.

Invest in a Swiss Insurance Company Annuity

Compared with investment in a Swiss bank, investment in a Swiss franc-denominated annuity policy offers the following advantages:

1. Your profits are not subject to Swiss withholding tax.
2. Insurance companies pay approximately double the rate of interest as Swiss banks. You can probably expect a return of from 3 to 5 percent annually. This rate of return is not exciting in and of itself, of course. However, your policy will be denominated in Swiss francs, which have been appreciating at an average rate of approximately 11 percent per year against the American dollar. Your total return then can come to approximately 14–16 percent per year, if recent trends continue. Furthermore, given the possibility of a ma-

jor social revolution some day in the United States, you may just find it handy to have some capital stashed abroad in one of the most stable societies in the world.
3. The mechanics are familiar and similar to establishing an American annuity or endowment policy.

How It Works

Swiss annuity policies are similar to American annuity policies. You deposit an amount of money into the annuity and have the option of (1) taking a regular periodic payment immediately for the rest of your life; (2) taking a regular periodic payment starting at some future date; or (3) in the case of an endowment policy, taking a lump sum payment at some specified point of time in the future. Persons at retirement age will probably opt to start taking payments immediately. Inasmuch as the Swiss franc has been an excellent hedge against inflation, a Swiss annuity can prove to be a hedge against loss of purchasing power of capital set aside for retirement. Persons still in active employment will probably opt to defer payments (deferred annuity) until some time in the future.

In the case of deferred annuities, you pay no income tax until you actually start to withdraw capital, at which time you pay income tax on that portion of your proceeds that represents a profit within the annuity. There is some question as to how capital gains arising from currency profits will be treated by the IRS taxwise, but certainly until you actually start to take capital out, your investment will be appreciating tax free.

Swiss insurance companies are highly regulated and are considered to be very safe. For further information on Swiss policies and regarding policies which can be denominated in other currencies, investors are directed to:

International Insurance Specialists (IIS)
P.O. Box 949
1211 Geneva 3
Switzerland
(Telephone 022-36-47-74)

Assurex S.A.
Volkmarstrasse 10
P.O. Box 290
8033 Zurich
Switzerland
(Telephone 01-60-2510)

Mr. Robert M. Edgar
Glanvill Enthovan Ltd.
144 Leadenhall Street
London, EC3P 3BJ
(Telephone 01-283-4622)

Recommended Further Reading

I strongly recommend the book *New Profits from Your Insurance Policy*, by Mark Skousen, Alexandria House Books, 901 N. Washington Street, Suite 605, Alexandria, Va. 22314. Mr. Skousen has emerged as one of the country's leading experts on matters relating to foreign investment, financial privacy, minimization of income taxes, and is particularly expert in matters relating to Swiss investment. His book provides many further details regarding the history of the fluctuations of the Swiss franc and regarding investment in Swiss annuity contracts.

14
COINS: THE ULTIMATE WEAPON OR THE ULTIMATE RIP-OFF?

Forbes magazine (December 15, 1974) carried a front-page headline, "Coin Mania—Are You Being Taken?" Its table of contents subtitled the piece, "Got Burned in the Stock Market? You Can Be *Murdered* in the Coin Market." General theme? That coins have become overpromoted, overpriced, and are due for a fall. That dealers are quite likely to turn out to be crooks, counterfeiters, charlatans, or worse. And that the typical investor is far better off keeping his money in the bank.

Along the way, the article did make note of the fact that coin turnover has grown from $100 million annually to $1 billion—a sure sign, according to *Forbes*, that the gilt is soon to rub off those gold pieces.

Naturally, the coin industry rose up in protest, with articles appearing in coin publications decrying the one-sidedness of the *Forbes* piece, claiming that the article contained not only misinformation, but misquotes, from persons interviewed.

In all likelihood, of course, exaggerations probably exist on both sides. The *Forbes* piece did, indeed, convey the impression that the honest coin dealer is rarer than the $500,000 Indian Head $20 piece that illustrated the attack. And, indeed, fake promotions, exaggerated claims, counterfeits, and general duplicity do plague the industry. But so have they plagued the stock market, condominum developments, commodities, and art. And, true, coin pieces have taken off in recent years with an unsustainable vengeance. But it's also true that over the past seventy-five years coin prices, despite temporary declines, have fared extremely well—easily outpacing inflation and the performance of the stock market.

Coin Performance Over The Past Six Years

And how have coins fared since the 1974 recession? The standard guide to coin values is the "Redbook," or *A Guide Book of United States*

Coins, published annually by the Western Publishing Company, 1220 Mound Avenue, Racine, Wisconsin 53404. The book is priced at approximately $4.95 and is available at virtually all coin dealers.

The catalog is naturally printed some months in advance of its dated year (e.g., the 1981 catalog came on sale during the summer of 1980), so its values do fall behind the times a bit as months pass. Values in the book tend to be somewhat overstated, and actual transactions, particularly if you are trying to sell your coins, will take place at lower values. The same situation prevails in the stamp market; almost any stamp can be purchased at from 60 to 70 percent of its Scott catalog printing.

Current coin price bids can be secured from *The Coin Dealer Newsletter*, P.O. Box 2308, Hollywood, California 90028. The price is $50 per year. Prices shown are dealer bid and asked prices. You will probably receive somewhat less if you try to sell to a dealer. The newsletter carries reports of price trends in coins, and generally has a rather upbeat tone to it.

The table below shows representative coin prices in 1974, 1975 (when I recommended a number of coins for purchase), and in 1980, from listings in the 1981 Redbook. You can see that coins have appreciated very well over the years, 1940-74. A selected group of coins, the "NFC Index," achieved a compounded growth rate of 18.7 percent for the twenty-seven years ending 1973, but a 26 percent growth rate, 1968-73, rising by 160 percent in 1973 alone. By comparison, the Dow Industrial Averages gained 5.9 percent per year during the comparable twenty-seven-year period (excluding dividends). The results of this study appear comparable to similar research conducted elsewhere.

However, prior to the 1940s coins increased in value at much more moderate rates. For example, the 1796 quarter appreciated at an annual rate of 17 percent, 1947-73, but only at a 4.0 percent rate until 1947. To restate, coin price rises have escalated very sharply in recent years, after moderate gains earlier in the century. However, gains have consistently outpaced inflation over the years and, long term, coins, on balance, appear to have been an excellent investment.

Coin	1974 Redbook Price	1975 Redbook Price	1981 Redbook Price
1840 Original Half Cent	$ 750.00	$ 825.00	$ 1,700.00
1886 Small Cent	67.50	70.00	115.00
1911 Nickel	60.00	77.50	325.00
1937 Dime	50.00	110.00	750.00
1828 Half-Dollar	200.00	350.00	800.00
1882 Silver Dollar	270.00	345.00	1,500.00
1900 Half Eagles	600.00	900.00	4,500.00
1866 Eagles	2,500.00	3,250.00	17,000.00

Annual Rate of Return
1973-1974

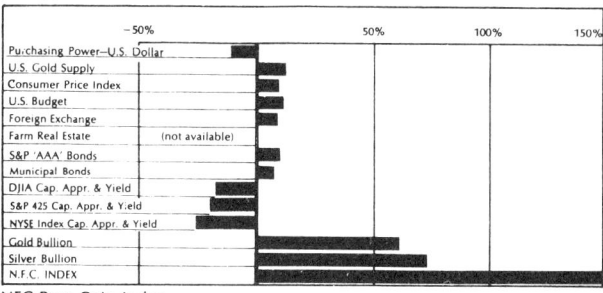

NFC Rare Coin Index

Annual Rate of Return
1969-1974

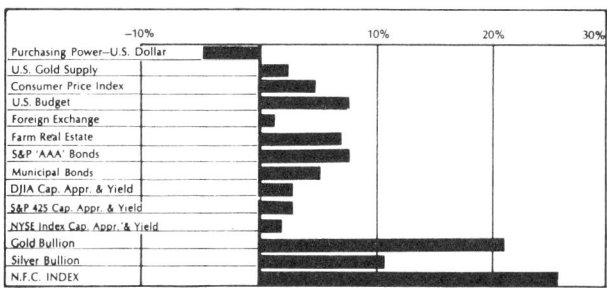

NFC Rare Coin Index

Annual Rate of Return
1947-1974

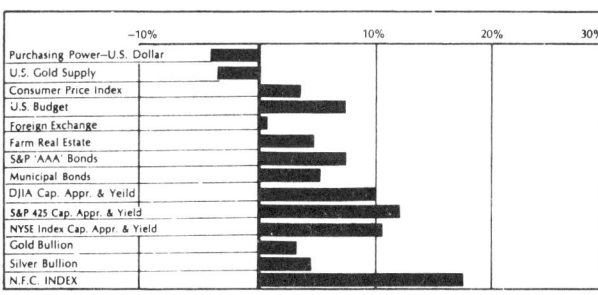

NFC Rare Coin Index

FIGURE 1
Coins have outpaced other forms of investment, particularly in recent years. (The N.F.C. Index includes a representative group of numismatic coins.) SOURCE: Numismatic Funding Corporation, 560 Broad Hollow Road, Melville, N.Y. 11747

The research department of a leading New York brokerage firm released a report in mid-1978 outlining the performance of various investments over the years. Using 1973 as a base year, it is clear that

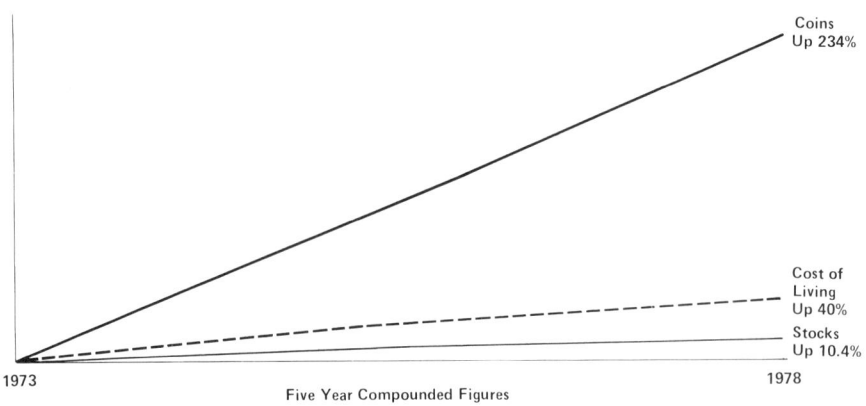

FIGURE 2
SOURCE: Numismatic Funding Corporation, Melville, N.Y. 11747.

coins outperformed all other forms of investments studied in the report. Below is a ranking of those investments and their *annual compounded rate of return:*

Rare Coins	28%
Rare Stamps	16%
Silver	16%
Gold	13%
Diamonds	13%
Housing	11%
Consumer price index	7%
Foreign exchange (strongest currencies)	6%
Bonds	6%
Stocks	2%
Chinese ceramics	down 2%

Buying Tips

Although virtually all *relatively scarce* coins have been rising in value, the outstanding gains have developed so far in truly rare coins. By and large you should obtain the highest quality coins you can secure, one or two excellent specimens likely to achieve better rates of gain than a diversified selection of commonplace items. Coins are graded from "good" to "proof," and any coin in less than good condition is generally of little interest to collectors. You *must* either learn to grade coins if you are to invest seriously, taking every coin purchased for separate verification, or risk getting badly stung by the purchase of overgraded coins. This is *not* a minor matter. For example, an 1853 Liberty Seated Half-Dollar has recently sold for $25 fine, $75 very fine, and $175 extra fine. Dealers have become prone to shine coins up, passing them off at a grade or two above their actual grading. Newcomers may want to purchase one of the many books available at coin dealers relating to the grading of coins. I personally recommend the *New Photograde* by James Ruddy, Bowers and Ruddy Galleries, 6922 Hollywood Blvd, Los Angeles, Calif., 90028, $2.95. *Never, but never,* purchase coins, either through the mail or in person, without first verifying the condition and authenticity of the coin—most mail order houses allow a free return period for this purpose.

Again, stay with high-quality coins, extra fine or better, in price ranges that show that the coin has already achieved some scarcity, if not rarity. Bruce M. Abrash, president of the Numismatic Funding Corporation, suggests that, as a minimum, coins purchased for investment should lie in the $30 range. However, considerable price appreciation has, at times taken place in less expensive coins.

You *can* buy from dealers or via the mail, providing you exercise proper precautions, but do exercise them. Should you purchase coins of any value at all, you may want to have the coin authenticated as to genuineness (not condition) by the *American Numismatic Association Certification Service*, P.O. Box 87, Benjamin Franklin Station, Washington, D.C. 20041. Fees for verification run from 3 to 6 percent of the coin's value; the higher the value, the lower the percentage. Some dealers will provide free verification if you purchase high-price coinage.

How to Avoid Being Taken

I recently reviewed a mail coin offering for *Boardroom Reports* (March 15, 1975). Some coin mail order service was offering a set of U.S. Morgan silver dollars for a price of $350, billing the set as "rare," the whole package presented in gilt print, complete with presentation case —"an heirloom to be passed along to your grandchildren." Good idea, passing it along for a couple of generations—it might take that long to retrieve your money. I priced the coins offered, separately, using nationally advertised mail order prices for comparison. You could have purchased that "350-dollar set," coin by coin, for a total price of $129! Be leery of fancy mail order ads; many, not all, are phony deals. And take the trouble to verify the condition of each and every coin you receive, comparison shopping along the way. You can readily obtain current quotes from such magazines as *Coins, Coinage,* and *Coin World*—all readily available at reasonable prices. *Coin World,* a weekly newspaper, offers just about all you'd want in the way of current prices and news, for $9.50 per year. You can order from *Coin World,* P.O. Box 150, Sidney, Ohio 45365.

In a similar vein, do not sign up for any coin investment program without first verifying the specifics of what the "experts," select for you and without actually determining your guarantees—and exercising them. Many are honest programs; others are not.

How to Set Up a Retirement Coin Fund

At least one company, Numismatic Funding Corporation Inc., 560 Broad Hollow Road, Melville, N.Y. 11747, has arranged for a Keogh Plan for coin collectors. They will ship coins to you for inspection and, if you are satisfied, you instruct the bank trustee (First National Bank of Glen Head, N.Y.) to pay the company from proceeds of the trust you have placed on deposit. NFC will submit to American Numismatic any coins priced at over $100 for verification at your request, no charge to you. Coins so purchased via Keogh are, of course, purchased with pretax dollars, but they draw no income while in your fund. I have comparison-priced NFC's offerings and have found that, in the past, their prices were competitive within the industry.

You May Prefer a Coin Trader

Independent coin traders or dealers do exist who will purchase coins for you, verify condition, and make suggestions. They generally can secure wholesale prices, but charge purchase and sale commissions of roughly 5 percent. John Kamin (19623 Ventura Boulevard, Tarzana, Calif. 91356) is one such dealer. If you mention this book and enclose a stamped, self-addressed #10 envelope, he will send you a complimentary copy of his newsletter, *The Forecaster,* which has called coin turns very well in recent years.

Which Investments to Avoid

Avoid commemorative or otherwise-styled trays, medallions, plates, statuary, and so forth, frequently offered via coin publications as investments. Generally created of gold or silver, these pieces sell at prices far above their intrinsic precious metal value and are probably one of the truly massive rip-offs to succeed in this country.

Gold coins, as a means of speculating in numismatics, are probably best avoided as well, particularly the very common gold coins that carry minimal numismatic value, and not fair gold value in view of their price. You can purchase gold coins of high numismatic value for their potential as collector's items, if the coins can stand on those merits alone.

Proof Sets

The U.S. Government Mint regularly offers proof sets to collectors via mail order. Proofs are particularly fine strikings of coins, issued for collection rather than for circulation. In many cases proof sets are put out in large quantities. Though relatively inexpensive, they offer little prospect for short-term price appreciation. However, over the long pull, proof sets do appreciate in value. You can put yourself on the Mint's mailing list by writing to the Bureau of the Mint, 55 Mint Street, San Francisco, Calif. 94175.

Sleeper Coins for the 1980s

This section was entitled "Sleeper Coins for the Late Seventies" in the first edition of this book. All of the following coins have appreciated very well since our recommendation for purchase in the first edition. I see no reason why they will not appreciate further in price, and all are recommended for continuing purchase. However, before making any purchases be aware that for the most part coins do not produce immediate profit; you should be prepared to hold them long term. You are, after all, buying at retail. When selling, between dealer discounts, auctioneering costs, commissions, and so forth, you have to plan on selling concessions of at least 20 percent, perhaps more. In other words, your coins must appreciate by at least 20 percent just for you to break even. Furthermore, coins, like all collectibles, provide no income, so you must consider the loss of income on funds so invested in measuring the merits of coins relative to income-producing investments such as bonds.

Caveats aside, here is the list of recommended coins exactly as they appeared in the first edition of *99 Ways to Make Money in a Depression*, following which is a table showing the results had you invested in these coins at that time. You may have missed the fine profit potential last decade. These coins should continue to appreciate in the coming decade.

1. With the Bicentennial just over the horizon, interest in Colonial Americana has been picking up, and coins from the period should develop increasing collector interest. In this area I suggest the *1652*

Pine Tree Shilling, selling in the $600 range and up, and the *Fugio Cent,* the first coin issued by authority of the United States Government. Prices for the Fugio run from $250 to 300, uncirculated.

2. In an altogether different league, the 1961–63 proof sets have served their apprenticeship as common coins, and now appear ready to increase in value. Listed in the 1974 Redbook at $4.25, the 1962s, for example, listed at $5.00 one year later, and could still be obtained at those prices at the time of this writing.

3. Various issues of the *Barber or Liberty Head* quarter (1892–1916) rose sharply in price during 1973 and 1974 and appear headed higher. For example, the proof ran from $325 to $400 within the year, gaining another $75 to $475 on the retail market by early 1975. Similar gains were recorded throughout the series, even in the lower grades.

4. As a group, the Morgan silver dollars (1878–1921) offer interesting potential for price appreciation. I particularly favor the 1882CC at around $25 uncirculated, the 1883S at roughly $350 uncirculated, and the 1891CC at around $50. These did *not* appreciate greatly during 1974, and only the 1883S has appreciated since. However, these coins are all on the lower fringes of the "scarce" category, and could become big movers.

5. Nor would I ignore the garden variety Morgans, for example, the 1881, 1881"0," 1884, 1885, and 1888, all selling in the $10 range, up, as a group, roughly 30 percent over 1973 levels. Downside risk in these coins appears slight.

6. Among the truly rare are our nation's first silver dollars, the 1794 "flowing hair" dollar. Uncirculated 1794s will set you back roughly $75,000, up, believe it or not, by nearly 400 percent since one year previous. Very fine specimens now sell at $10,000, "good" condition items going for $1,750. Prices *have* been rising. The 1795s, not nearly as rare, currently run at $12,000 uncirculated, but only (only?) $1,600 extra fine.

7. Trade dollars, minted between 1873 and 1878, are low-mintage coins, beginning to wander into the upper price regions. Issued originally to compete with other trade coins in the Orient, the coin was also afforded the status of legal tender within the United States. Such status, however, was eliminated in June 1876, when production of the coin was restricted to export demand only. From 1879 to 1885 only proofs were struck. The 1885 proofs, only five existing in all, were recently offered at $300,000. Trade dollars have recently really begun to climb in price. A proof 1873 now goes for roughly $1,500, up from $475 (1973). Other coins in the series have shown similar gains. Some of these are truly low-mintage items. For exam-

ple, only 900 trade dollars were struck during 1878, all proofs, and their value has tripled since late 1973.

8. The lowly penny, of all things, may soon rise to stardom. One of the few coins to lose value between 1973 and 1974, the 1939D Lincoln penny, uncirculated, has recently surpassed its late '73 levels, now selling at $3.50 uncirculated. Copper pennies, you may recall, were recently threatened with extinction when it appeared that copper prices were going the way of oil. However, no successful copper cartel ever got started. demand faltered, and the copper penny, a speculator's dream, temporarily turned into a nightmare, prices falling. (No, Virginia, coin collecting is *not* a one-way street.) However prices of the menial coppers do appear to be rising once again, even in the lower grades—and it's certainly one way to get started cheap.

The above list, of course, barely scratches the surface, and presuming that the surfaces aren't scratched, your coins should appreciate very nicely in the years to come. I suggest that you secure back issues of the *Guide Book* to study price trends yourself. (Incidentally, older issues of the *Guide* are becoming collector's items in themselves.)

And now, here are the results had you invested in the above selection of coins as per my recommendation some six years ago.

The above values all represent the highest-grade coins in the litter. The usual rules of collecting apply in coins; buy less of the best rather than more of the ordinary.

Some Further Tips on Coin Collecting

Rare coin collections have been prime targets for burglary, loss, and even small children mistaking a Fugio cent for a 1944 Lincoln. *Do* store

Coin	Price, 1975	Price, 1980
1652 Pine Tree Shilling	$ 600	$ 1,300
Fugio Cent	275	500
1961–63 Proof Sets	5	23
Liberty Head Quarter	475	600
1882CC Silver Dollar	25	125
1883S Silver Dollar	350	2,500
1891CC Silver Dollar	50	350
Morgan Silver Dollars	10	150
1794 Flowing Hair Dollar	10,000	17,500
1873 Proof Trade Dollar	1,500	2,000
1939D Lincoln Penny	3.50	4.50

your coins out of sight, preferably in bank vaults. There have been a number of scandals recently involving "coin exchanges" selling on the installment plan, or selling silver coins on margin, supposedly storing coins for their customers. Do *not* buy coins on margin. Either take full possession or wait until you can. Many of these outfits have gone broke, taking their customers' money down the slot with them.

Coins have been minted at Philadelphia; Charlotte, N.C.; Dahlonega, Georgia; New Orleans; Carson City, Nev.; San Francisco; and Denver. Philadelphia coins carry no mint mark, except for the 1942–45 nickels, which carry a "P." The Charlotte and Dahlonega mints (marks "C" and "D") minted gold coins only, between 1838 and 1861. New Orleans ("O") minted coins from 1838 to 1909; Carson City ("CC") from 1879 to 93. San Francisco coins are marked "S"; Denver coins, "D."

Coins should always be held by the edges, never with the fingers on the face. Storage of coins in paper envelopes is destructive; the sulfur content in the paper encourages oxidation and tarnishing. Keep your coins cut off from oxygen.

You can obtain free sample copies of *Numismatic News Weekly* and-/or *Coins* magazine by writing to the publisher at Iola, Wisconsin 54945.

Although "fine"-grade coins are the most widely collected, the best-obtainable-condition coins struck for circulation are "uncirculated." Such coins should show no abrasive wear; however, some tarnishing may be present. The full design must be present, no wear on any portion. The next grade down, extremely fine, should show only slight wear on the highest points of the design. Another source to the study of grading is *A Guide to the Grading of United States Coins* by Martin R. Brown and John W. Dunn.

And, finally, do consider joining the American Numismatic Association, P.O. Box 2366, Colorado Springs, Colo. 80901.

15

ART, ANTIQUES AND AUTOGRAPHS— NO "A"s, HOWEVER, DURING THE COMING DEPRESSION

If 1972 was a banner year for art, antiques, and such, 1973 saw the first rumblings of trouble and 1974 the first major crack in a grossly inflated market that had risen to ridiculous heights during the economic boom of the sixties.

Actually, the fine arts market, like commodities, like stocks, and like wine, ran through the inevitable cycle. Fueled by soaring stock market profits and general prosperity during the fifties and early sixties, the art market continued to soar into the early seventies. A couple of art funds emerged; art was billed as an investment virtually second to none, and, indeed, the upward price momentum, at least for major works, carried on for several months after the stock market topped out in early 1973. A number of factors were involved: worldwide prosperity that brought in Japanese and European bids; inflation, which led to a flight from cash into various "storehouses" of value; publicity given to fanciful auction pricing as museums competed for major pieces; and the luring in of the public by clever mail order promotions. Ultimately the bubble had to burst, and of course burst it did.

Nor was the debacle surprising. In my book *Double Your Money Every Three Years* (Windsor Books, 1974), I cautioned readers that any further rise in art prices would bring out the sellers. Auctions in Europe during mid-1973 had already demonstrated resistance among buyers, with mounting turnover as foresighted collectors distributed their wares to less sophisticated latecomers.

But that was in Europe. The bell began to toll loudly here as well last year as the recession (depression?) deepened. In October, following disappointing sales at Christie's in London, a series of crucial auctions at Sotheby Parke Bernet in New York confirmed the downtrend in art prices, pieces changing hands at well below presale estimates. One sale, in fact, saw fully 37 percent of the offerings returned to their owners because of insufficient bids. In 1973 the average ratio of pieces bought in was roughly 10 percent.

Nor do I expect matters to improve particularly in the years immediately ahead. It has been steadily rising prices rather than intrinsic value that has brought out the buyers in recent periods—any weakening at all can lead only to more cautious bidding: a buyer's market, if, indeed, buyers are to be found at all.

In short, art is *not* an investment for the coming depression.

The Odds Are Clearly Against You

The accumulation of artwork for profit has always, in fact, probably been a stacked deck, and I don't need to say on whose side the deck has been stacked. As a collector-investor you are paying retail prices for goods that have to be sold wholesale to dealers, or at auction, with auctioneering fees in the area of 15–20 percent of the sales price. In other words, you require a markup of at least 20 percent just to break even.

In the meantime, your art, antiques, or whatever draws no income for you while their value supposedly grows. In fact, you are liable for continuous expense during the life of your holding—insurance, burglary prevention devices, etc. Nor, again, as a matter of fact, have gains, even in the best of times, amounted to all that much, a few exceptions aside. For example, the rate of gain of a piece, purchased for $150,000 and sold five years later for $250,000, comes to only 10.3 percent per year, *before* auctioneering and other costs. Have fortunes been made in art? Yes, by a few specialized collectors able to accumulate schools of painters *prior* to their becoming fashionable. Are the odds on your side? Definitely not, unless you have rare foresight, luck, and judgment. And, again, the odds are likely to prove even more steep during the economic climate I see directly confronting us.

The Secret Is in the Buying

Presuming that you do hope to cash in by collecting artwork, your major chance for success lies, again, in accumulating works before they become fashionable. Interest has tended to move forward in time, from the old masters (recently weak) to the impressionists to art nouveau—only certain contemporaries drawing much interest. In recent years considerable attention has been paid to the Hudson River school of American art: Thomas Cole, Sanford Gifford, Worthing Whittredge, and Caleb Bingham. Prices along the Hudson have soared recently, so it's already too late to get in real cheap.

Later nineteeth-century artists may still offer room for price appreciation, although there have already been markups of 500 percent and more for some American artists of the period over the past eight or nine years alone. For example, "Steelworkers Noontime" (1880–82) by Thomas Anshutz fetched $250,000 at auction in 1972. The work was originally sold by the artist for $150. Interest is beginning to center heavily in ethnic work, western scenes, and certain still lifes.

Do authenticate any major purchase. Forgeries have been rife in the world of art, forgeries of signatures as well as overlays of details to enhance the value of the work. For example, in the United States, paintings of sailing ships including the American flag are more valuable than paintings in which the flag does not appear. Given this fact, is it surprising that many old-time ships found Old Glory added posthumously? In the same vein, where styles of old masters are similar, the signature of the more valuable is frequently substituted for the signature of the lesser. An instance: William Harnett is frequently substituted for John Peto. (Small wonder, Harnetts have been priced as high as $350,000, which is, after all, a lot of money for one signature.)

Try, if possible, to buy privately, *after* studying and learning something regarding one or two particular schools of art. Haunt the auctions, pester dealers, read, and develop access to experts who can advise you regarding, and are able to authenticate, any purchase. At the least, Sotheby Parke Bernet in New York City will provide a ball-park appraisal for most items.

For Further Information:
Graphic Art in the 20th Century, by Wolf Stubbe, Praeger.
How To Identify Prints, Bell & Sons Ltd., London.
Encyclopedia of Modern Art Auction Prices, by Michele Berard, Arco.
Art As An Investment, by Richard H. Rush, Bonanza.
Art News, 750 Third Ave., New York, N.Y.
Art Investment Report, 54 Wall St., New York, N.Y.
The Print Collectors Newsletter, 205 E. 78 St., New York, N.Y.10021

The Proper Economic Climate

Obviously, art is no investment for the depression. As an investment, art is only moderately liquid, requires long-term holding for profit, and will thrive only in climates of economic prosperity. It is not a game for periods when pessimism is high. The sharpest gains are likely to be recorded during the tail ends of economic booms—when prices, in general, are rising and optimism runs rampant.

Antiques

Whatever is true for art is, broadly speaking, true for the collection of antique furniture as well. Again, the truly big money is made either by dealers who buy wholesale and sell retail, or by truly sophisticated collectors who buy what they enjoy, hold for years, and ultimately resell.

In both areas—in fact, in all collector media—a major key to success is the purchase of quality, items that are already demonstrating a pattern of rising prices, but *before* pricing has run away. Try to locate and accumulate out-of-fashion quality pieces. Sooner or later tastes once again will run in your direction.

The *London Financial Times* sponsored a two-day conference in October 1974 on the World Antiques and Fine Arts Market, in which Otto Wittman, director of the Toledo Museum of Art, proposed ten rules for successful collection. These were:

1. Purchase the best you can afford. You are better off owning one fine piece than ten mediocre ones.
2. Do *not* purchase art as an investment. Although prices *may* rise, there are better investment media.
3. Learn by attending museums, particularly museums that are highly selective for quality.
4. Become familiar with major dealers, collectors, and auctions in your area of interest and consult experts as often as possible.
5. Observe sound and cautious business practices. Deal only with recognized dealers. Limit your bargaining tactics when bidding for unique pieces, but do demand a full bill of sale attesting to the legitimacy and authenticity of the work.
6. Study, observe, read, and travel. Review auction pieces.
7. Be willing to take risks in collecting. Buy out-of-fashion material whenever possible.
8. Purchase only work that is in excellent condition.
9. Buy what you like, not for price alone.
10. Remember *"caveat emptor,"* let the buyer beware.

Some Sleepers for 1976

With Chippendale prices sky-high, investors in antiques might look into later American periods for price appreciation in the years to come. The Federal period (post-Revolution to the 1820s) is most likely to show the next big move. Prices run at roughly 65 percent of Chippendale.

If you want to get a jump on the crowd, you might move directly into Empire (post-1820) and Victorian (1850 on)-prices going at half the levels of Federal. Chippendale pieces have been appreciating (predepression) at roughly 20 percent per year. Antique furniture, according to *Barron's* (January 6, 1975) headed the appreciation parade during 1974. Fine Chippendale chairs, attributed to Benjamin Randolph, sold for $207,500 during the year. French furniture also showed strong gains.

In another league entirely collector-investors who find Persian a bit rich might take positions in a bit of Americana-hooked pictorial rugs dating back to the 1850s. Look for original artwork, particularly for animals, family scenes, and scenes dealing with whaling. Avoid the mass-produced rugs made from stencils that were plentiful during the 1890s.

For Further Information:
American Furniture, Queen Anne and Chippendale Periods, by Joseph Downs, Viking.
American Furniture: The Federal Period, by Charles F. Montgomery, Viking.
Fine Points of Furniture, by Albert Sack, Crown.
American Chairs, by John Kirk, Viking.
The Complete Antiques Price List, by R.&T. Kovel, Crown.
Antiques As An Investment, by Richard H. Rush, Bonanza.
Collecting Antiques in America, by Thomas H. Ormsbee, Deerfield Books.

Shopping Tips

Private home sales are by far your best bet. Private owners will part with their possessions at in-home sales for prices above wholesale but well below dealer retail. Second-best bets are auctions—learn to recognize the dealers at auctions; they bid frequently but surreptitiously, frequently by a slight nod to the auctioneer.

If a series of similar items are put up for auction, the middle items will sell at the most reasonable price. The first item put up will set the upper limit. The middle items will go for the least. The last piece will usually sell midway between the opening and mid prices as those shut out of earlier sales get in their final licks.

Try Traveling for Better Prices

You can frequently purchase antiques abroad at a fraction of their American prices. For example, prices on Portobello Road, the London antique district, run roughly one-half the prices on Third Avenue in New York City. I was able to secure a set of brass and wood scales on Portobello for $75; equivalent price at Bloomingdale's, $225.

Avoid Auctions of Well-Known Estates Unless You Want to Pay Top Dollar

Auction prices at well-known estate auctions frequently run high—the pedigree of the previous owners adding to the price, if not the value, of the offerings. An example: An auction was held of the Morgan estate on Long Island, N.Y., summer of 1974. Prices ran as high as almost 1,000 percent of preauction estimates, and during a weak antiques market at that. Obviously the Morgan name drew the crowds, foreign buyers as well as American.

If you do happen to make a purchase at such an auction, *do* keep proof of the previous ownership of your purchase—that proof will be worth cash in the years to come.

Autographs

Runaway inflation, which leads investors into tangible inflation hedges, has benefited autographs as well as antiques in recent years. Specimen signatures, however, bear the same burdens as art and antiques during depression periods: low liquidity, falling prices in general, and the twin handicaps of no income drawn—selling expense at disposal time.

Nonetheless, autographs have shown a high rate of appreciation over the past decade, probably too high to be sustainable. Estimates place the price appreciation for autographs at up to 2,500 percent since about 1960—a rate of increase that cannot continue indefinitely.

Probably the best known of autograph dealers is Charles Hamilton, of Charles Hamilton Galleries, Inc., 25 East 77 Street, New York, N.Y. 10021. He conducts approximately ten auctions each year at New York's Waldorf-Astoria Hotel. Hamilton emphasizes the historical significance of any letter or document purchased for investment purposes.

A signature, in and of itself, has relatively little value. However, a manuscript by George Washington in which he refused pecuniary rewards for services to his nation sold, in 1973, for $37,000. Less significant letters by our first President might change hands in the $1,000-$3,000 area. Among the Presidents, manuscripts by Washington, Lincoln, and John Adams are appreciating well. And add to those the signature of—Zachary Taylor! Why Taylor? He was in office only a short time, and Presidential letters signed by him are quite scarce.

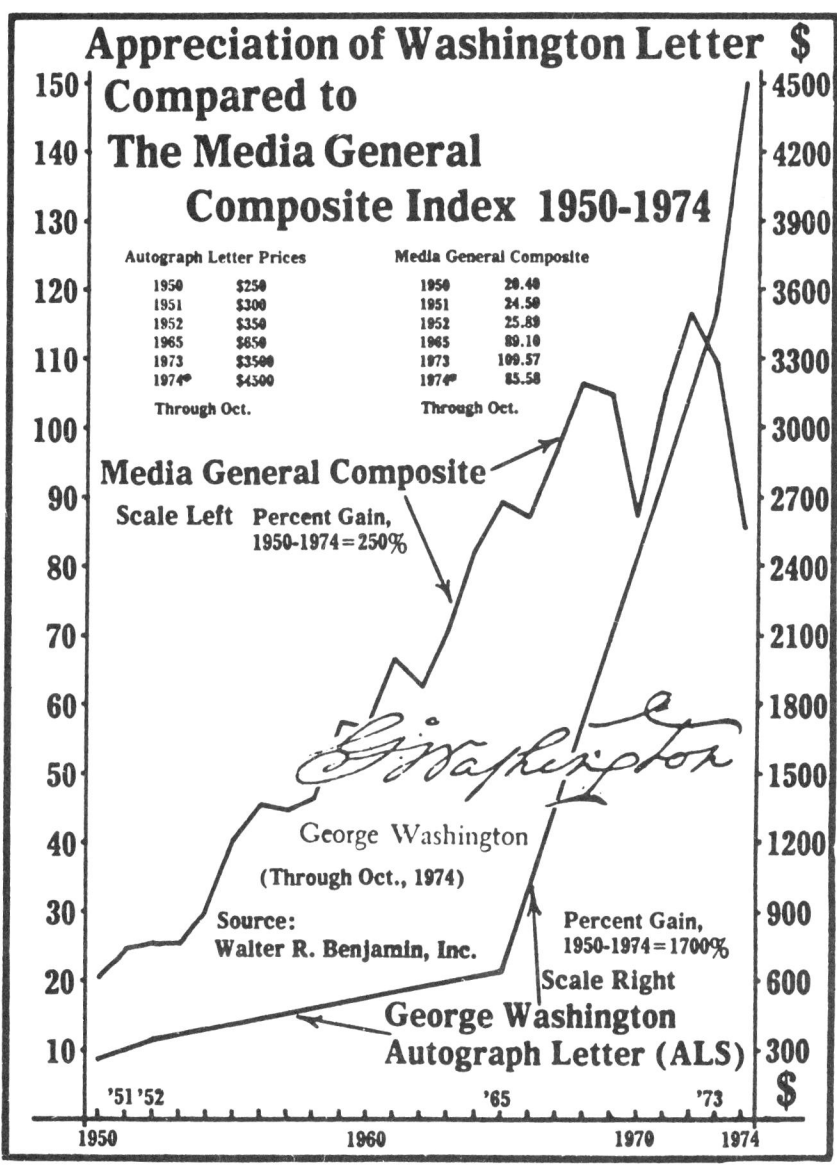

FIGURE 1
The George Washington Autograph Letter has recently outperformed the stock market, as measured by the Media-General Composite Index. SOURCE: *Media-General Financial Weekly,* Richmond, Va. 23261.

Other potential winners? Noted scientists such as Freud and Einstein. Forget about plain celebrity signatures. Also beware of Presidential signatures forged by secretaries or signed by the autopen (which duplicates signatures), recognizable because all signatures are exactly alike.

The Blots on the Paper

Unfortunately, dealer markups run very high in the world of autographs. Expect to pay from 20 to 50 percent dealer commissions. Nor have autographs been a particularly good hedge against inflation—the *Media-General Financial Weekly* reported (November 25, 1974) that autograph prices plunged by 95 percent during the Great Depression, not to recover until the 1950s.

Shopping and Storage Tips

Never, but never, purchase an autograph except from a reliable dealer, and then only with fully guaranteed verification of authenticity.

Do not pay extra for frills such as framing, or, if you must, open the frame before purchase to check the back of the manuscript. Do not attempt to repair damages yourself-and never with cellulose tape.

Keep autographs out of bright sunlight and away from extremes in temperature and humidity.

Avoid temptations to dispose of autographs (or art, for that matter) shortly after the creator's death. The death of a personage frequently brings out his work for sale on the theory that prices will immediately rise. Wait until the rash of offerings has been absorbed.

In addition to content, the condition, age, length, and clarity of an autograph determines its value. Age assumes considerable significance if a European autograph predates 1400; and an American, 1675.

Diversify a bit. Autographed letters do not appear all that frequently. By diversifying, you'll secure better chances of finding something of value for yourself.

The most valuable class of autograph is the "ALS," autographed letter, signed—a letter written in longhand by the personality and signed by him. Next most valuable is the "LS," letter written or typed by someone else, signed by the personality. Again, the most valuable will be letters with significant content.

Autographed photographs of celebrities have relatively little value—figure roughly $50 to $100, on average, for luminaries such as Charlie Chaplin, Lillian Gish, and Sarah Bernhardt.

It might pay to study pricing history *before* you take your own personal plunge into penmanship. Dealers frequently offer price lists, sometimes at a price, sometimes for free. We have already mentioned the Charles Hamilton Galleries, Inc. Others include:

Bruce Gimelson, Autographs
96 S. Limekiln Pike
Chalfont, Pa. 18914

Walter R. Benjamin Autographs, Inc.
Scribner Hollow Road
Hunter, N.Y. 12442

For Further Study:
A Key to Collecting, by Mary A. Benjamin (Walter R. Benjamin Autographs)
Collecting Autographs and Manuscripts, by Charles Hamilton (University of Oklahoma Press)

16
FROM BATMAN TO BORDEAUX—COLLECTIBLES AND SUCH

We'll say it just one more time. No collectible is a safe investment during depression climates. Stay in gold, cash, currencies, or on the short side of the stock market. But since half the fun is knowing what to do with your money when the time is right, and since many investors prefer to combine profits with pastimes, here goes . . .

Antique Photographica

Yes, photography buffs do collect as well—and prices have been rising. For example, the mid-nineteenth-century daguerreotype view camera, wood and brass, brings over $2,000 today on the collector's market. So, for that matter, does the Leica 35mm Model B, circa 1920. These illustrate the kingpins of two diverse elements of collector photographica—the nineteenth-century wood, leather, and brass pieces, and twentieth-century technological innovation, including some surprisingly inexpensive starter sets for the investor who prefers to start small.

On the antique trail, besides the daguerreotype (dates 1839–60), collector interest centers on late nineteenth-century stereoscopic cameras; Thornton Pickard field cameras; "detective cameras" (small, easily concealed cameras, 1883–1900), particularly cameras disguised as watches, satchels, and so forth; early Kodak box cameras (1888 and later); and various sundries such as the Kinora (a hand-cranked movie viewer) and the Phenakistoscope (a spinning device that gives the illusion of motion). Collector pieces have achieved status in recent years as Christie's, Sotheby's, and Sotheby Parke-Bernet have admitted the genre to auction. Prices have been moving up. Usual antique rules apply.

The Leica has reigned supreme among the modern collector cameras, only the very common Leica III F refusing to gain much ground. Early-model Leicas are in particularly high demand, ranging from the Leica A (1925) to the Leica II (1932). In recent years Nikon rangefinder cameras have gained in value, with interest beginning to develop as well in Japanese postwar, fine rangefinder equipment, still usable as well as collectible.

In between are some of the modern exotica: the Compass (1937), a range finder camera manufactured in England, worth nearly $1,000 today, and the Kodak Six-20, the first fully automatic still camera. Introduced at the World's Fair in 1939, the camera, originally priced at $225, sells currently in collector land for roughly $500.

Virtually all high-quality equipment fifteen to twenty years old, in fine condition, represents modern collectibles, sometimes available dirt cheap. Not the Leicas and Nikons to be sure—their value is too well publicized. But second-line equipment: the Olympus, Aires, Konica, Minolta, Rolleicord, Ciroflex—all are frequently obtainable at garage sales for $10 to $20 and all offer high potential in the years to come.

Photographic Sleepers For 1976

Nikon S-2	Kodak Folding Cameras
Olympus 35 S	Kodak Retina II S and III C
Contax II	Voightlander Prominent
Early model Polaroids	Konica III A

The Nikon, Retina, and Contax will run at approximately $100–$150. The others can be secured for $25–$75. Collect only cameras in excellent condition, and do try to obtain cases and instruction booklets if possible. Antique cameras are particularly fine display items, usually very striking when mounted on old-style wooden tripods.

For Further Information:
"Time Exposure," a series of articles by Eaton S. Lothrop, Jr., appearing regularly in *Popular Photography*.
"The Camera Collector," a series of articles by Jason Schneider, appearing in *Modern Photography*.
A Century of Cameras, by Eaton S. Lothrop, Jr., Morgan and Morgan, Inc., Dobbs Ferry, N.Y.

Dealers:
Shutterbug Ads, P.O. Box 730, Titusville, Fla. 32780. The publication lists cameras for sale and articles on collecting. Heavy on Leicas and other modern equipment.
The Daguerrian Era, Pawlett, Vt. 05761 offers mail catalogs four times each year. Write for latest price.
Olden Camera and Lens Company, 1265 Broadway, New York, N.Y. 10001. Large selection of Leicas, Nikons, and Contax. Some antique pieces as well. In London, try Brunning's, 133 High Holborn, Lon-

don W.C.1. The establishment specializes in vintage microscopes (another excellent collector item) and photographic equipment.

Considerable exchange of equipment takes place at local hobby and collector shows, sponsored by various societies. The best known is the Photographic Historical Society of New York, Inc., 520 W. 44th St., New York, N.Y. 10036. The organization sponsors lectures as well as shows.

Antique Photographs

One of the few items really to take off in recent years, antique and later quality photographs, have been rapidly emerging as an art form in their own right. Dr. Franz Pick has estimated that prices of vintage photography soared by 200 percent during 1974 alone, a claim backed by auctioneering tallies. For example, a presentation album of prints by Julia Margaret Cameron, among others, went for $100,000 at a Sotheby auction. One single print by Mrs. Cameron (a hot name on the circuit) has sold for as high as $3,000.

Nor are investment opportunities limited to the big leagues. Nineteenth-century stereoscopic cards are becoming scarce and eventually may even become rare. Still available at from 50¢ to $50.00 or so (some higher), they have been steadily growing in value. Lockets containing old daguerreotypes, circa 1850, command prices of roughly $100, give or take, likewise appreciating rapidly. Outdoor daguerreotypes of the Old West have been escalating as well. Favorite names on the vintage photography scene: L. J. M. Daugerre, N. Niepce, Mathew Brady, J. Gurney, M. A. Root, A. Bogardus, A. Claudet, and, of course, Julia Margaret Cameron.

The daguerreotype (1840–60) was the first commercially successful photographic process. Daguerreotypes were made from silver copper plates and are recognizable because the image upon them changes from positive to negative as the angle of view is altered. The *ambrotype* (1854–63), a later process, was produced on a glass negative, blackened on one side. Because of the limited time in which they were in production, ambrotypes are likely to become scarce. Ferrotypes, or tintypes, images produced on tin, are still quite plentiful, but worth accumulating at the price. Specimens are generally available at antique shows, at auction, or through the Daguerrian Era, address above. I was recently able to acquire an autographed photograph of General Sherman, taken by Mathew Brady—cost $75.

In the later genre, photographs by more recent masters—Edward Weston, Henri Cartier-Bresson, Ansel Adams, and Eugene Atget—are rapidly rising in price as well. Original collector prints are obtainable from the Museum of Modern Art, Lending Library, 21 West 53 Street, New York, N.Y. 10019, as well as from galleries.

From Bibliophiles to Bibliopoles (Collecting Rare Books)

A depression hedge? Hardly. Prices of high-quality merchandise dropped by as much as 80 percent during the depression. However, for ultimate recovery, an excellent vehicle for long-term investment; prices of *rare books* climbed at an average rate of roughly 50 percent annually in recent years (less the inevitable selling costs, of course).

Rare books have one tried and true ingredient for long-term price appreciation: Their number is fixed for all time, and as time passes, the floating supply can only diminish. Antique buffs, in fact, are now literally purchasing morocco-bound volumes by the inch to line the shelves of antique bookcases. Will the rush continue? Over the long pull, probably yes—with, again, our usual caveats.

What to Buy

The upper level is certainly beyond my reach, and, very possible, well beyond yours as well. For example, Chaucer's *Canterbury Tales* recently changed hands at $216,000; Audubon's *Birds of America* at $155,000. (Old books that include finely rendered color plates have become quite valuable. Reprints of the Audubon, in fact, sell for nearly $7,000 per set of four.)

Leaving the legendary, what about the garden variety of collector works. First rule of thumb: stay with established authors such as Hemingway, Joyce, Faulkner, and Steinbeck. Don't bother with current favorites—the print runs today are too large. Second, only first editions, preferably signed by the author, have any value to speak of. Generally you can tell a first edition by the fact that the year of printing matches the copyright date. However the rule of thumb does not pertain if the initial printing was so popular as to warrant more than one printing in the first year. In short, best sellers are vulnerable on two counts: The first editions are too large, and it may be just a bit difficult (but not impossible) for neophytes to verify such a first edition.

Taken all told, your best bet will lie in some specialization—learn one or two areas and learn them well. As usual, stay with high-quality books, in good condition. Auction sales are good bets, and, if you're diligent, you may be able to turn up a good find at garage sales, second-hand bookstores, or flea markets. Occasionally such finds do actually develop. Be prepared to purchase a lot complete if the lot includes one or two items of value. Some damages to books are reparable, but do not try to do the job yourself. If the book is good enough for investment, it should be good enough to hire an expert for the repair.

Fortunately, a number of sources exist for pricing and identification. Newcomers to the field may want to read:

Book Collecting: A Beginner's Guide, by Seumas Steward (Sutton)
New Gold in Your Attic, by Van Allen Bradley (Fleet Press)
American Book Prices Current (American Book Prices, New York)
The Book Collector's Handbook of Values, by Van Allen Bradley (G. P. Putnam's Sons)
The Antiquarian Bookman (Box 1100, Newark, N.J. 07101—a weekly newsletter)
First Editions of Today and How to Find Them, by Henry Boutell (Peacock Press)

Should you prefer to start by browsing through dealer shelves, you might try H. P. Kraus, 16 East 46 Street, New York, N.Y. 10017, or The House of El Dieff, Inc., 139 East 63 Street, New York, N.Y. 10021.

And finally, local dealers may be found by writing to the Antiquarian Booksellers Association, 630 Fifth Avenue, New York, N.Y. 10020. The Association publishes lists of dealers and their specialties.

Comic Books and the Ilk

Yes, Batman did finally make the big time in Gotham City. *Barron's* (January 13, 1975) decided to cover the comic book convention at the Commodore Hotel, New York City. Sandwiched between an article on last week's market trading and a serious editorial on New York City's financial crises, "Funnies Money" by Margaret D. Pacey noted that the prices of vintage comics had soared by 400 to 500 percent over the past decade, prices of rarer editions running as high as $3,000—and for a ten-cent comic at that.

Insofar as past issues go, Batman and Superman rank high, with the E. C. Comics series of crime, gore, and horror (circa 1950) coming up fast. Early Captain Marvel goes for $2,000 nowadays, when buyers can be found, a category shared by prewar items such as Marvel Mystery and Detective Comics.

Should you chase the crowd? I think not. The market for comics, except for dealers and a handful of well-heeled nostalgia buffs, is basically limited to teen-agers and young adults—most of whom simply do not have the cash to keep bidding up such exotica (?). And Walt Kelly's signature is, after all, not quite George Washington's.

Still, should you happen to have a youngster who collects comics, why not begin to set aside *now* the issues that will make collector pieces in the future. In particular, stash away introductory issues and issues in which new heroes are introduced for the first time—these are the comics that can ultimately be turned into cash.

In the meantime, funnies do make fun reading.

Profits in Politics

In 1956 you could have purchased an Adlai Stevenson-Estes Kefauver campaign button for exactly one nickel. By 1974 the price of that button had climbed to $75—a 150,000 percent profit! No sooner had McGovern dumped Senator Eagleton as his running mate (1972) than the price of McGovern-Eagleton buttons soared, spawning immediate counterfeiting operations.

In short, there can be pay dirt in political campaigns, very frequently on the loser's end, and all the more if the loser were short on funds and unable to supply buttons in any great quantity.

Jugates, buttons on which appear photos of both the Presidential and Vice-presidential candidates, are the most valuable. But do not confuse jugates, which show actual photographs, with buttons showing only sketches of the candidates; the latter are worth much less. Rising in value have been the Roosevelt-Garner (1932), the Davis-Bryan (1924), and the Theodore Roosevelt-Hiram Johnson Bull Moose Progressive Party (1912).

A good bet in future years: Nixon-Agnew or any memorabilia, in fact, from the Nixon period. Charles Hamilton, the autograph dealer, has stated that he considers Nixon autographs to be excellent investments for the years ahead. The same will, no doubt, be true for any Nixon souvenirs.

For More Information

The American Political Collectors, 66 Golf Street, Newington, Conn. 16111, policies the sale of campaign buttons to eliminate dealers in "cheats" or fakes. However, Congress has recently passed the Hobby

Protection Act, which requires manufacturers of replicas to stamp "Copy" on replicas of coins, medals, or paper money. The rule also applies to political posters, campaign buttons, and advertisements, so your chances of being stuck with a forgery have diminished.

The APIC also conducts auctions and conventions, setting price guides and issuing *The Keynoter*. Other publications include *The Button World*, R.E. #4, Young Street, Easton, Pa. 18042 and *The Political Collector*, 2509 Huntington Drive, Aptos, Calif. 95003. Also *The Illustrated Political Button Book* by Dick Bristow, Dick Bristow Publications, Box 1741, Santa Cruz, Calif. 95060 and *The 1972 Presidential Campaign In Buttons* by Tom French, Political Collector Publications, Box 80816, San Diego, Calif. 92138.

Come the depression, you might just go out sporting that old Hoover button once again. Unless, of course, you live in a Republican neighborhood.

Profits in Imbibing

Whisky

From time to time whisky—not in the bottle, but in the cask—has proven a sound investment play. At other times, the spirit has proven quite ephemeral indeed. Whisky, however, is not a good depression play, though hard times do frequently drive normally sober men to drink.

The essential play in whisky investment involves the purchase of raw, fresh, preblended Scotch malt or grain whisky, generally through a broker or dealer. The whisky is not delivered to you, but is kept at your expense in a warehouse in Scotland until it is ready for blending and bottling—at 4-, 8-, and 12-year ages. Theoretically at least, in the interim, the stuff gains in value and is ultimately sold to a blender at a profit.

Obviously, the profit potential depends upon the supply-demand picture, worldwide, at the time you're ready to sell. Post-World War II shortages of whisky pushed prices up rapidly during the fifties. Investors who purchased whisky in, say, 1954, saw their holdings gain 330 percent in value by 1958; 468 percent by 1962. Those were the good years. Had you purchased whisky, however, in 1964, you would have shown losses of nearly 10 percent a year, or 80 percent after expenses by 1972. On average, from 1954 to 1964 whisky investments returned approximately 12 percent per year after expenses, but keep in mind that this rate of return is heavily influenced by the strong gains recorded early in the period.

What Are the Prospects?

Whisky merchants are prone to point out rising rates of worldwide whisky consumption—and, indeed, imbibing has been increasing on an international scale. However, though demand has been increasing, whisky production frequently does run ahead of itself, and, in recent years, there seems to have been no shortages to speak of. (In fact, rumors have been spreading that the producers have been pouring surplus whisky down sewers.) Whisky promotions in the United States have frequently bordered on the shady, only relatively recently attacked by the SEC. One outfit, Strathmore Distillery, regularly sold whisky in the United States at $3 per gallon, when the going rate was closer to $1–$1.50. The SEC ultimately closed out the firm's operation here—investors able to get back only 40¢ on the dollar.

You have to keep in mind that whisky, although a fluid, is *not* a liquid investment. It is difficult to resell whisky before it reaches its blending age, and, furthermore, you will *not* receive the going market rate when you sell in small quantities. (For any chance at all, purchase at least $2,500 worth at a time.) And, still further, whisky draws no income and involves expenses for storage, insurance, and an outlay of money (refundable) for the casks in which the whisky is stored—not to mention brokerage commissions (roughly 5 percent each way). All told, you'll need a rise in the price of whisky of from 60 to 80 percent before you can break even. This is *not* a play for getting rich overnight.

The Other Side of the Coin

On the other hand, whisky, as a commodity, does represent some form of inflation hedge, with an indirect currency play to boot. As a whisky owner, you can receive payment for your whisky in either pounds sterling or dollars, so if the dollar is weak, you may prefer the British currency at the time.

There is also a favorable tax-play possibility available. Suppose you purchase new whisky, hold for four years, and wish to liquidate. You can trade in the aged whisky, now having increased value, for the same dollar value of new fillings. You will not be obligated for taxes until you accept cash, so your holdings are, in effect, appreciating tax free.

Table of Representative Grain Prices During the Indicated Years

	1.	2. GRAINS	3.
Whisky bought in Spring 1961 cost	£0.48	($1.15)	$1.34
Value in Spring 1964 cost	£1.73	($4.15)	$4.86
Value in Spring 1965 cost	£1.80	($4.32)	$5.02
Value in Autumn 1971 cost	£2.00	($4.80)	$4.82
Value in Spring 1973 cost	£1.25	($3.00)	$2.95
Value in Spring 1974 cost	£0.75	($1.80)	$1.66
Whisky bought in Spring 1962 cost	£0.58	($1.39)	$1.62
Value in Spring 1965 cost	£1.33	($3.19)	$3.71
Value in Spring 1966 cost	£1.13	($2.71)	$3.16
Value in Autumn 1971 cost	£1.15	($2.76)	$2.77
Value in Spring 1973 cost	£0.60	($1.44)	$1.41
Value in Spring 1974 cost	£0.73	($1.75)	$1.62
Whisky bought in Spring 1963 cost	£0.63	($1.51)	$1.76
Value in Spring 1966 cost	£0.78	($1.87)	$2.18
Value in Spring 1967 cost	£0.60	($1.44)	$1.67
Value in Autumn 1971 cost	£0.65	($1.56)	$1.56
Value in Spring 1973 cost	£0.50	($1.20)	$1.18
Value in Spring 1974 cost	£0.72	($1.73)	$1.59
Whisky bought in Spring 1964 cost	£0.70	($1.68)	$1.96
Value in Spring 1967 cost	£0.50	($1.20)	$1.39
Value in Spring 1968 cost	£0.33	($0.79)	$ .79
Value in Autumn 1971 cost	£0.52	($1.25)	$1.25
Value in Spring 1973 cost	£0.45	($1.08)	$1.06
Value in Spring 1974 cost	£0.76	($1.82)	$1.68
Whisky bought in Spring 1965 cost	£0.63	($1.51)	$1.75
Value in Spring 1968 cost	£0.29	($ .70)	$ .69
Value in Spring 1969 cost	£0.54	($1.30)	$1.29
Value in Autumn 1971 cost	£0.50	($1.20)	$1.20
Value in Spring 1973 cost	£0.45	($1.08)	$1.06
Value in Spring 1974 cost	£0.76	($1.82)	$1.68
Whisky bought in Spring 1966 cost	£0.53	($1.27)	$1.48
Value in Spring 1969 cost	£0.50	($1.20)	$1.19
Value in Spring 1970 cost	£0.55	($1.32)	$1.32
Value in Autumn 1971 cost	£0.50	($1.20)	$1.20
Value in Spring 1973 cost	£0.45	($1.08)	$1.06
Value in Spring 1974 cost	£0.80	($1.92)	$1.77
Whisky bought in Spring 1967 cost	£0.44	($1.06)	$1.22
Value in Spring 1970 cost	£0.55	($1.32)	$1.32
Value in Spring 1971 cost	£0.45	($1.08)	$1.08
Value in Autumn 1971 cost	£0.50	($1.20)	$1.20
Value in Spring 1973 cost	£0.50	($1.20)	$1.18
Value in Spring 1974 cost	£0.80	($1.92)	$1.77
Whisky bought in Spring 1968 cost	£0.40	($ .96)	$ .96
Value in Spring 1971 cost	£0.45	($1.08)	$1.08
Value in Autumn 1971 cost	£0.50	($1.20)	$1.20
Value in Spring 1972 cost	£0.50	($1.20)	$1.28
Value in Spring 1973 cost	£0.50	($1.20)	$1.16
Value in Spring 1974 cost	£0.84	($2.02)	$1.86
Whisky bought in Spring 1969 cost	£0.49	($1.18)	$1.17
Value in Spring 1972 cost	£0.52	($1.25)	$1.33
Value in Spring 1973 cost	£0.52	($1.25)	$1.22
Value in Spring 1974 cost	£0.85	($2.04)	$1.88

Table of Representative Grain Prices During the Indicated Years (Cont.)

	1.	2.	3.
		GRAINS	
Whisky bought in Spring 1970 cost	£0.49	($1.18)	$1.18
Value in Spring 1973 cost	£0.60	($1.44)	$1.41
Value in Spring 1974 cost	£0.87	($2.09)	$1.93
Whisky bought in Spring 1971 cost	£0.50	($1.20)	$1.20
Value in Spring 1974 cost	£0.85	($2.04)	$1.77
Whisky bought in Spring 1972 cost	£0.60	($1.44)	$1.54
Value in Spring 1974 cost	£0.80	($1.92)	$1.77
Whisky bought in Spring 1973 cost	£0.65	($1.56)	$1.53
Value in Spring 1974 cost	£0.72	($1.73)	$1.59

1. Sterling value in new pence
2. Sterling converted at $2.40
3. Sterling converted at January conversion rate for the year.

SOURCE: Accrued Equities Inc., 295 Northern Blvd., Great Neck, N.Y. 11021.

Table I shows the appreciation (or depreciation) of grain whisky purchased during various periods. Insurance, storage, and other costs are not included.

Miscellaneous

Whisky is sold in quantities measured in original proof gallons (o.p.g.). Allowance for evaporation is made, 11 percent considered normal for four-year whisky. In other words, if you start with fifty gallons, your buyer of four-year-old whisky anticipates the receipt of 44.5 gallons.

Lloyds of London offers "all risk" insurance, cost ½ of 1 percent of your holdings per annum. Your broker or dealer will arrange coverage for you.

Investors may choose between grain and malt whisky. Grain is a neutral spirit, carries no taste, and is essentially of one quality, brand to brand. Malts vary considerably in quality and are more expensive than grain. Prices vary considerably from dealer to dealer; comparison shop *before* you buy, verifying the *exact* malt offered at the exact price. If the dealer won't specify, go elsewhere.

Among the finer malts: Smith's Glenlivet, Glen Grant, Balmenach, Mortlach, Macallan-Glenlivet. Lower grade: Glenfiddich, Macduff, Ardmore, Dufftown, and Tomatin.

Malts have shown more consistent price growth than grain, but, overall, the rate of gain for both averages out similarly over extended periods of time.

When you do decide to sell, allow several weeks for the consummation of the transaction and the receipt of your money.

For More Information:

Harper's Wine and Spirit Gazette, Southback House, Black Prince Road, London S.E.1, England

Ridleys' Wine and Spirit Trade Circular, Wheatsheaf House, Carmelite Street, London, E D 4, England

Wine and Spirit Trade International, Gillow House, 5 Winsley Street, London, W1A 2HG, England

Accrued Equities Inc., 122 East 42 Street, New York, N.Y. 10017 (Accrued Equities was the first dealer to register with the SEC. Their free prospectus is quite informative. The firm specializes in grain whisky, and their prices appear to moderate for the trade.)

Wine

Speculation in fine wine is essentially similar to speculation in whisky—you accumulate parcels of fine wine, store the goods, and auction the wine after aging has improved its value.

Wine prices, particularly for French Bordeaux, shot up to intoxicating heights during the 1970–73 period, but prices collapsed during the recession of 1974, aided and abetted by scandals in France (dealers substituting inferior wine for fine, falsely labeling the bottles). Price recovery may take some time, but over the long pull prices of quality wine do tend to rise with age.

Local ordinances may prevent your dealing in wine locally, liquor licenses being required. For this reason many investors sell at auction overseas; your dealer will make arrangements for a commission, generally 3–10 percent.

Only the Best Wines Qualify

You must collect only the finest-grade wines, wines that age gracefully and continue to improve with time. Inferior wines reach their peaks relatively early in life and offer little in the way of investment appreciation. Among the Bordeaux, favored wines include Chateau La-Fitte, Chateau La Tour, Chateau Margaux, Chateau Haut Brion, Chateau Mouton Rothschild, Cheval Blanc, and Petrus. Top Burgundies include La Romanée, La Toche, and Romanée Conti.

Wines must be stored undisturbed in cool cellars, away from light. Some dealers will store for you.

For More Information:
The First Book of Wines, by Alexis Bespaloff, World Publishing, New York, $7.95

Encyclopedia of Wine and Spirits, by Alexis Lichine, Alfred A. Knopf, New York, $15

Wines of France, by Alexis Lichine, Alfred A. Knopf, New York, $8.95

Interested parties should contact fine wine merchants such as Sokolin & Co., Morrell & Co., and Sherry-Lehmann, all in New York City. Representatives there will discuss the current wine market and investment opportunities. Nor do they seem to push their goods at all costs. Sokolin, for example, was recommending the sale of wine, not the purchase, in 1973, just before the bubble burst.

Summing Up:
No, not for the depression, for obvious reasons. But a very chic investment when the living becomes easy.

If Not Batman, Babe Ruth

Back on the nostalgia scene, sound investments are being made, believe it or not, in baseball cards—those cardboard squares enclosed with bubble gum. Just the sort of item you might be able to acquire virtually for nothing at an attic sale some day.

The older the card, of course, the better. Babe Ruth and Lou Gehrig cards dating from the thirties run at more than $5 per card. Ty Cobb is worth roughly $500—few of his pictures ever appeared. Latter-day cards, sold as sets, go for up to $100 per set.

Just in case the scene has some appeal, contact:

American Card Catalog
Nostalgia Press, Box 293
Franklin Square, N.Y. 11010

You can buy and sell through *Card Collector's Company,* address above.

If Not Babe Ruth, How About Bing?

So comics never turned you on and baseball's a bore. How about music? Consider investing in and collecting original Broadway show albums, which, incidentally, provide more profit to collectors when they flop than to the original backers.

The logic is simple enough. Pressings of *My Fair Lady* must run into the millions. But did you ever hear of a flop called *Kwamina?* Or something called *Jimmy?* The secret to converting discs into dollars is to pick up original cast albums at below list price when they are issued, storing them carefully in their original cellophane wrappers, and putting them up for sale years later to collectors.

Price appreciation can occasionally prove fancy, indeed. For example, items such as *The Boys From Syracuse, Golden Rainbow, New Girl In Town,* and *Saratoga* now run at $20–$30 in the collectors' market, or at about 400 percent of their original price.

Cutouts

Cutouts are records unsold by retailers, returned to the manufacturer. He, in turn, distributes them at knockdown prices to cutout distributors. Such distributors often sell them at considerable discount via retail shop or by catalog. Once the supply is exhausted, these out-of-print issues gradually rise in value.

You might write to dealers for catalogs of cutouts. Among them are:

Apex Records, 1134 West Elizabeth Avenue, Linden, N.J. 07036

Candy Stripe Records, 17 Alabama Avenue, Island Park, N.Y. 11558

Scorpio Music Distributors, P.O. Box 2902, Philadelphia, Pa. 19126

Dealers in collector records include:

The Record House, Inc., 1101 Polk Street, San Francisco, Calif. 94109 (free catalog)

Broadway/Hollywood Recordings, Georgetown, Conn. 06829 (catalog, 50¢)

Richard d'Honau, writing in *The Capitalist Reporter* (March–April, 1975) "Broadway's Greatest Hits," recommended the following as current sleepers, still available at list price or below:

SHOW	*LABEL*
Canterbury Tales	Capitol SW-229
Cry For Us All	Project 3 TS-1000
Cyrano	A & M 3702
Grass Harp	Painted Smiles 1354
Lorelei	MGM/Verve 5097
Oh! Calcutta	Aider 9903
Seesaw	Buddah 95006
Two Gentlemen of Verona	ABC-1001

Free Enterprise (formerly *The Capitalist Reporter*), 150 Fifth Avenue, New York, N.Y. 10011, incidentally, is one of the best sources for information regarding investment in collectibles, as well as other vehicles. Subscription rates have been moderate, and, if you have any interest at all in exploring diverse avenues for investment, the magazine is highly recommended. (P.S., I have been the financial editor of *FE*.)

Selling
Your collector records can be sold at auction, via advertisement in audio or high fidelity magazines, or at wholesale prices through dealers.

Stamps

Stamps, like coins, tend to appreciate in value over the years, but the rate of increase has been far less, the penalties paid at disposal time probably greater. Still, if stamps are your thing, you might want to follow these rules for maximum profit:

1. Try to purchase whole collections at one time, preferably from a private party. Dealer markups run to 100 percent and more.
2. Stay with stamps that have already demonstrated significant price appreciation. Common stamps are of little value and will show little in the way of appreciation.
3. Complete sets will have more value than partial.
4. Obtain only stamps in top condition—these will show the greatest appreciation.
5. Specialize! Learn one group of stamps well.
6. Be patient. It takes time for stamps to appreciate in value.

Two Techniques

One method of determining the growth rate of stamps is to compare prices in past and present catalogs—usually available at public libraries. The Scott catalogs (Scott Publishing Co., Omaha, Nebraska) are the recognized price guides, available in U.S. and foreign categories at virtually all stamp dealers. Besides prices, the catalogs show mint marks, numbers issued, and current list prices. Never pay list price for stamps! They are widely available, generally, at 60 to 70 percent of catalog prices. Purchase issues showing the most rapid rise.

A second technique involves the purchase of full-numbered sheets or coils of newly issued stamps at the post office as they are issued. The trick here is to invest in high-priced stamps, stamps with a face value of $1 or more each. Since a roll of these can run to more than $100, few casual collectors will be able to afford the rolls, which will eventually become scarce on the market. Do not expect instant profit, but, in due course, you should make out very nicely indeed.

For Further Information:
Basic Knowledge for The Stamp Collector, by Sid Pietzch, Linn's Stamp News, Sidney, Ohio 45364
The Dictionary of Stamps In Color, by James A. Mackay, Macmillan, New York

High Fidelity Equipment

A new collector's market is beginning to emerge in vintage high fidelity equipment, particularly top-quality, tube-type units from 1955 to 1963 or so, just prior to the introduction of transistor units.

Many of these units can be obtained very inexpensively from private owners. Immediately have the pieces brought up to factory specification (while parts are still available), and carefully store them for future resale.

My best bets for sleepers in this area are the Marantz, McIntosh, and early Fischer and Scott stereo receivers. The Fischer 500C, circa 1964, was the last of the Fischer tube-type receivers and has been rising steadily in value in recent years.

Any hobby item, of course, may ultimately develop into investor-collector fare. The key to success lies in learning one or two areas, preferably for your own pleasure, seeking investment profit only secondarily. Why not try it yourself? As we said for starters, what can be more gratifying than to convert your pastime into profit?

17
MISCELLANEOUS MONEY MATTERS: SOME WAYS TO SAVE DOLLARS NO MATTER WHAT

How to Save Income Taxes on Securities Profits: The Bargain Sale

You are entitled to give up to $3,000 per year to each of your children ($6,000 if the gift is made jointly with a spouse) without paying gift taxes—up to a $30,000 ($60,000 joint) lifetime gift-tax exemption. For any number of reasons you might prefer not to give your child that large a gift at one time. Here's how you can give something to him or her (say, as a down payment on college expenses) and save income taxes at the same time.

Let's presume that you have purchased some securities for $5,000 and that you sold them within six months for $5,600. Kept in your name, presuming you are in the 50 percent tax bracket, you will be liable for $300 tax on the profit. Nor can you give the shares outright to your child—the gift would exceed the $3,000 gift-tax exemption.

Why not handle it this way? *Sell the Shares* to your child for your cost basis—$5,000. You take a note from your child for $5,000, an amount he or she officially owes to you. He or she, in turn, sells the shares immediately, receiving $5,600, from which he or she pays you the $5,000 you laid out. The profit accrues to him or her and is therefore transferred from your higher tax bracket to his or her lower—very possibly no taxes will be due at all. Even if IRS should rule that the profit is a gift, it will remain well within the parameters of the gift-tax exclusion.

On smaller stock purchases you can transfer the shares in their entirety to a minor, making certain that you present him or her with shares you hold at a profit, marking the gift to your cost basis. Any profits accruing will be taxed to him or her at the lower tax rate.

While we're on the subject of taxes, the odds are that you're better off avoiding an IRS audit if at all possible. One certain way to invite audit is to claim deductions in excess of the averages. If your claim is

Table I

Adjusted Gross Income	Average Deductions For Contributions	Average Deductions For Interest	Average Deductions For Taxes	Average Medical Deductions
$ 15,000–20,000	$ 434	$1,477	$ 1,407	$397
20,000–25,000	553	1,338	1,781	396
25,000–30,000	705	1,556	2,185	456
30,000–50,000	1,050	2,015	2,989	537
50,000–100,000	2,132	3,581	5,140	688
100,000–200,000	6,072	7,649	10,081	980

legitimate, by all means declare all that you are entitled to. However, if you do happen to estimate certain deductions without holding full substantiation, you should know what are the average filing claims—after all, there really is no point in pressing the panic button on that IRS computer.

Business Week Letter (April 7, 1975) printed average deductions for differing classes of income, year 1973. It *is illegal* to claim deductions to which you are not entitled, but, still, it might be useful for you to know the averages.

Incidentally, should you be audited and have to revise your federal returns, be certain to file a corrected return immediately with your state or city, should you be subject to such taxation. The federal authorities will, in all probability, notify your state of the change, in any event, and you might as well report to them before they come to you.

Take Advantage of Bank Regulations

Many banks offer day-of-deposit to day-of-withdrawal interest credit on deposits held in account. Others will credit you with a full quarter's interest if you deposit by the tenth of the month—giving, in effect, ten grace days.

If your neighborhood has two such banks nearby, close enough to each other to justify the effort, you can add to your interest return by the following procedure:

Start by depositing funds in one or the other bank. Let's presume that you start by placing your funds in a day-of-deposit to day-of-withdrawal bank. Hold the money there until the tenth day of the following quarter. Then, on that day, move the money into the bank that offers grace days. *For the first ten days of the quarter, you will be receiving duplicate interest on your funds!* At the end of the quarter, move the money back to the day-of-deposit to day-of-withdrawal bank, repeating the process.

By the end of the year, you'll have accumulated forty free interest days, thereby raising your effective bank interest by 11 percent. On a $20,000 savings account, the extra return will amount to more than $115 per year, or to nearly $29 free money in your pocket per transaction.

While we're on the subject of banks, don't forget that increasing numbers of money or cash management funds now offer check-redemption privileges, giving you, in effect, interest-bearing checking accounts, generally at higher rates of interest than you could secure in a bank savings account—not to mention the fact that some checking accounts pay no interest at all.

Just one more point. If you can maintain the discipline of not overdrawing your credit, make as many purchases as you can via credit or charge account card, keeping the cash you otherwise might have used in the bank, gathering interest. Pay up before the charge card charges you interest, however. By getting in the habit of handling finances this way, you will be drawing interest, in effect, on money you've already spent.

Ever Wonder How Much You'll Be Worth Some Day?

The following tables should be of some help. Table II, *One Dollar Principal*, shows the amount to which a given amount of money will grow, compounding over different periods of time at different rates. For example, you would like to know to how much $20,000 will grow if you leave it in a long-term savings account, compounding at 7½ percent per year for twenty years.

By moving over to the 7½ percent column and going down to year 20, you can see that one dollar will grow to $4.248. Multiply the $4.248 by $20,000 and you'll have your result.—$84,960. Which does prove that you can get rich slowly, but steadily, if you'll stay patient.

Table III, *One Dollar Per Annum*, is useful in computing potential retirement resources. It shows what will happen if you add a fixed amount of money each year, say, to a retirement fund, and the money compounds at a given rate of return.

For example, let's presume that you set aside $3,000 per year in a Keogh account, compounding the funds at 7½ percent per year for twenty years. Again, you look under the 7½ percent column, down to the twenty-year line. There you see that for one dollar deposited annually, compounding at 7½ percent, you will end up with $46.553. Multiply that by $3,000, and you'll see that your retirement fund will have grown to $139,659.

Savings on Stock Commissions

If you can do without some of the frills associated with brokerage firms who are members of the New York and American Stock Exchanges, you might prefer to deal with "discount brokers" who trade in the Third Market, where listed securities change hands over the counter through dealers. Such houses offer commission savings, frequently ranging up to 50 percent of member-firm charges. They generally offer no or little research, however, nor other side services. Some do not hold securities in custody; others do not allow margin.

These firms advertise regularly in the financial press, but you might start by contacting any or all of the following for the details of their latest arrangements.

Blinder, Robinson & Company
55 Post Road
Westbury, N.Y. 11590

Source Securities Corp.
70 Pine Street
New York, N.Y. 10005

Daley, Coolidge & Co.
1010 Euclid Avenue
Cleveland, Ohio 44115

Letterman Transaction Services, Inc.
2043 Westcliff Drive
Newport Beach, Calif. 92660

Marquette de Bary Co.
30 Broad Street
New York, N.Y. 10004

Odd Lot Securities, Ltd.
60 East 42 Street
New York, N.Y. 10017

Thrift Trading, Inc.
164 Northstar Center
Minneapolis, Minn. 55402

Clayton Polleys & Co.
141 Milk Street
Boston, Mass. 02109

On May 1, 1975, member firms introduced negotiated commission rates, finally forced by the SEC to abandon the long-standing structure of uniform, fixed commission rates. Should you prefer to deal with a member firm, do shop around. However, the discount houses are fully insured and, up to the time of this writing at least, have delivered generally satisfactory service—and their commission rates have remained low. (Some discount houses are now offering savings on exchange as well as Third Market transactions.)

Table II

MISCELLANEOUS TABLES

COMPOUND INTEREST TABLE

ONE DOLLAR PRINCIPAL

Will increase to the following amounts at the rates of interest and in the terms designated.

4%	4½%	5%	6%	7%	Years	7½%	8%	10%	12%	15%
$1.040	$1.045	$1.050	$1.060	$1.070	1	$1.075	$1.080	$1.100	$1.120	$1.150
1.082	1.092	1.103	1.124	1.145	2	1.156	1.166	1.210	1.254	1.323
1.125	1.141	1.158	1.191	1.225	3	1.242	1.260	1.331	1.405	1.521
1.170	1.193	1.216	1.262	1.311	4	1.335	1.360	1.464	1.574	1.749
1.217	1.246	1.276	1.338	1.403	5	1.436	1.469	1.611	1.763	2.011
1.265	1.302	1.340	1.419	1.501	6	1.543	1.587	1.772	1.974	2.313
1.316	1.361	1.407	1.504	1.606	7	1.659	1.714	1.949	2.211	2.660
1.369	1.422	1.477	1.594	1.718	8	1.783	1.851	2.144	2.476	3.059
1.423	1.486	1.551	1.689	1.838	9	1.917	1.999	2.358	2.773	3.518
1.480	1.553	1.629	1.791	1.967	10	2.061	2.159	2.594	3.106	4.046
1.539	1.623	1.710	1.898	2.105	11	2.216	2.332	2.853	3.479	4.652
1.601	1.696	1.796	2.012	2.252	12	2.382	2.518	3.138	3.896	5.350
1.665	1.772	1.886	2.133	2.410	13	2.560	2.720	3.452	4.363	6.153
1.732	1.852	1.980	2.261	2.579	14	2.752	2.937	3.797	4.887	7.075
1.801	1.935	2.079	2.397	2.759	15	2.959	3.172	4.177	5.474	8.137
1.873	2.022	2.183	2.540	2.952	16	3.181	3.426	4.595	6.130	9.358
1.948	2.113	2.292	2.693	3.159	17	3.419	3.700	5.054	6.866	10.761
2.026	2.208	2.407	2.854	3.380	18	3.676	3.996	5.560	7.690	12.375
2.107	2.308	2.527	3.026	3.617	19	3.951	4.316	6.116	8.613	14.232
2.191	2.412	2.653	3.207	3.870	20	4.248	4.661	6.727	9.646	16.367
2.279	2.520	2.786	3.400	4.141	21	4.566	5.034	7.400	10.804	18.822
2.370	2.634	2.925	3.604	4.430	22	4.909	5.437	8.140	12.100	21.645
2.465	2.752	3.072	3.820	4.741	23	5.277	5.871	8.954	13.552	24.891
2.563	2.876	3.225	4.049	5.072	24	5.673	6.341	9.850	15.179	28.625
2.666	3.005	3.386	4.292	5.427	25	6.098	6.848	10.835	17.000	32.919
2.772	3.141	3.556	4.549	5.807	26	6.555	7.396	11.918	19.040	37.857
2.883	3.282	3.733	4.822	6.214	27	7.047	7.988	13.110	21.325	43.535
2.999	3.430	3.920	5.112	6.649	28	7.576	8.627	14.421	23.884	50.066
3.119	3.584	4.116	5.418	7.114	29	8.144	9.317	15.863	26.750	57.575
3.243	3.745	4.322	5.743	7.612	30	8.755	10.063	17.449	29.960	66.212
3.373	3.914	4.538	6.088	8.145	31	9.412	10.868	19.194	33.555	76.144
3.508	4.090	4.765	6.453	8.715	32	10.117	11.737	21.114	37.582	87.565
3.648	4.274	5.003	6.841	9.325	33	10.876	12.676	23.225	42.092	100.700
3.794	4.466	5.253	7.251	9.978	34	11.692	13.690	25.548	47.143	115.805
3.946	4.667	5.516	7.686	10.677	35	12.569	14.785	28.102	52.800	133.176
4.104	4.877	5.792	8.147	11.424	36	13.512	15.968	30.913	59.136	153.152
4.268	5.097	6.081	8.636	12.224	37	14.525	17.246	34.004	66.232	176.125
4.439	5.326	6.385	9.154	13.079	38	15.614	18.625	37.404	74.180	202.543
4.616	5.566	6.705	9.704	13.995	39	16.785	20.115	41.145	83.081	232.925
4.801	5.816	7.040	10.286	14.974	40	18.044	21.725	45.259	93.051	267.864
4.993	6.078	7.392	10.903	16.023	41	19.398	23.462	49.785	104.217	308.043
5.193	6.352	7.762	11.557	17.144	42	20.852	25.339	54.764	116.723	354.250
5.400	6.637	8.150	12.250	18.344	43	22.416	27.367	60.240	130.730	407.387
5.617	6.936	8.557	12.985	19.628	44	24.098	29.556	66.264	146.418	468.495
5.841	7.248	8.985	13.765	21.002	45	25.905	31.920	72.890	163.988	538.769
6.075	7.574	9.434	14.590	22.473	46	27.848	34.474	80.180	183.666	619.585
6.318	7.915	9.906	15.466	24.046	47	29.936	37.232	88.197	205.706	712.522
6.571	8.271	10.401	16.394	25.729	48	32.182	40.211	97.017	230.391	819.401
6.833	8.644	10.921	17.378	27.530	49	34.595	43.427	106.719	258.038	942.311
7.107	9.033	11.467	18.420	29.457	50	37.190	46.902	117.391	289.002	1083.657

SOURCE: Systems and Forecasts, P.O. Box 1227, Old Village Station, Great Neck, N.Y. 11023.

Table III

COMPOUND INTEREST TABLE

ONE DOLLAR PER ANNUM

Paid in advance at the beginning of **each year** will increase to the following amounts at the rates of interest and in the terms designated.

4%	4½%	5%	6%	7%	Years	7½%	8%	10%	12%	15%
$ 1.040	$ 1.045	$ 1.050	$ 1.060	$ 1.070	1	$ 1.075	$ 1.080	$ 1.100	$ 1.120	$ 1.150
2.122	2.137	2.153	2.184	2.215	2	2.231	2.246	2.310	2.374	2.473
3.246	3.278	3.310	3.375	3.440	3	3.473	3.506	3.641	3.779	3.993
4.416	4.471	4.526	4.637	4.751	4	4.808	4.867	5.105	5.353	5.742
5.633	5.717	5.802	5.975	6.153	5	6.244	6.336	6.716	7.115	7.754
6.898	7.019	7.142	7.394	7.654	6	7.787	7.923	8.487	9.089	10.067
8.214	8.380	8.549	8.897	9.260	7	9.446	9.637	10.436	11.300	12.727
9.583	9.802	10.027	10.491	10.978	8	11.230	11.488	12.579	13.776	15.786
11.006	11.288	11.578	12.181	12.816	9	13.147	13.487	14.937	16.549	19.304
12.486	12.841	13.207	13.972	14.784	10	15.208	15.645	17.531	19.655	23.349
14.026	14.464	14.917	15.870	16.888	11	17.424	17.977	20.384	23.133	28.002
15.627	16.160	16.713	17.882	19.141	12	19.806	20.495	23.523	27.029	33.352
17.292	17.932	18.599	20.015	21.550	13	22.366	23.215	26.975	31.393	39.505
19.024	19.784	20.579	22.276	24.129	14	25.118	26.152	30.772	36.280	46.580
20.825	21.719	22.657	24.673	26.888	15	28.077	29.324	34.950	41.753	54.717
22.698	23.742	24.840	27.213	29.840	16	31.258	32.750	39.545	47.884	64.075
24.645	25.855	27.132	29.906	32.999	17	34.677	36.450	44.599	54.750	74.836
26.671	28.064	29.539	32.760	36.379	18	38.353	40.446	50.159	62.440	87.212
28.778	30.371	32.066	35.786	39.995	19	42.305	44.762	56.275	71.052	101.444
30.969	32.783	34.719	38.993	43.865	20	46.553	49.423	63.002	80.699	117.810
33.248	35.303	37.505	42.392	48.006	21	51.119	54.457	70.403	91.903	136.632
35.618	37.937	40.430	45.996	52.436	22	56.028	59.893	78.543	103.603	158.276
38.083	40.689	43.502	49.816	57.177	23	61.305	65.765	87.497	117.155	183.168
40.646	43.565	46.727	53.865	62.249	24	66.978	72.106	97.347	132.334	211.793
43.312	46.571	50.113	58.156	67.676	25	73.076	78.954	108.182	149.334	244.712
46.084	49.711	53.669	62.706	73.484	26	79.632	86.351	120.100	168.374	282.569
48.968	52.993	57.403	67.528	79.698	27	86.679	94.339	133.210	189.699	326.104
51.966	56.423	61.323	72.640	86.347	28	94.255	102.966	147.631	213.583	376.170
55.085	60.007	65.439	78.058	93.461	29	102.399	112.283	163.494	240.333	433.745
58.328	63.752	69.761	83.802	101.073	30	111.154	122.346	180.943	270.293	499.957
61.701	67.666	74.299	89.890	109.218	31	120.566	133.214	200.138	303.848	576.100
65.210	71.756	79.064	96.343	117.933	32	130.683	144.951	221.252	341.429	663.666
68.858	76.030	84.067	103.184	127.259	33	141.560	157.627	244.477	383.521	764.365
72.652	80.497	89.320	110.435	137.237	34	153.252	171.317	270.024	430.663	880.170
76.598	85.164	94.836	118.121	147.913	35	165.820	186.102	298.127	483.463	1013.346
80.702	90.041	100.628	126.268	159.337	36	179.332	202.070	329.039	542.599	1166.498
84.970	95.138	106.710	134.904	171.561	37	193.857	219.316	363.043	608.831	1342.622
89.409	100.464	113.095	144.058	184.640	38	209.471	237.941	400.448	683.010	1545.165
94.026	106.030	119.800	153.762	198.635	39	226.257	258.057	441.593	766.091	1778.090
98.827	111.847	126.840	164.048	213.610	40	244.301	279.781	486.852	859.142	2045.954
103.820	117.925	134.232	174.951	229.632	41	263.698	303.244	536.637	963.359	2353.997
109.012	124.276	141.993	186.508	246.776	42	284.551	328.583	591.401	1080.083	2708.246
114.413	130.914	150.143	198.758	265.121	43	306.967	355.950	651.641	1210.813	3115.633
120.029	137.850	158.700	211.744	284.749	44	331.065	385.506	717.905	1357.230	3584.128
125.871	145.098	167.685	225.508	305.751	45	356.969	417.426	790.795	1521.218	4122.896
131.945	152.673	177.119	240.099	328.224	46	384.817	451.900	870.975	1704.884	4742.482
138.263	160.588	187.025	255.565	352.270	47	414.753	489.132	959.172	1910.590	5455.005
144.834	168.859	197.427	271.958	377.999	48	446.935	529.343	1056.190	2140.981	6274.405
151.667	177.503	208.348	289.336	405.529	49	482.530	572.770	1162.909	2399.018	7216.716
158.774	186.536	219.815	307.756	434.986	50	518.720	619.672	1280.299	2688.020	8300.374

SOURCE: Systems and Forecasts, P.O. Box 1227, Old Village Station, Great Neck, N.Y. 11023.

18

HOW TO TELL WHEN THE DEPRESSION'S COMING TO AN END AND HOW TO TAKE ADVANTAGE OF THE TURN

Obviously, it's one thing to follow a master plan for depression survival, policies that will not hurt you even in the best of times, and quite another to pick the precise moment to begin actively to move your capital into investments that will prosper with the coming business resurgence. Are there means of ascertaining the turn? Fortunately, yes —and here are some that should stand you in good stead in the years to come.

Contrary Opinion—Still One of the Best of All Indicators

If the peaks of business cycles are marked by unbridled optimism, then the troughs of depressions (and recessions) are accompanied by rampant pessimism. Watch the public media. When popular magazines, Sunday supplements, and daily newspapers headline reminiscences of the Great Depression; when "superbears" becomes a public watchword; when unemployment figures make the headlines; when consumers positively refuse to purchase anything; when fear, uncertainty, and foreboding are the order of the day—then the depression is probably close to an end.

In short, operate against crowd sentiment—the majority is nearly always wrong at major turning points. Be ready. You will have at least several months' time to scoop up bargains, but, if you wait until the upturn is confirmed, you will be, at the least, somewhat late.

Track Interest Rates

The cost of money soars during business booms as corporations compete for available funds to meet expansion campaigns. The results:

inflation, high costs for borrowed money, excessive inventory. As the recession starts, businesses begin to cut back on borrowing, inventories of unsold goods peak, and then are reduced at cut-rate prices (remember the auto rebates in early '75?) until, finally, excess inventories are slashed to the bone. Accompanying this process is likely to be federal intervention—the Federal Reserve Board pouring money into the banking system to lower borrowing costs. Interest rates fall because, at first, businesses are loath to borrow, still fearful. Eventually, corporations step in to take advantage of available funds. Interest rates begin to firm and then, slowly at first, to climb. This is a sign, probably, that the business upturn is already under way.

Check the Economic Indicators

Major financial newspapers regularly carry the latest data on major economic indicators. These include housing starts (housing starts affect the lumber, construction, plumbing, hardware, appliance, and paint industries); automobile sales (oil, auto companies, tire industries, plastics, and related industry groups); unemployment figures (look for a slowing of trend or a reversal); durable goods orders (major appliances, etc.). Also, study the rate of inflation (depressions are generally marked by deflation). When prices once again start to firm, when the shortage of goods becomes more pronounced than the shortage of buyers, a turn is probably close at hand.

A Major Economic Indicator

The stock market, as it turns out, is a major lead indicator, turning up, generally, several months before economic recessions actually come to an end. Even if you miss the early rise in the stock market, or even if you stay out of the market altogether, the first strong rallies in stocks should help you plan for other areas of investment: real estate, art, coins, and so forth. The rule that the stock market points the way is, of course, not infallible. The market staged a strong recovery in 1930, following the crash of '29, only to settle back for many years until the depression ran its course. Nonetheless, by and large, the stock market does remain a major lead indicator.

How to Recognize a Stock Market Bottom: Ten Rules for Catching the Turn

With some luck, the ability to buck the crowd, and an awareness of telltale omens of selling climaxes, intense public liquidation of stocks, you should be able to take positions in the stock market at least relatively close to low points. Look for these signs:

1. The public is either intensely pessimistic regarding the stock market or, at best, apathetic.
2. The financial pages regularly feature articles relating to the demise of Wall Street. A number of brokerage houses fail.
3. The mutual funds are heavily in cash. In recent years this means that cash represents 12–14 percent of mutual fund assets.
4. The favorite glamour issues (IBM, Coca-Cola, Xerox, Polaroid) show sharp and sustained price declines. These issues are generally the last to be unloaded by institutions.
5. Stocks provide yields in excess of savings accounts. Investors demand high dividends to compensate for the risk of further price declines.
6. Liquidation of stocks takes place across a broad front. There will be at least several weeks in which at least 1,000 issues reach new lows. This data is available weekly in *Barron's*.
7. The market will hit bottom with a thump! Following several weeks of protracted and sharp decline, an immediate and sharp rally will take place, at first greeted with disbelief. This will be followed by a secondary decline, *on lower volume*. Although the popular market averages (such as the Dow Industrials) may reach new lows, the number of issues reaching new low levels will decline in relation to the earlier spike down. Following this test, the market will turn up sharply.
8. The most actively traded stocks will suddenly come to life! Following weeks in which less than four of the twenty most actively traded issues are able to rise, we will see weeks in which fifteen or better are up. (Data available weekly in *Barron's*.)
9. Short-term Treasury bill yields will decline below the yields provided by long-term, high-quality bonds. (During bear markets short-term yields often exceed long-term.)
10. You, yourself, will feel hesitant to place any money in the stock market. You will feel fear overtaking greed.

How to Maximize Profits from the Upturn

Buy Low-Priced Stocks!
History has shown that low-priced stocks, on average, gain by larger percentages during bull markets than higher-priced issues. In particular,

seek out low-priced issues that show a pattern of rising earnings despite the depression. The potential doublers and triplers are more likely to come from the ranks of issues trading at under $10 than from the high-priced ranks.

Purchase Stocks Before the Economic Upturn Is Confined

As we noted above, stocks begin to rise in price in advance of the upturn in corporate profits. By the time the upswing is confirmed by other indicators, the best portion of the market advance will have passed.

The Wall Street Journal (April 18, 1975), for example, printed the following table, which shows what the Dow Industrial Average has done, measured from its low points during business slumps. The table also shows what this average did in the twelve months following actual upturns in the economy.

You can see that the greatest gains are achieved, again, before the actual business upturns have taken place. However, although the rate of gain does slow, you will still have plenty of room in which to profit from the stock market, even if you do miss the first several months.

Purchase LOW-Quality Bonds

Research has demonstrated that, with the exception of actual depression periods, the returns from low-quality bonds far exceed returns from higher-quality bonds, even allowing for the occasional defaults involved. During depression periods stay either in government paper or in the very best of corporates. During better times the odds favor your side if you speculate a bit.

For example, W. B. Hicknan (*Corporate Bond Quality and Investor Experience*) studied the relationship between rates of return provided by low- and high-quality bonds for the period 1900–43. The top-rated group of bonds provided returns for large issues of 5.1 percent, if held to maturity. The larger issues of grade 7 bonds, low-quality, provided actual rates of return of 23.4 percent! Only during the Great Depression

Table I

	DJIA During the Slump, Gains from Low Point	DJIA in the 12 Months Following the Onset of Business Recovery
1969–1970	+25.8%	+ 4.6%
1960–1961	+16.9	+ 6.1
1957–1958	+ 8.5	+32.2
1953–1954	+37.1	+33.6
1948–1949	+17.7	+18.2
1945	+22.8	−12.7
1937–1938	+40.3	− 3.8
1929–1933	+52.7	+61.5
Averages	+27.7%	+17.5%

did higher-rated issues outperform lower-rated. However, on balance the ownership of common stocks has outperformed the ownership of bonds, particularly high-grade. The exception: depression periods, of course.

Buy Low-Rated Bonds on Margin!
For the ultimate in speculation—and possible reward, and only if you can truly afford the hazards involved—purchase a few low-quality bonds on margin.

The odds are that the yields from these bonds will greatly exceed the margin costs (interest paid to the broker for the loan) involved in their purchase. You can purchase straight (nonconvertible) corporate bonds at most brokerage houses by putting only 30 percent down, borrowing 70 percent of the purchase cost from the broker. At the start of business upturns interest rates are generally low—the spread between what you receive in interest and what you pay out, the lowest. For example:

How To Achieve a 29.7 Percent Return from an A-Rated Bond!

To update a ploy mentioned earlier, in April 1975 the American Financial 9½s 1988 bonds were priced at $625 per bond, for a current yield of 15.2 percent. At the time you could have purchased them on margin, paying margin interest of roughly 9 percent. Suppose you had purchased one of these bonds, putting down 30 percent of its cost, or $187.50. You would have received $95 per year in interest for the bond you held. You would have had to pay out 9 percent interest on your margin debit, or $39.38 (9% X $437.50). Your net return would have come to $55.62 or 29.7 percent annually—and that does not include the capital gain deriving from the fact that you paid only $625 for a bond for which you will receive $1,000 back upon maturity in 1968. This amounts to a capital gain of $375 in 13 years, a 200 percent increase based upon the $187.50 you originally placed in the deal. (These bonds, by the way, are A-rated by Fitch.)

And that, in the end, is what's so nice about preserving your capital during depression periods. There are so many opportunities for the person with money in his pocket when the upturn finally does arrive.

19
EPILOGUE

The preparation of a book of this nature does, of course, involve many months of research, preparation, and actual writing. I began during the late fall of 1974 and essentially completed the work in May of 1975.

During that period events have developed that appear to indicate that the world may have stepped back from the brink of economic disaster after all—at least this time around. Or to put it another way, it now appears that the free world may not yet go bankrupt, that the flow of money to the Arabs via the oil pipeline may slow, that business may recover. Certainly, the rapid rise in stock prices points to an economic recovery in the years ahead. I certainly do hope so.

But is everything really all that sanguine? Unfortunately, no. New York City's credit rating has just dropped another notch or so; layoffs of city personnel continue, attesting further to the growing plight of our big cities. The Treasury has recently announced that it will need to borrow $80 billion, a record amount, to finance deficit government spending. Machine tool orders, a lead indicator, remain low. So do housing starts—in fact, private home ownership has been virtually priced out of working-class reach. The stock market? Booming, as I write these words, following the usual period of gloom, doom, and dumping; as I said, indicating a general sense that the worse may not come to pass after all.

But for how long can we survive on deficit spending, mounting labor costs, lower productivity, and a changing picture of international power? I really do *not* know, but I am glad for this interlude—you will now have a second chance to read the signs and to take productive action while you still can. When I sat down to write the earlier chapters, I said I hoped that we would see this opportunity. Apparently we now will.

Some Forecasts of Events to Come

1. By 1976 government spending, heavy corporate borrowing, and consumer demand will once again fuel inflation. The rising cost of

living will once again supplant depression as the major national concern.
2. The stock market will peak either during 1976 or early in 1977, at which time we will see a resumption of the bear market. Stay alert to the danger signals.
3. The government will have to increase taxation to finance continued deficit spending. This is already taking place at state and local levels.
4. An economic downturn will begin sometime later in 1977 or early in 1978, providing it does not start sooner.
5. Gold, which is now out of favor, will return to prominence once again as investors seek known storehouses of value.
6. Commodity prices will once again rise, pointing the way to inflation at the consumer level.
7. The money funds will provide increasing yields once again, and will retain their popularity as cash havens.
8. Unemployment will stabilize at higher levels than in the past. Seven percent unemployment will be considered "normal"—during recessions the figure could climb higher.
9. The public, as usual, will enter the stock, realty, art, antique, and collector markets at the very peak.

You have been warned, and you have been shown how to protect yourself. I have done what I can. The rest is up to you.

20
EPILOGUE TO THE EPILOGUE

As you have no doubt gathered by now, the first edition of this book was prepared during 1974 and early 1975 and published in mid-1975. Just prior to publication date, I prepared Chapter 19—my predictions of events to come for the next several years. Let's review some of the predictions that appeared in that epilogue, and then let's consider some predictions for the 1980s.

1. I predicted that by 1976 government spending and heavy corporate borrowing would fuel inflation. I further stated that the rising cost of living will once again supplant depression as the major national concern. Events have, of course, borne out this prediction, although my timetable might have been just a bit premature. By 1980 inflation had, indeed, become a national preoccupation—rates of inflation rising to approximately 20 percent per year, before entering into a period of minor decline. And, indeed, the inflation was fostered by heavy government and private borrowing.
2. The stock market will peak either during 1976 or early in 1977, at which time I predicted a resumption of the bear market. The Dow Industrial Average reached a recovery peak of 1014.79 on September 21, 1976, thereafter declining to as low as 743 by the end of February 1978.
3. The government will have to increase taxation to finance continued deficit spending. This has, likewise, taken place. Tax shelters have come under increasing attack by the Internal Revenue Service, as well as by Congress. Inflation has pushed wage earners into higher tax brackets, resulting in higher taxation on dollars that are already losing purchasing power.
4. An economic downturn will begin during late 1977 or early 1978, providing it does not begin sooner. Here, my timetable was again a bit premature. Heavy use of debt appears to have propped up the economy until roughly the start of 1980, at which point a very serious recession got under way. At the time of this writing, this recession has not yet graduated into a full depression—but it could.

5. Gold will return to prominence once again as investors seek known storehouses of value. Gold, selling at approximately $200 an ounce at the time of the first edition, has since reached over $800 an ounce. Need I say more?
6. Commodity prices will once again rise, pointing the way to inflation at the consumer level. I suppose that I could have not been more right on that score either.
7. The money funds will provide increasing yields once again, and will retain their popularity as cash havens. During 1980 money fund yields rose to well over 16 percent. Their growth was so spectacular that, partially to protect the banking system, the Federal Reserve Board temporarily restricted the funds' right to invest. The public demand for shares of money funds became so great that many of these funds had to curtail the taking of new orders until new computer facilities could be developed to handle the inflow of fresh capital.
8. Unemployment will stabilize at higher levels than in the past. Seven percent unemployment will be considered normal. This has already come to pass; the rate of joblessness has exceeded 30 percent among certain minority groups within the country. The overall national rate of unemployment has reached 9 percent.
9. The public, as usual, will enter the stock, realty, art, antique, and collector markets at the very peak. A safe prediction—one that has been borne out over many a century.

All told, I think that just about all of you will agree that my forecasts of 1975 have proven somewhat more than moderately accurate. That, frankly, I think is an understatement, but I leave the conclusions to my readers.

Predictions for the 1980s and Beyond

The following are my fearless forecasts for the 1980s. Needless to say, past performance is no guarantee of future success—but those of you who remain unprepared for trouble are most likely to suffer the full consequences.

1. Inflation will stabilize during quiet periods at approximately 10 to 12 percent per year, but will, by 1981–82, threaten the 20 percent level once again. (The Administration started to administer the proper belt tightening medicine early in 1980, but backed off quickly at the first sign of blood. The enormous debt structure in

this country has not yet unwound. Our labor force is still not oriented to increasing productivity. As a result, the prices of our goods will continue to increase in ever mounting leaps of prices. This does not even take into account worldwide inflation and the worldwide increases in the prices of raw materials and energy.

2. A bear market will get under way either late in 1980 or relatively early in 1981. It will continue for approximately one to two years and should end some time during 1982.

3. Recessions during the 1980s will become more and more severe as the nation adjusts to a generally declining standard of living. New homes will become smaller in size, matching reductions in the sizes of the American automobile. Our auto industry, already in a decline, will show a secular deterioration, taking many segments of the economy down with it.

4. Gold will periodically show sharp increases in price. Investors will be well advised to accumulate gold during periods of quietude.

5. Silver will shortly emerge as the coming speculative vehicle.

6. The money market funds will continue to grow and prosper. However, inasmuch as a major danger does exist of an international bank catastrophe arising out of an overextension of world credit, investors should not place all of their capital into such vehicles.

7. Economic recoveries will become more transient than in the past. Many years may be required before mature American industry will show any real growth.

8. America will continue to lose preeminence and influence in the world.

9. The most favorable investments are likely to be investments in hard metals, highly liquid debt instruments, coins, and other inflation hedges. We may face a doubly disastrous period of recession coupled with continuing inflation.

10. Real estate may face a major shakeout. Purchases of investment property should be made only with the utmost caution.

11. There is at least a reasonable chance of major social disorder if the worst expectations regarding the economy come to pass. The prudent investor will place at least some investment capital overseas in foreign havens.

INDEX

Abrash, Bruce M., 173
Advance–Decline line, 77–79, 80, 82
Aetna Life & Casualty, 44
Ambrotype, 190
American Financial Corporation, 46
American Home Products, 44
American Hospital Supply, 44
American Numismatic Association Certification Service, 173, 174, 178
American Stock Exchange, 72, 75, 118, 120, 123, 124, 206
Anshutz, Thomas, 181
Antiques, 7, 13, 17, 18, 50, 179, 182–84, 191
APL, 42
Arabs, 3, 5, 6, 19, 28, 57, 60, 70, 153, 154, 156, 214
Argus, 4
Arkansas, 34
Armstrong Cork Company, 143
Art, 7, 13, 14, 17, 18, 50, 179–81, 210
ASA Ltd., 68, 69
Atlantic Richfield, 118, 119
AT&T, 13, 36, 38
Auctions, 179–84, 190, 191
Autographs, 13, 179, 184–86
Automobile industry, xi, xii, 3, 6, 34, 75, 210, 218
Avon, 74

Bache, 60
Balance of payments, 151–52, 153, 157, 159
Balance of trade, 151
Bank for International Settlements, 164
Bank of Japan, 161
Bank of New York, 44
Bankers' Acceptances, 51
Bankruptcy, 2, 3, 4, 43, 50, 214
Banks, Canadian, 165–66
Banks, Mexican, 152

Banks, Swiss, 147, 148, 159, 166
Barron's Financial Weekly, 2, 8, 10, 17, 36, 55, 57, 74, 75, 77, 79, 80, 88, 90, 101, 111, 123, 165, 183, 192, 211
Bendix Corporation, 110
Beter, Peter, 6
Bingham, Caleb, 180
Bent, Bruce R., 53
Bethlehem Steel Company, 2
Boardroom Reports, 173
Boise Cascade, 143
Bond ratings, 33–34, 36
Bonds, American Financial, 213
Bonds, convertible, 26, 40–47, 72
Bonds, corporate, 36–39, 45–46, 212, 213
Bonds, government agency, 16, 30, 52
Bonds, municipal, 26, 31–33
Bonds, New York City, 34
Bonds, U.S., 19, 85, 212
Bonds, U.S. Treasury, 15, 19, 28, 29, 45, 88, 113, 211
Books (comic), 192–93
Books (rare), 191–92
Borrowing, 6
Bretton Woods Agreement, 58, 151
Bristol Myers Company, 44
British pound, 57, 147, 149, 150, 151, 155, 159
Browne, Harry, 4, 12
Business Week, 4, 10, 30
Business Week Letter, 204
Button World, The, 194
Buttons (Presidential campaign), 193–94

Cabot, J. P., Short-term Fund, 55
Call options, 113, 117, 118, 119, 120, 122, 123
Campaign buttons (Presidential), 193–94
Campbell Red Lake Mines Ltd., 69
Canadian Deposit Insurance Company, 165

Canadian dollar, 147, 149, 160–61, 164
Capital gain rates, 38
Capital Preservation Fund, 50, 52, 53, 55
Cartier's, 22
Cash, 12, 13, 14, 50, 130
Cash equivalents, 12
Cash management funds, 205
Central Selling Organization, 19
Certificates of Deposit, 51, 52, 53, 165, 166
Chase Manhattan Bank, 54
Chase Manhattan Corporation, 44
Chicago Board of Trade, 67
Chicago Board Options Exchange (CBOE), 118, 120, 121, 123, 124
Chicago Mercantile Exchange, 67, 148
Chippendale, 182, 183
Christie's, 13, 179, 188
Chrysler Corporation, xi, 4, 29, 75, 101, 108, 109
City Investing, 143
Coca-Cola, 211
Coin Dealer Newsletter, 170
Coinage, 174
Coin World, 174
Coins, xii, 7, 13, 50, 169–78, 210, 218
Coins, gold, 61–63, 175, 178
 $20 St. Gaudens, U.S., 62, 63
 $20 Liberty, U.S., 62, 63
 $10 Liberty, U.S., 62
 Sovereign, Great Britain, 62
 20 Franc, Switzerland, 62
 50 Peso, Mexico, 62, 63
 20 Peso, Mexico, 62
 10 Peso, Mexico, 62
 100 Korona, Austria, 62, 63
 100 Korona, Hungary, 62, 63
 10 Guilder, Netherlands, 62
 Krugerrand, South Africa, 62, 63, 71
Coins, grading, 173, 178
Coins (magazine), 174
Coins, silver, 18, 178
Coins, U.S.
 Barber quarter, 176
 1937 Dime, 170
 1866 Eagles, 170
 1794 Flowing hair dollar, 177
 Fugio cent, 176, 177
 1828 Half dollar, 170
 1900 Half eagles, 170
 Liberty head quarter, 176, 177
 1853 Liberty Seated half-dollar, 173
 Lincoln penny, 177

Morgan silver dollars, xii, 173, 176, 177
 1911 Nickel, 170
 1840 Original half-cent, 170
 1652 Pine Tree Shilling, 176, 177
 1882 Silver dollar, 170
 1886 Small cent, 170
 Trade dollars, 176–77
Cole, Thomas, 180
Coleigh, Ira U., 11
Collector's items, 188–202
Commercial paper, 51, 52
Commodity Exchange, Inc., 67
Commodity exchanges, 60, 123, 149
Commodity prices, 2, 215, 217
Consolidated Foods, 44
Continental Oil Company, 44
Credit, 1, 5, 205, 214, 218
Currency, 147–60, 164, 172
Currency futures, 147–60, 164
Currency, spot, 150
Cycles, 9–11, 209
Cyclical securities, 102–09, 143

Daguerrotype, 188, 190
De Beers Consolidated Mines Ltd, 19–21, 22
Debt, xi, 5, 6
 Corporate, xi, 6
 Federal, xi
 Personal, xi, 3
Deposits (bank), 5
Depression (1929), 3, 34, 50, 150, 186, 209, 212
Detective camera, 188
Detroit, 34
Devaluation, 151, 152, 153
Diamonds, 18–25, 26, 57, 172
Dines, James, 4, 7, 57
Dines Letter, 4
Discount rate, 87
Dow Jones Industrials, 6, 7, 8, 50, 74, 75, 77, 78, 79, 80, 82, 83, 85, 88, 106, 170, 211, 212, 216
Dow Jones Stock and Bond Yields, 86
Dow Theory Letters, 4
Dow Utility Average, 82, 83
Dreyfus Equity Fund, 50
Dreyfus Liquidity Assets, 49, 50, 53, 55
Du Pont, 36
Dutch guilder, 147, 149, 150, 156–57

Earnings, 6
Eastman Kodak, 2
Emhart Corporation, 143
Equity, 7, 8
Equity financing, 6
Equity securities, 40
Evans Products, 143
Export-Import Bank, 30

"Fannie Maes" (Federal National Mortgage Association), 30
Federal Deposit Insurance Corporation (FDIC), 53
Federal Homes Loan Banks, 30
Federal Housing Administration, 30
Federal Land Banks, 30
Federal National Mortgage Association, 30, 44
Federal Reserve Bank, New York, 28
Federal Reserve Banks, 27, 87
Federal Reserve Board, 84–88, 152, 210, 217
Fidelity Daily Income Trust, 49, 55
Financial World, 4
First National Bank of Glen Head, N.Y., 174
"Flower bonds" (U.S. Treasury), 29
Forbes, 169
Forecaster, The, 174
Foreign currency. *See* Currency, British pound, Canadian dollar, Dutch guilder, French franc, German mark, Italian lira, Japanese yen, Mexican peso, Swiss franc.
Foster Wheeler, 94, 95, 96
Foreign exchange rates, 150, 151
Four Seasons, 43, 101
Foxboro, 94, 97
France, 5, 60, 64, 70, 75, 157
Franklin National Bank, 3, 5
French franc, 149, 157–58

Gardner-Denver, 94, 96
Gaunt, Harry, 21
Gemological Institute of America, 22, 23, 25
General American Transportation, 44
General Electric, 36
General Foods, 36
General Motors, 1, 2, 3, 6, 13, 18
Georgia Pacific, 143
German mark, 58, 59, 147, 149, 150, 154, 156, 157, 159

Germany, 60, 75, 148, 154, 156, 157
Giant Yellowknife Mines Ltd., 69
"Ginnie Mae pass throughs," 30
Gifford, Sanford, 180
Golconda Investors, 64
Gold, xii, 17, 18, 50, 57ff., 61, 66, 150–51, 153, 155, 159, 172, 174, 215, 217, 218
Gold auction, U.S. Treasury, 70
Gold bullion, 18, 58, 59, 63, 64–65
Gold futures market, 65–67, 69
Gold Reserve Act of 1934, 58
Gold shares. *See* Gold futures.
Gold Standard Act of 1900, 57
Government National Mortgage Association, 30
Government spending, 6
Great Britain, 2, 3, 5, 10, 75, 151, 155, 156, 161
Guide Book of United States Coins, 169, 170, 176, 177

Haller, Gilbert, 79
Hamilton, Charles, 184
Harnett, William, 181
Hass, Gilbert, 10
Hazlitt, Henry, 6
Helmerich & Payne, 110, 111
Hirsch, Yale, 9
Hobby Protection Act, 194
Housing industry. *See* Real Estate.
Houston Light & Power, 44

IBM, 211
Illinois Bell Telephone, 36
Illustrated Political Button Book, 194
Indicator Digest, 80, 81
Inflation, xi, 7, 8, 14, 19, 27, 38, 45, 50, 70, 125, 126, 127, 150, 151, 152, 153, 154, 156, 157, 159, 161, 167, 179, 184, 210, 214, 216, 217
Institutional Investor, 128
Insurance. *See* Swiss Insurance Company Annuity.
Insurance policy (life), 15, 16
Interest, 6, 8, 27, 33, 38, 39, 42, 46, 54, 82, 85, 143, 144, 152, 156, 157, 159, 165, 166, 207, 209–10
Bank, 204–05
Interest rates. *See* Interest
Internal Revenue Code, 32
Internal Revenue Service, 32–33, 139, 144, 167, 203–04, 216

International Investors, 64
International Monetary Fund, 58
International Monetary Market, 66, 67, 148ff.
Inventory, 8, 210
Investment Diamonds Incorporated, 21
Iran, 5
Israel, 5
Italian lira, 147, 151, 152, 163–64
Italy, 2, 3, 10, 151, 152, 163
IT&T, 73

Japan, xi, 4, 154, 161
Japanese yen, 147, 149, 150, 161–62
Jersey City, 34
Johns-Manville, 143

Kamin, John, 174
Kaufman & Broad, Inc., 143
Keogh Plan, 52, 174
Kodak cameras, 188, 189
Keynoter, The, 194
Kimmel, Murray M., 48
Kinora, 188
Kondratieff, Nikolai, D., 9
Kondratieff Wave, 9, 10
Kohinoor International Ltd., 21–22

Labor, xii, 6, 7, 214, 218
La Jolla Diamond, Inc., 21
Lebenthal & Company, 34
Leica cameras, 188, 189
Letters of credit, 51
Levin-Townsend, 43
Levitz, 101
Libya, 5
Lindsay, George, 10
Liquid asset funds, 72
Liquidity, 3, 12, 51–52, 63, 71, 150, 166
Lloyd's of London, 5
Loans (automobile), 15
Loans (bank), 5
Loans (insurance), 15
Lockheed, 75
Loews, 120, 121, 122, 123
London, 5, 59, 60, 61, 75
London Financial Times, 182
LTV Corporation, 40–42, 117

Master Card, 15
Mattel, 102, 105, 106
McCrory Corporation, 39
Media-General Financial Weekly, 185, 186

Merrill Lynch, 18, 30, 43, 63, 164
Merrill Lynch Government Securities, 30
Mexican peso, 147, 148, 149, 150, 153, 162–63
Mexico, 152, 153, 162
Middle East, xi, 3
Milgo Electronic Corporation, 102, 107
Milton Bradley, 102, 104, 105, 106
Minnesota Mining and Manufacturing, 44
Money funds, 17, 49ff., 149, 166, 205, 215, 217, 218
Mortgage interest, 129, 130
Money management funds, 53, 54–55
Money Market Management, 55
Morgan, J. P., Company, 44
Morgan Silver Dollar, xii, 173. *See also* Coins.
Mortgage payments, 33
Mutual funds, xii, 51, 63–64, 70, 72, 89, 90, 211
Myers, C. V., 4, 12

National Gypsum, 143
Netherlands, 156
New Photograde, 173
New York City, 2, 5, 27, 34, 214
New York Journal of Commerce, 150
New York Mercantile Exchange, 67
New York Stock Exchange, 3, 30, 69, 72, 77, 79, 90, 206
New York Times, 1–2, 3, 9, 17, 77, 80, 123
Newark, 34
NFC Index, 170, 171
Nikon cameras, 188, 189
Nostalgia. *See* Collector's items.
Numismatic Funding Corporation, 173, 174
Numismatic News Weekly, 178
Numismatics, 61, 169–78

Ohio Bell Telephone, 36
Oil, xi, 2, 5, 60, 153, 154, 155, 157, 160, 161, 162, 163, 177, 214
Oil embargo, (1973), 99
OPEC, 5, 153, 155
Oppenheimer Monetary Bridge, 49, 55
Owens Illinois Company, 44

Paris, Alexander, 4
Pennies, 67, 177. *See also* Coins.

Pension funds, 1
Peters, Harvey W., 6
Peto, John, 181
Petroleum, 2
Pfizer Company, 44
Photographic Historical Society of New York, 190
Photographica, antique, 188–91
Pick, Franz, 12, 190
Polaroid, 74, 101, 114, 115, 149, 189, 211
Political Collector, 194
Ponderosa System, Inc., 97, 98, 100, 101
Portobello Road, 183–84
Postal service, 30
Price-earning multiples, 110–11
Prices, 14
Prime rate, 46, 86
Proctor & Gamble, 36
Productivity, xi, 154, 214
Profit margins, 6
Put options, 113–17, 122, 123

Rapid American, 39
Raw land, 139–49
Raw materials, 3, 6, 156, 160, 161
RCA, 13
Real estate, xii, 7, 12, 13, 14, 18, 19, 50, 125–36, 137–46, 210, 214, 218
Real estate investment trusts (REITs), 125–26
Real estate syndicate. *See* Real estate.
Redbook. *See* Guide Book of United States Coins.
Recession, xii, 3, 4, 8, 10
Republic National Bank (New York), 63
Reserve Bank of South Africa, 63
Research Capital, 64
Reserve Fund, 49, 50, 51, 52, 53, 55
Retirement fund, 205
Reuters, 164
Rosenau, David R., 9, 22
Roulac, Stephen, 128
Rowe Price New Income Fund, 55
Ruddy, James, 173
Russell, Richard, 4

Santa Fe International Corporation, 97, 98
Sav-A-Stop, Inc., 97, 99
Savings, 19, 53, 205, 211
Saxon Industries, 92–94, 95, 96, 97, 98, 99
Schaefer, Alfred, 2
Schultz, Harry, 4

Scott catalogs, 201
Seaboard World Airlines, 47
Sears, Roebuck, 3, 36
Securities, 8, 17
Securities and Exchange Commission, 124, 206
Short selling, 72–91, 92–112, 114, 115, 117, 118, 119
Shuman, James B., 9
Silver, 59, 60, 172, 174, 218
Simon, William E., 3, 5
Social security, xi, xii
Sotheby Parke Bernet, 13, 22, 179, 181, 188
Sotheby's, 188, 190
South Africa, 60, 62, 63, 69–70
South West Bell Telephone, 37
Soviet Union, xi, 5, 10, 19, 60
SPL, 74
Sprague, 43
Stamps, 13, 14, 170, 172, 201–02
Standard and Poor's, 2, 34, 59, 111
Standard Oil of Indiana, 36
Stereoscopic camera, 188
Sterling Drug, Inc., 107, 108
Stock market, 1, 8, 13, 14, 17, 26, 43, 88, 89, 149, 150, 210, 211, 214, 215, 216
Stock options, 113–24
Straddles, 122, 123
Strategic Investments, 64
Sunbean Corporation, 143
Swiss franc, 147, 149, 150, 158–60, 166, 167, 168
Swiss Insurance Company Annuity, 166–68
Switzerland, 60, 64, 147, 148, 159

Tax rates. *See* Taxes.
Taxes, xii, 16, 26, 115, 116, 130, 131, 137–38, 139, 167, 215, 216
  Gift, 203–04
Tax-exempt securities, 16, 27, 144
  Municipal bonds, 16, 31–35, 144
Tax shelters. *See* Taxes
Tele-Com Company, 39
Telex, 39
Third Market, 206
Thornton Pickard field camera, 188
Tiffany's, 20, 22
Tiger International, 47
Tonka Corporation, 102, 106
Trading ranges, 110
Travelers Corporation, 44

223

Treasury bills, U.S., 27–28, 53, 113, 211
Treasury issues, U.S., 16, 26, 27, 52, 116
Treasury notes, U.S., 28–29, 88, 113, 114
TVA, 30

Unemployment, 1, 3, 4, 7, 8, 34, 210, 215, 217
Union Bank (Zurich), 2
Union Pacific Railroad, 37
United Brands, 39
United Service Fund, 64
U.S. Government Mint, 175
U.S. Treasury, 30, 214. *See also* "Flower bonds," Treasury bills, Treasury issues, Treasury notes.
Utilities, 82

Value Line, 4

Wall Street Journal, 2, 10, 17, 36, 70, 80, 88, 90, 101, 123, 124, 150, 165, 212

Warner Communications, 39
Warrant, 124
Warren, Gorham & Lamont Real Estate Investors Report, 140
Washington National, 44
Welfare, 1, 128
Whisky, 194–98
Whittredge, Worthing, 180
Will Ross, 44
Wine, 7, 13, 14, 17, 50, 179, 198–99
Wisconsin Telephone, 37

Xerox, 44, 73, 211

Yamashita, Eimei, 4
Ythrium aluminum garnets (YAG), 25

Zurich, 5, 60, 147

The Mallory Library